Strategic Management of Human Knowledge, Skills, and Abilities

Eugene B. McGregor, Jr.

Strategic Management of Human Knowledge, Skills, and Abilities

Workforce Decision-Making in the Postindustrial Era

 Jossey-Bass Publishers

San Francisco • Oxford • 1991

STRATEGIC MANAGEMENT OF HUMAN KNOWLEDGE, SKILLS, AND ABILITIES
Workforce Decision-Making in the Postindustrial Era
by Eugene B. McGregor, Jr.

Copyright © 1991 by: Jossey-Bass Inc., Publishers
350 Sansome Street
San Francisco, California 94104
&
Jossey-Bass Limited
Headington Hill Hall
Oxford OX3 0BW

Library of Congress Cataloging-in-Publication Data

McGregor, Eugene B.
  Strategic management of human knowledge, skills, and abilities :
  workforce decision-making in the postindustrial era / Eugene B.
McGregor, Jr. — 1st ed.
      p.   cm. — (The Jossey-Bass public administration series)
  (The Jossey-Bass management series)
  Includes bibliographical references and index.
  ISBN 1–55542–307–8
  1. Personnel management. 2. Manpower planning. I. Title.
II. Series. III. Series: The Jossey-Bass management series.
HF5549.M33957 1991
658.3'01—dc20   90–20738
                                                               CIP

Manufactured in the United States of America

The paper in this book meets the guidelines for
permanence and durability of the Committee on
Production Guidelines for Book Longevity of the
Council of Library Resources.

JACKET DESIGN BY WILLI BAUM
FIRST EDITION

Code 9109

*A Joint Publication of
The Jossey-Bass
Public Administration Series
and
The Jossey-Bass
Management Series*

Contents

ix

Preface

Postindustrial organizations are founded on complex systems of knowledge and information management that have replaced the smokestacks, mass production lines, and organizational structures of an earlier industrial age. In the postindustrial era, the accumulation and deployment of human knowledge, skills, and abilities have an enormous, and perhaps controlling, impact on the ability of complex social systems to achieve productivity goals and objectives. Thus, the choices that managers make affecting the capacity of a workforce to master knowledge disciplines, develop abilities, and acquire productive skills become the key to the vitality and success of public and private enterprise. In this respect workforce decision making has become a strategic discipline.

Strategic Management of Human Knowledge, Skills, and Abilities is an attempt to create an intellectual roadmap for a strategic approach to human resource management. In particular, it is for executives and general line managers who are attempting to think systematically and concretely about managing human resources in the postindustrial era, an age when organizational effectiveness is increasingly synonymous with the knowledge, skills, and abilities possessed by people. When the primary asset of an organization is stored in people rather than physical assets such as buildings and machines, the executives who guide the overall strategy of an organization must include personnel factors in their decisions. In such an environment, "personnel" is no longer the province of one isolated department; it forms the core of business and public agency strategy.

It has become increasingly obvious that top line managers must think strategically about decisions involving human resources. Witness the relatively recent elevation and expansion of the personnel function within many corporations and some public agencies. The creation of enlarged human resource management portfolios, higher salaries for top human resource managers, and direct access to line decision making are all testimony to the fact that personnel have become, as never before, a strategically significant resource on whose management the success of public and private enterprise now depends. Additional evidence is found in the intellectual ferment of journals, some recently established to capture the magnitude and direction of change. Scholars are now being challenged by the pace of events and shifting standards of professional practice to create in short order a knowlege base that has both theoretical rigor and practical utility. In short, the foundations of public and private management have permanently and fundamentally shifted, and this book is simply one attempt to contribute to the still emerging agenda of workforce management.

The turbulence and change that have created the need for a new approach to workforce management have many sources. Three specific developments make this book both possible and necessary. One is that the postindustrial economic systems that characterize all Western countries and Japan are based on competitive management of the intellectual capital—knowledge, skills, and abilities—stored in people. Workers and the knowledge they possess or control are no longer simply *a* resource; in many cases, they are *the* resource without which productivity does not occur. This development changes our view of human resources in a fundamental way. "Human resource management" ceases to be merely a staff service whose effects can be ignored. Strategic planners and line managers must be involved as never before in successful management of the human resource pool that forms the organized workforce. In effect, line management decision making has been fused to human resource management, and the resulting merger has created the subject of what is referred to here as "workforce management decision making."

The second development is the revolution in management technology. Within two decades, computers, information systems, and planning tools have become available in user-friendly configurations that redefine the possibilities for management decisions. The rapid development of powerful, inexpensive micro- and minicomputers means that computer technology can be widely distributed within organizations and at all management levels. Commercially available software programs now offer managers an enormous variety of ways to code, store, retrieve, and analyze human resource data without the requirement that they be highly trained computer specialists. Managers can query and manipulate information systems in an interactive "what if?" manner that approaches the requirements of real-world decision making.

A third development is more difficult to characterize. It originates with the discovery that when confronted with large and difficult undertakings in turbulent environments, thoughtful managers can often generate diverse alternative ways to organize and manage human resources. Public and private managers, under pressure to adapt practices to suit new realities and rising demands for productivity, have many options for action. It is no surprise, therefore, that the interests of public and private managers converge around a search for new instruments of organized productivity coupled with strategies for effective workforce management. Prospectively, the costs of management experimentation are relatively low when compared to the risks of living with outdated systems. If an experimental strategy works, then it deserves immediate adoption and emulation. If it does not work, little is lost because traditional, "tried and true" practices will be better appreciated.

This finding of workforce management variability establishes a basic premise on which this book is founded. Managers do not have to search for the imaginary "one best way," for there are many ways to direct human talent toward organized objectives. Furthermore, the number of experimental options is growing, not shrinking. If one set of assumptions, designs, and procedures does not work, then managers are authorized to try something new. The *managerial problem* is to understand in concrete and specific terms the range of choices from which management might fashion a winning strategy.

It is premature to attempt to produce the complete handbook of postindustrial human resource management—that accomplishment must await further developments. For example, at this writing the list of case problems that might sustain an extensive discussion of management applications is still short. The literature on scientific technologies and methods of analysis has only recently come into its own in the area of workforce forecasting and planning. Tentative and tendentious beginnings are appearing in the areas of management information, decision support systems, and applications of artificial intelligence. The factors that affect individual and organizational learning are just starting to be understood. Human resource accounting is still an exploratory exercise that has not yet reordered in any significant way standard accounting practice; this must occur before anything approaching a concrete benefit–cost evaluation of human resource options can be developed. Absent a fully developed knowledge base, the goal here is to take a first step: a complete statement of the issues and problems—the agenda—that must be confronted if the theory and practice of modern workforce management decision making are to be advanced.

"Workforce Management" Defined

A modest investment in jargon is needed at this point. The term "workforce management" is used here to distinguish this book from other works packaged under such labels as "personnel administration," "human resource management," and "industrial relations," all of which typically concentrate in varying levels of detail on *personnel operations*—the policies, procedures, routines, and actions used to manage the *individuals* employed by an organization. Thus, personnel offices, regardless of title, exist to manage the processes by which people are hired, promoted, paid, trained, and retired, or otherwise acted upon by personnel policy and procedure.

The notion of *workforce management,* by contrast, refers to strategic and tactical choices—decisions made by senior executives and line managers—that establish the policies within which personnel operations are conducted. Executives make decisions about organizational goals and objectives, the instruments and technologies of production, and the constraints on resource availability. Managers make decisions about organizational and personnel system design, the allocation of resources, and the work processes through which productivity occurs. These decisions establish the choices available to personnel operations. Indeed, one of the premises of this book is that a finite and identifiable set of executive and managerial decisions preempts most of the choices available to personnel administrators.

"Workforce management" is a useful shorthand to describe a function born of necessity. The terminology is not widely used. There is not, for example, an Office of Workforce Management in either the public or private sector. In some cases, workforce management problems will be tackled by entrepreneurial personnel consultants who have enlarged the franchise of an auxiliary staff function to include issues that classically have been the responsibility of general managers and executives. In other cases, new offices carrying such titles as "human resources planning" will become the first line of attack on workforce management problems. In still other cases, the problems will remain where they have always been—a responsibility of operating line managers whose job it is to figure out how human resources get organized and deployed to meet the requirements of large and complex enterprises. I leave to others the wordsmith's task of deciding what to call those who work on problems of workforce management.

The Publicness Issue

Much of this work applies to managers in both the public and private sectors. Despite the substantive differences separating them, both sets of managers confront the problem of knowledge management in the postindustrial era. Both confront the problem of balancing labor demand and supply. Both must deal with complex information needs that support decision making. Both must confront the agonies of making decisions and implementing choices that, on paper, might look good but have complex implications. Furthermore, both types of managers operate in competitive environments under conditions of risk where the failure to apply the right human capacities to work on key problems at the right time can result in losses of markets, missions, and organizational leverage, and perhaps even the collapse of the organization itself.

At the most general level, the problems of postindustrial workforce management are not restricted to either public or private managers, nor to the service or the manufacturing sector, nor to profit-making or nonprofit enterprises. The challenge cuts across departments, sectors, and industry groupings. Although corporate examples are used, this book concentrates on the challenge of workforce management as it appears to public executives and managers. The emphasis on public-sector case material is not entirely arbitrary. As we will see, public workforces turn out, in the aggregate, to be the most sophisticated pool of human resources found in an increasingly sophisticated mixed economy. Also, in the public sector we find dimensions of management complexity not found in the private sector; thus, in the public arena we can explore the most complex conditions confronting modern management. Regardless of substantive emphasis, however, a basic set of questions guides the inquiry about managing something so complex as a postindustrial workforce. They are neither public nor private questions, but essentially management questions.

Only at the level of concrete case application is the public/private designation required. For example, the link between public policy and human resource management is simple and direct: government "products" are, with only the rarest exceptions (such as the U.S. mint), services rather than manufactured products. Furthermore, simple and routine services are often contracted to the private sector, leaving government with the difficult and risky tasks of implementing public policy. Almost without exception, however, the complex public services—education, health, police, fire, and human services, to name only a few—are the products of human skill and energy. In essence, in the vast majority of public service delivery systems, people *are the product*. Thus, to manage people is to manage the final product itself.

Nonetheless, I hope this book will be valuable to private-sector managers. The common problems, logics, information needs, and decision dilemmas will be recognizable even if there is a dearth of corporate case study contained herein. The impatient and selective private-sector practitioner and scholar may wish to dive directly into the middle two sections of the book and then backfill until concepts, jargon, and discussion direction are clear. Chapter Two on managing human capital should not be skipped. Those interested exclusively in public management should start with the first chapter and read the first five chapters in order before jumping around.

The Audience

This book defines a list of problems that must be confronted if the challenge of workforce management is to be met. The audience is best characterized as an agglomeration of instructors, practitioners, and researchers. First, instructors of advanced undergraduate and graduate courses in personnel may find that the book complements standard personnel administration texts. Instructors who offer an advanced course on strategic human resource management should find this a useful resource, because I define a new knowledge base that establishes the connection between human resource management on the one hand and strategic management, information systems, and operations management on the other.

For practitioners, I hope to stimulate thinking about the strategic connections between human resources and organizational productivity. The argument here is designed to focus attention on some of the most difficult workforce management issues that command the attention of human resource managers and general managers. In the public sector, for example, managers have for years been forced to operate increasingly complex public programs under conditions of fiscal scarcity and against shifting sets of goals that are often hard to define. They can be easy marks to attacks from critics charging misfeasance and malfeasance, exacerbating the enormous complexity that represents the true challenge of public management. Yet, complexity does not by itself preclude effective and thoughtful management, and the practical aim of this book is to show how public-sector effort can be directed toward productive ends. Workforce management becomes a case illustration of how public-sector complexity can be managed.

The extent to which general managers should be involved in the problem of workforce management will vary from organization to organization. Much depends on how the personnel manager in the enterprise construes the human resource management portfolio. In general, the more narrow and operational the personnel function, the more general managers will need to worry directly about the issues raised in this book. The more broadly and imaginatively the personnel portfolio is defined, the more general managers can turn their attention to other matters, confident that someone is minding the human resource store. Virtually all managers will need to develop a common vocabulary about workforce management, however, and be concerned about the strategic management of a strategic resource.

The third audience is the research community. One can view this book as a compilation of the research available on key issues now confronting human resource managers and scholars. The agenda established in these twelve chapters then becomes an organizing rubric, a logical framework for thinking about research findings and issues. In the end, the book is not an attempt either to describe what human resource managers now do or to prescribe how they ought to do it. It is an analysis of what we think we now know about an emerging problem. Throughout, I have attempted to identify areas where research can contribute to the agenda, and research issues abound.

Overview of the Contents

The following questions form the overall structure of the book:

1. What are the real issues associated with managing a workforce in an age when knowledge management is the strategic requirement for success?
2. What basic logic can be applied to the art and science of workforce management?
3. What information is required to support workforce management decisions?
4. What are the important choices that managers make about a workforce?

These questions are addressed in the four parts of this book. Part One deals with the challenge to management excellence in postindustrial societies. Part Two develops a scheme for meeting the challenge by presenting a logic for thinking strategically about workforce management. Part Three explores workforce information systems that support multiple levels of complex decision making. And finally, Part Four deals with applications—how managers can use the ideas to make and implement workforce management decisions.

The argument is cumulative. In Part One, Chapter One defines the workforce management challenge, while Chapter Two explores what I have called the "double strategic" dimension of postindustrial workforce management. In Part Two, Chapters Three, Four, and Five develop a generic logic associated with balancing workforce availability and requirements. Chapter Three examines the complex connections between strategic decision making and personnel operations; the aim is to develop a line management perspective of the strategic significance of human resources. Chapter Four shows the effect of employment system design on workforce availability—the supply side of workforce management. Chapter Five shows the direct link between strategy and workforce requirements—the demand side of the challenge.

Part Three comprises four chapters on information systems. Chapter Six defines the user need for workforce information. Chapter Seven examines the alternative ways to convert raw data into information and knowledge ʰat is useful to managers. Chapter Eight explores the tools and technologies available to satisfy management's seemingly insatiable appetite for information. Chapter Nine discusses the pivotal role of data base management and crosswalk schemes.

Part Four is concerned with applications. This is where the preceding discussion in Chapters One through Nine is applied to management decision making. Chapter Ten discusses the analytic uses for workforce information—analysis that cuts through the information morass and produces knowledge on which decisions can rest. Chapter Eleven shows the application of this analysis to workforce decision making. Finally, Chapter Twelve examines the often overlooked and complex issues surrounding the actual implementation of workforce management improvements; without implementation, "workforce management" becomes an imaginery exercise rather than a force for improvement.

To enhance accessibility, technical issues and scholarly sources are relegated to five appendixes. Appendix A lists the dominant characteristics of several information systems software packages. Appendix B provides an example of a classification crosswalk to illustrate how operational, tactical, and strategic levels of workforce information can be linked. Appendix C contains an annotated bibliography on workforce forecasting and planning. Appendix D offers a quantitative illustration of the application of simple forecasting and planning models to the case of mental health services. Appendix E provides a brief technical explanation of the learning curve, a phenomenon that has new relevance to the role of human resource management in postindustrial economies.

What follows are four short books in one that collectively show why workforce management is important to the success of modern enterprise and how the basis for management decision making might be formulated. The argument is presented by explaining how the workforce decision-making agenda can be defined, supported, and implemented through appropriate use of available technologies and tools of analysis. In this way, it is hoped that a measure of clarity is brought to the complex choices and issues implied in the attempt to deal seriously with the strategic management of human knowledge, skills, and abilities.

Bloomington, Indiana Eugene B. McGregor, Jr.
February 1991

Acknowledgments

In so ambitious an undertaking, large debts of knowledge, assistance, and support are inevitable. Many people have both wittingly and unwittingly contributed their time and ideas to this work. One group consists of colleagues with whom I have trained, taught, and conducted research over the past twenty years. An extended management consultancy at the National Aeronautics and Space Administration's Goddard Space Flight Center in Greenbelt, Maryland, gave me a thorough introduction to the practical nature of management in technologically advanced organizations; in particular, Raymond Sumser and Michael Vaccaro provided many valuable insights about human resource management. A great debt is owed Jean Couturier and Richard Schick, formerly of the National Civil Service League; we spent much time together in the late 1970s, during the era of federal civil service reform, researching the structure of federal labor markets. Further debts are owed George Maharay and Richard Chapman of the National Academy of Public Administration, with whom a productive year was spent delving into the arcane art of standardized occupational classification.

During the 1980s my research emphasis shifted, focusing on the structure and operation of state and local government systems and the application of emerging information management technologies. An eight-year project with the Indiana Department of Mental Health provided an ideal laboratory in which to develop, test, and apply new workforce management ideas and technologies in the context of state government. To the National Institute of Mental Health and officials of the Indiana Department of Mental Health, including Dennis Jones and Priscilla Crawford, and numerous managers and clinicians of Indiana's large and complex mental health care system, a great debt is owed for long-term patience, encouragement, and funding. During that time, we developed a prototype workforce management information system and demonstrated the feasibility of the end-user computer applications discussed in this book. John Daly served as research assistant for part of this multiyear effort, and the compilation of software availability, discussed in Chapter Eight, resulted as a collaborative research spinoff.

Another group of contributors has faithfully attempted to rescue me from committing foolishness and error to print. Jossey-Bass editors Lynn D. W. Luckow and Alan Shrader were invaluable in suggesting how a very rough idea could be developed and distilled. Alan, particularly, was unusually perceptive and helpful in finding ways to improve and focus the original manuscript. In addition, the anonymous reviewers of the manuscript spotted several opportunities for improving precision, clarity, and organization. Surviving errors cannot be fobbed off on others. They are the sole property of the author.

Still other contributions came from colleagues and students who provided forums over the years. The late Charles H. Levine provided two opportunities to present and publish papers on key components of the workforce management theme. H. George Frederickson stimulated some early thinking and my prospectus on "manpower management" in the *Public Administration Review*. Undergraduate and graduate students in my public personnel administration and human resource management courses were partial hostages to my determination to work through the logic and implications of what I now call workforce management decision making.

The act of writing can result occasionally in antisocial behaviors and attitudes paradoxically visited most frequently on those closest to the writer. Serious writing sometimes requires strange hours, absentmindedness, and an occasional misanthropic mien. In this case, two daughters—Kelly and Alison—and my wife, Carol, are the most aggrieved parties. While completed work cannot be atonement, it does mean that what has come in our house to be known, sometimes affectionately, as "Dad's boring book" no longer haunts family life. I can only hope that acknowledgment of the social price paid by others will be understood as a heartfelt "thank you" for patience and kindly forbearance.

Finally, thanks must be extended to long-time faculty colleagues in the School of Public and Environmental Affairs at Indiana University who have reviewed and commented on previous work and who are this year shouldering burdens so that I can take a sabbatical leave in Europe to reflect on the postindustrial transition in the United States and the rest of the world. New colleagues in the public administration departments of Erasmus University of Rotterdam and Leiden University have made matching commitments of money, office space, and computers so that I can continue to conduct sabbatical research on the broader issues that surround workforce management.

The sabbatical has provided time to do some final editing at a pivotal point in the integration of the European community, the end of the Cold War, the collapse of the Iron Curtain, and an accelerating global experimentation with new ways to manage human affairs. Events to date appear to reinforce the premise with which this book was originally undertaken: that skillful workforce management is strategically important to the management experimentation now underway in the United States, Europe, Japan, and much of the rest of the world. Whether this premise is correct will be judged soon enough. Critics can properly assess the quality of the message that follows, and events will determine whether the message is timely. An author can merely express willingness to defend the former and wait with everyone else to discover the outcome of the latter.

EBM

To
Carol Carew McGregor,
who understands human capital

The Author

Eugene B. McGregor, Jr. is professor of public and environmental affairs at Indiana University, Bloomington. He received his A.B. degree (1964) from Dartmouth College in government and his Ph.D. degree (1969) from the Maxwell School, Syracuse University, in political science. His dissertation studied the career mobility of bureaucrats, and he has spent more than twenty years consulting and conducting research in public-sector human resource management. Research papers have been published in *American Political Science Review, Brookings Dialogues in Public Policy, Public Administration Review, Journal of Politics, Policy Studies, The ANNALS of the American Academy of Political and Social Science, Administration and Society, Policy Studies Journal, Review of Public Personnel Administration,* and numerous edited volumes. He has consulted for several levels of government, including the City of Bloomington and Monroe County, Indiana, the state of Maryland, the United Nations, universities and consulting organizations, and such agencies and organizations as the National Aeronautics and Space Administration (Goddard Space Flight Center), the U.S. Department of Labor, the U.S. Office of Personnel Administration, the U.S. General Accounting Office, the Indiana Department of Mental Health, the Indiana House of Representatives Judiciary Committee, and the National Academy of Public Administration. McGregor's current research focuses on the role of information management technology in public management decision making. He has taught at the University of Maryland and Syracuse University and has been a visiting professor at Erasmus University of Rotterdam and Leiden University.

PART ONE

THE STRATEGIC MANAGEMENT
OF A STRATEGIC RESOURCE

Human resource management is currently under pressure from two challenges. The first derives from general management's concern with strategic management. The second is based on a shift in the role of human resources where postindustrial systems increasingly regard human capital as their strategic resource. The result is an agenda built around a double strategic: strategic management of a strategic resource.

Chapter One

The Challenge to Traditional Management Practice

A transformation has reordered the relationship between people and organized productivity. Production processes along with products are being vested with ever-increasing amounts of intelligence. Goods and services are complex, rather than simple, and increasingly "smart," resulting from substantial investments in research and development. Production processes are increasingly automated and are being redesigned to be flexible rather than rigid in order to respond quickly to the shifting demands of turbulent environments that constantly change markets and human needs. The result has been the creation of a postindustrial order founded on the management of knowledge and information.

In such a transformation, the capacity of people to bring knowledge, skills, and abilities to the task of productivity becomes a critical variable. Indeed, a massive transformation of the United States workforce has been underway for some time as labor markets and managers struggle to develop increasingly computerized production processes, invent state-of-the-art technologies and products, market research and development spinoffs, and repair and maintain the information systems servicing the new postindustrial order. The transformation is not limited to the United States, because the emerging strategic significance of human capital has become obvious in all the economically advanced nations of the world and appears to have gained recognition in less advanced countries as well.

The role of human knowledge, skills, and abilities in modern organizations has redefined the criteria by which the practice of human resource management is judged. In essence, the decisions that link general management practices to the management of people have become pivotal to the success of modern public and private organizations. This book aims to discover why such a transformation has taken place and what it means for management decision making. In essence, at least two strategic issues are involved in what we refer to here as workforce decision making: first, people are a strategic resource in postindustrial organizations; second, only a strategic approach to human resource management can create the close working relationship between the goals of organizations and the management of people. This chapter attempts to chart the nature of the "double strategic" problem: the strategic management of a strategic resource.

Thus, a challenge is presented: if one takes seriously the desirability of creating a new and close relationship between general management decision making and human resource management, it is not self-evident how the integration can occur. Historically, standard organization designs created functionally separate disciplines. Corporate or strategic management, middle management, financial management, and operations management, for example, were clearly differentiated from the specialized business of human resource management. Each discipline had its own purposes, knowledge base and skill requirements, and standards of performance. Overcoming the functional insularity thus created will not be easy. One goal of this book is to explain both the necessity and the basis for changing the practice of human resource management.

In traditional organizations, it is not unusual to find the specialized claims of human resource managers standing at the end of the decision chain. Personnel managers were historically the last to contribute to the management of enterprise.

One particularly strong assessment sums up their traditional contributions (Mercer, 1989, pp. 12–13):

> Most human resources action models merely play tag-along with the plans created by other departments. For instance, the personnel and management succession plans flow out of an organization's annual and long-range business plans that are created by other departments. The training plan drafted by the human resources department stems from the technical and managerial needs expressed by non-human-resources departments. Even the recruiting, compensation, and benefits plans come out of the needs generated by other departments' requirements to attract and retain talent.
>
> None of these traditional human resources planning models show a proactive stance on the part of the human resources staff. All of them come into existence as useful adjuncts *after* another corporate department creates a profit-oriented plan that needs human resources input. These planning models do not noticeably directly improve the bottom line. For years, executives have called for human resources to become more proactive and involved in the guts of business operations. Until now, few, if any, planning models have emerged to do just that.

That frank appraisal would be equally appropriate in public or private settings.

The cost of obscuring the direct connection between the general management agenda and the management of people is the organizational breakdown that results. One general class of breakdown is lowered prospects for productivity. This is particularly true in service-based economies, where productivity is defined by the activities performed by people rather than by the goods produced or the natural resources extracted. The dependence on people as the key agent of productivity particularly characterizes public-sector endeavors, where many an ambitious management plan has foundered simply because of the failure to connect the goals of public policy to the human capacity to produce what policy requires (Meier, 1989). A simple demonstration can be found in a recent federal report (U.S. General Accounting Office, 1989, pp. 19–21). A sampling of six cases illustrates the point.

- *Prison security:* Staffing shortages at a time of dramatic increases in prison populations invite trouble both in the criminal justice system and in society at large.
- *Air traffic control:* An explosion in air travel requires air traffic controllers with substantial and special aptitudes for managing complex radar systems and flight patterns. Shortages loom.
- *Environmental protection:* Cleaning up the environment requires a well-trained and sophisticated workforce, particularly attorneys, chemists, and engineers. They are not being hired.
- *Thrift institution oversight:* Weak oversight of governmentally insured banks and loan guarantee programs invites a policy of insuring weak and possibly corrupt institutions and creates slow detection of failures. A cadre of trained bank examiners is required to prevent an enormous accumulation of bailout costs.
- *Drug enforcement:* A drug war strategy that seizes the assets of drug traffickers requires a workforce knowledgeable about real property law and management. Government does not now have such people in adequate numbers.
- *Tax processing:* Shortages of trained personnel capable of modernizing and automating tax collection places government revenue generation at risk because government makes incorrect calculations, issues slow refunds, and creates incentives to dodge paying taxes altogether.

These are but a few examples of problems currently plaguing the federal government; other lists could easily be developed for state and local government services.

In private firms, evidence of the rising significance of human skill is ample. Successful production strategy, for example, requires a flexible production system linking organizations that make a "range of customized products or services on the same production line using advanced technologies that minimise down-time between product lines" (Rajan, 1990, p. F1). Such a strategy can be supported only by a cycle (research–design–production–marketing–distribution) under increasing pressure to accelerate as customization shortens the shelf life of products. More and more, as human ingenuity is used to reconfigure production systems, the skill content of work will be a company's key strategic factor.

A second type of breakdown lies in what Wallace Sayre (1948) has referred to as the triumph of technique over purpose. When left alone, specialized staff activities become understandably enamored of the administrative techniques associated with their portfolios—personnel operations, budgeting, procurement, and so forth. In the case of human resource management, important decision making can be hidden in the myriad details of hiring, compensation, appraisal, and employee relations systems. Yet clearly enterprises do not exist to do job analyses, promulgate compensation plans, or produce performance appraisals. They exist to create the products and services—final products—desired by customers and clients. Public and private organizations are identical in this regard even though their aims, products, and production methods differ.

The inevitable result of separating organization purpose from specialized "management" technique is that enormous resources are devoured in the course of producing intermediate staff products. Talent is wasted on relatively mundane, and possibly purposeless, activity. Michael W. Mercer (1989, pp. 5–6) puts the point directly and pointedly: "Many human resources managers also spend a lot of their time carrying out high-class clerical duties. For example, many aspects of typical compensation or benefits work are more administrative than managerial. That is, quite a few components of such human resources endeavors can be explained in a straightforward manner so that a clerk, secretary, or administrative assistant could handle them. Nevertheless, many human resources managers spend their time sifting through administrative duties instead of creating and implementing profit improvement solutions to business problems." Furthermore, many of the administrative functions of human resource management can be at least partially computerized. In the automated environment, as we see in Chapter Eight, the traditional divisions between executive decision making, general management, human resource administration, and the clerical functions of the personnel office break down. Indeed, virtually all the specialized aspects of personnel management are now positioned to be radically redesigned.

The New Significance of Human Resources

Preventing and reversing the functional separation of management disciplines are not automatically or easily achieved. Pioneering attempts have been made, particularly in the private sector (Beer and others, 1984; Fombrun, Tichy, and Devanna, 1984; Odiorne, 1984; Douglas, Klein, and Hunt, 1985), to reforge the connection between human resources and general management, but the results and conclusions are general rather than specific. They provide few explanations about precisely how the connection can be made and are largely limited to the private sector. In fairness, it should also be said that recognition of the problem has been recent and that the basis for a more strategic approach to human resource management is only beginning to emerge. The practical reality for both public and private sectors, however, is that there is still a dearth of literature describing what the new human resource agenda entails.

One reason for this dearth is the sheer difficulty of clearly defining and analyzing the subject. Unlike money and physical assets, with which management can form some tactile relationship, the essence of modern human resource management lies with managing an invisible resource. In one sense, of course, this is nonsense; people are tangible beings and can be counted. But the *strategic* feature of modern human resource management lies with the knowledge, skills, and capabilities that reside

within people—the part of the human resource pool that cannot be seen (Hall, 1989). The commodity being analyzed—the
human capacity to perform and produce—is neither obvious
nor easily measured.

Second, modern personnel management choices are made
difficult by the absence of a clear logic that connects people to
productivity. In the public sector, the logic is particularly and
inherently complex because it requires theoretical links among
public policy choices, employment systems, and the management of people. These links do not now exist. They have to be
forged for the first time.

Because of the nature of public work and the conse-
quent makeup of the public workforce, human resource management issues in the public sector lie in the vanguard of the
social and economic shift, not in the rear. Thus, while it may
be true that public-sector *practice* currently lags what is happen-
ing in the private sector, this may be due to the complexity of
public management problems. Public organizations face the same
double challenge as private ones—strategic management of a
strategic resource—but they must do it in a public environment for a public purpose. Precisely why the entire human
resource management agenda has changed is worth a short ex-
cursion. We will return to the problem of public-sector strategy
in Chapter Two.

The Awakening. Awareness of the strategic role of human resources in modern organizations has penetrated management
literature and practice (Meyer, 1978; "Personnel Widens," 1979;
Douglas, Klein, and Hunt, 1985; Fombrun, Tichy, and Devanna, 1984; Odiorne, 1984). A few prescient analysts (Machlup, 1962; Chorafus, 1968; Drucker, 1968; Schultz, 1971)
grasped early the significance of human resources in information-based societies and economies. For the most part, however, social scientists and practitioners have been slow to understand the profound changes required when trained
intelligence is the critical ingredient required in what is now
commonly referred to as the postindustrial age.

The strategic importance of human resources has resulted from massive changes in production systems for goods and services. In earlier industrial systems, people were merely operational or tactical resources, not strategic. For example, people are operational resources when they serve as interchangeable forms of common labor from which physical products or other routine services are derived (Cleveland, 1985, pp. 20–21). In early industrial and office operations, the human contribution consisted of simple, specialized, and repetitive routines *(Scientific American, 1982)*. These operations were appropriate subjects for industrial engineers such as Frederick W. Taylor, whose observations about work methods and organizational efficiency were implicitly based on the widespread existence of simple organizational forms and products (1947). Over time, with mass production of complex manufactured goods and services, people became *tactically* significant as more intelligence was programmed into products and organizations. Human labor was more highly trained, more varied, less easily interchangeable, and subject to more complex organizational arrangements than in early industrial systems. Those organizing the human input had to make more complex decisions. Variables such as human learning (Belkaoui, 1986), morale and human relations (Roethlisberger and Dickson, 1939), job design (Herzberg, 1966), supervisory style (McGregor, 1960; Likert, 1961), and organization design (Galbraith, 1973) define many human resource decisions. The literature on "contingency management" (Fiedler, 1967; Lawrence and Lorsch, 1967; Hellriegel and Slocum, 1974; Mintzberg, 1979) documents how diverse are the designs that have arisen to link people, positions, and productivity in complex organizations.

Because industrially based productivity required that people be properly organized and assigned to specialized tasks, large numbers of middle managers were required. Work had to be carefully coordinated. Worker performance had to be appraised and rewarded. Resources had to be administratively allocated rather than left to markets and prices (Williamson, 1975). Predictably, middle management systems became more complex after World War II, culminating in a rich array of contingency management schemes (Mintzberg, 1979). At the same time, "human resource management" developed further as a specialized function concerned with complicated resource deployments in large organizations.

The Discontinuity. In postindustrial systems, however, the relationship between people and productivity shifts dramatically once again. Simply put, "productivity" no longer refers to the manufacture of things (Cleveland, 1985). When final products are brute physical things or routine services (guards at the gate, custodial health care, line operations processing of criminal justice cases), the workforce is significant only operationally or at most tactically. When the final products are "smart" products and complex services, however, humans become *the* critical input. This occurs when knowledge—often formal knowledge developed through rigorous theoretical training—is embedded in final products and services. In effect, human knowledge becomes inseparable from final outputs and the processes by which they are produced. Thus, what is *strategic* about strategic human resource management is the management of the workforce's knowledge so that this resource is converted into final knowledge products and ever-changing production techniques (Brickner, 1981; *Scientific American,* 1982; Reich, 1983).

In an economy where products are simple and production techniques either do not change or change very slowly, work patterns are stable and amenable to routine specialization. In such a setting, job skills can be transferred from one generation to the next through apprenticeships and other types of on-the-job training, and repetitive experience is the basis for labor productivity (Murname, 1988). When final products derive from investments in knowledge and production techniques are constantly changing, however, muscle power and job experience are an insufficient basis for productivity.

This finding is a discontinuity (Drucker, 1968) with earlier practice. It means that productivity is increasingly linked to the trained human intellect. In postindustrial systems, "occupation" refers less to a position in a production process and more to classes of work based on knowledge and skill requirements. These are what we call "knowledge jobs" (Drucker, 1968, chaps. 12 and 13). In effect, theoretical knowledge replaces experimental learning and apprenticeship as the basis for productivity (Drucker, 1968). Research-based industries supplant natural resource and craft-based industries (Lambright and Teich, 1981), and knowledge of such things as symbolic logic, plasma physics, fiber optics, molecular and submolecular structures, and social science serves as the source of future productivity (Drexler, 1986).

Knowledge and the learned capacity to accumulate and manipulate new knowledge become the coin of the postindustrial realm. The stock of human capacity to produce goods and services from that knowledge is termed "human capital" (Thurow, 1970, p. 15). The strategic importance of human capital changes forever the way both public- and private-sector managers must think about workforce management.

The Grace Commission Challenge

The awakening of private-sector management has happened in the last two decades. Precisely why and when public-sector managers recognized the new environment of human resource management is not clear. There were no official declarations, no dramatic legislative acts. There were, however, distant rumblings advertising approaching storms. One such storm is worth further discussion.

For years, managers of all governmental agencies have operated under continuous suspicion that their practices are fundamentally flawed. The absence of competitive markets leads many analysts, with few exceptions (Bragaw, 1980), to the contestable conclusion that public management excellence may be an oxymoron. Government is not alone in this; suspicion plagues all ventures whose productivity is not defined by a convenient measure of profitability. The latest and most serious public-sector challenge was posed by the President's Private Sector Survey on Cost Control (known as the Grace Commission), commissioned in 1982 by President Reagan. The commission's mandate was simple: find the sources of waste in the federal government and come up with specific recommendations to increase management efficiency. The president was desperate. His administration had made a fiscal mistake that had generated a structural deficit (that is, a shortfall built into the budget) of roughly $200 billion a year, or nearly $1 trillion between 1981 and 1986. The political need was to find money with which to project a retrieval of the deficit without raising taxes. Thus, the task of the Grace Commission was to retrieve as much as possible in short-term savings from government operations (McGregor, 1985).

The commission proceeded with a zeal that lent credence to the suspicion that large-scale management misfeasance was at work throughout the federal establishment. Indeed, between March 1982 and January 1984, more than 2,000 Grace volunteers in 36 task force groups dashed about federal agencies, assembled over 2,500 recommendations in 750 issue areas, and drafted a 49-volume report outlining improvements in federal government efficiency. Clearly, the commission's work was not an exercise in dispassionate scholarly analysis, and no one was surprised when the report concurred with founding assumptions that "management improvements" were needed and that they would save large amounts of money. Whether the commission's estimates were precise, whether the research was of uniform quality, or whether a "private" bias dominated the analysis is not the focus of attention here. The compelling point for our purposes is that within twenty-one months, an experienced group of private managers had concluded that federal management in general, and personnel practice in particular, was a leading source of waste (Grace, 1984). More specifically, after auditing federal personnel operations, the commission reported that

- The federal administration incurred some unusual personnel costs in its packaging of wages, salaries, and fringe benefits.
- The government could take advantage of more cost-effective ways to design employment systems and manage federal personnel.

- Governmentwide management of the federal workforce did not exist, though some innovative management could be found in particular agencies and bureaus.
- The size of personnel costs and the savings possible with effective workforce management justified a careful scrutiny of federal personnel practices.

In its report, the commission avoided operational detail and fixed its attention instead on what it regarded as the key weakness in an otherwise sophisticated system of federal personnel administration: that governmentwide workforce management did not exist. The system did not have a way of determining human resource requirements or a way of managing the skill mix needed to deliver its final products and services.

Insights. The Grace Commission clearly understood the strategic issues that separate workforce management from personnel operations (Grace, 1984). Its conclusions, however, are deceptive, for they are packaged as standard pleas for eliminating waste. For instance, the commission suggested reducing payroll costs by introducing true comparability into compensation packages. It advocated eliminating overstaffing and overgrading managerial positions. It urged the use of incentives for productivity improvement. It advised eliminating unnecessary overtime pay and payroll padding with temporary positions. These are the standard "volume up, costs down" recommendations that public managers expect from the business community. Indeed, most productivity improvement reports that apply simple efficiency solutions to complex organizational problems are as unreliable for private business as they are for public agencies (Judson, 1982).

The commission went beyond simple labor efficiency analysis, however. The general question for this commission was whether large-scale inefficiency and waste could be documented on a governmentwide basis. One of the subsidiary questions was whether projected savings from improvements in personnel management could retrieve a measurable share of the federal deficit. To attract the attention of policymakers chronically bored by small numbers, the commission quite understandably attached the biggest numbers it could to its recommendations. Thus, the Grace plan to retrieve $424 billion in three years (including $91 billion through personnel management improvement) can at least be credited with getting policy-level attention.

How are personnel insiders to respond to an external review by private management outsiders who project more than $400 billion in overall "waste"? Some would discredit the report by raising questions about the applicability, precision, and accuracy of the findings and the motives of the commission members. This option is tempting because the report is clearly vulnerable. Others would discount the value of the recommendations by the extent to which improvements depend on changes in public policy that would require the unlikely cooperation of Congress. Then career public managers can hide in the intricacies of the policy process and ignore the substance of the report. Courageous managers, however, would consider the report seriously, bearing in mind the constraints placed on the commission. From this perspective, what is striking is the direct way the commission tackled the "big" personnel management issue. The opening paragraph of the report makes the point (Grace, 1984, pp. 228–229).

> Work force management determines the number of people and skills necessary to accomplish an organization's objectives, and the actions necessary to obtain, develop, and motivate the work force. Work force requirements, however, have received little attention in Government because budget decisions are usually overriding, there is lack of leadership from the Office of Personnel Management (OPM), and there is insufficient information to develop complete and integrated management systems. As a result, there is a need for human resource planning procedures that would allow for uniform decision making throughout the federal

Government regarding the size, composition, allocation, and development of work force needs.

The finding is significant for all the recommendations in
the commission's personnel report. In effect, the commission
found that the federal government is attempting to manage a
large and expensive workforce by using only the leverage of
the Office of Personnel Management's control of personnel
operations and the Office of Management and Budget's allocations of cost, average grade, and employment ceilings. Yet
federal managers have no identifiable system for managing a
workforce of 2.1 million people (not including postal workers
or military members) that, at the time of the report, cost $51
billion annually in direct wages and salaries and $41.7 billion
in fringe benefit costs connected with retirement, health benefits, and life insurance. Missing, or at least obscure to the Grace
Commission and everyone task force members talked with, was
a method—any method—for formulating federal personnel
operating requirements. How could federal managers know
what kind of workforce was needed? This question is central
to workforce management; requirements determine the adequacy of on-board staffing levels from which, in turn, are derived future decisions.

The commission also discovered that no information system existed to support managerial decision making. A helpful
information system would classify the workforce according to
its contribution to productivity, its cost, and its chief characteristics compared with the competitive alternatives. Current federal information systems still do not produce such information.
Indeed, I know of very few government information systems that produce truly managerial information, although some
installations have developed very advanced systems. Current
government personnel information systems *do*, however, collect, store, and generate lots of raw *data* and generate many
reports about people (such as personnel bio-data), performance appraisals, payroll status and costs, the characteristics of
an applicant pool, and employment histories of on-board or
recently employed personnel. But they only rarely attach the

characteristics of personnel to final products or costs in ways that inform public management decision makers about alternative courses of action.

In effect, most government personnel information systems are still designed with personnel operations and not executive-level management in mind. The failure to establish an information link between human resource operations and productivity means that many important questions about federal personnel simply cannot be answered. In some cases, the system may fool itself. For instance, the Grace Commission charged that the federal workforce was overgraded, underproductive, and overpaid compared with private-sector counterparts. The absence of productivity measurement systems that would justify the "overpayment" was used to reinforce the suspicion of inefficiency.

The Grace Commission concluded that federal personnel practices should be pulled into line with "more efficient" private practice. The conclusion is both plausible and forceful. Only the executive levels of the federal workforce were considered systematically underpaid and, even then, the issue is the compensation owed to true executives (as opposed to highly graded specialist employees). Recent attrition rates do indeed suggest that an inadequate set of rewards has resulted in the loss of executives crucial to the operation of the federal government. The absence of attrition at lower levels of the white-collar service suggested to some that the rewards were more than adequate. If it is true that the federal workforce is excessively layered, overstaffed in highly graded positions, and overpaid compared with nonfederal workforces performing similar work, corrections should be made. For example, the public work load can be moved to other parts of the economy at enormous potential savings.

Critique. There was, however, another response to the commission's report: federal grading, staffing, and pay had changed to reflect more demanding federal goals and responsibilities. An increasingly sophisticated workforce must be graded higher and paid more than the private sector in many cases. This is a requirements-side response to the commission's supply-side generalizations.

The argument is only partly speculative. Massive changes in the federal skill mix have indeed occurred since World War II. Also, many changes in the federal workforce are driven by the federal role at the cutting edge of a highly advanced post-industrial economy (McGregor, 1988). This line of argument implies that much federal work is really unlike much of the general economy and requires adequate compensation packages to attract and retain a highly trained professional workforce. In other words, the Grace Commission was probably dead wrong: Rising pay structures really reflect the richer skill mix of the growing white-collar federal workforce and *not* the bureaucratic layering and consuming overhead that have nearly crippled parts of American industry—the experience base of most of the task force members.

Which position is correct? The significance of the commission's personnel report is its finding that "nobody knows" (Grace, 1984, p. 232). Neither the commission nor its critics can document allegations about the strategic basis for federal personnel practice. There is no solid information base that documents the human resource requirements of federal work and compares the requirements with on-board availability. No validated classification crosswalk connecting the many different government personnel definitions and systems permits a direct comparison of federal and nonfederal workforces. The salary survey was, and is, too narrow to be useful for comparative analysis. The commission was not even able to penetrate the aggregate computation of average grade to realize what a 61.5 percent average grade increase from 1949 to 1981 might conceivably mean. The report ignores the fact that in the thirty-two–year span under review, federal operations changed enormously, and personnel requirements were not left untouched. After all, the rise of the research and development agencies, the growth of computerized entitlement programs, and the vast contracting of federal missions to remote instrumentalities requires a vastly more sophisticated and professional workforce than that required by a simpler and smaller federal mission.

In short, a detailed factual basis for the commission's conclusions cannot be found—and that itself is the key insight of the commission. What the Grace Commission documented was the extent of the federal government's ignorance about its own operation. The commission could not be more discriminating in its analysis of federal personnel management because federal managers themselves do not have the information, and perhaps not the data, that would demonstrate the adequacy or inadequacy of their own practices.

That insight leads to another question about the state of the public personnel art. If the data on the federal workforce will not sustain a managerial investigation of its structure, why not? One brief answer is that there is not a central management office in government that wants to know the answers to questions about how to convert the program goals of government into personnel requirements. The two obvious candidates—the Office of Personnel Management and the Office of Management and Budget—have traditionally dealt with, respectively, personnel operations and budget examination. The most active agency currently pressing for a genuine managerial agenda is the General Accounting Office (GAO), which is in the wrong institutional position to design and operate a system for federal human resource management. Thus, except for the occasional presidential query that generates an awkward White House foray into civil service management, there appears to be no institutional interest in governmentwide examination of the federal workforce. The result is unfortunate. Without publicly defended analyses of federal operating requirements, the whole system is vulnerable to perennial and politically motivated suspicions that too much is being spent on the wrong kinds of employees. The finding highlights what is more than a federal problem. Most general-purpose units of government would not receive favorable marks from a Grace type of review—nor would, perhaps, much of American industry during the late 1970s and early 1980s.

Implications. The federal experience with the Grace Commission represents a general problem confronting all public-sector human resource managers. From time to time, financially pressed presidents, governors, and mayors will wish to review the management practices of their administrations. The justification is even more compelling than in the federal case because state and local payrolls claim such a large proportion of operating budgets (anywhere from 40 to 85 percent of operating costs, depending on program area). Furthermore, in the name of economy and efficiency the temptation is irresistible to apply some standard—any standard—in order to estimate government's "real" staffing requirements. Without specific guidelines from public executives and program managers, groups such as the Grace Commission will reach out to grasp private-sector staffing standards. The private yardstick is obviously suspect: Government operations are not business operations. But if public management cannot or will not provide an alternative basis for assessing its own requirements, it is understandable (even if unjustifiable) that ill-fitting measures will be applied. Indeed, until public managers can establish a connection between productivity and personnel operations, comparisons between public and private sectors will continue, and government workforces will most likely suffer from the comparison.

Public managers, particularly, are under pressure as never before to assess personnel operations based on productivity. Such assessments would compare personnel requirements with personnel availability and formulate strategies for balancing the two sides of the equation. This is easier said than done. Literature that describes in practical terms how to accomplish the tasks of balancing workforce requirements and availability is scant, presenting a state-of-the-art management challenge to any who would tackle the problem.

The key to meeting the challenge lies with linking strategic planning with operational details of personnel management. Yet the links cannot be based, as in the Grace Commission case, on simple efficiency analysis. For one thing, efficiency analysis often has a counterintuitive side in which short-term improvements can undermine long-term productivity. A good example is contained in the report's conclusion that reform of the federal retirement system carried a potential savings of more than $58 billion. Clearly, lowering the pension benefit level, extending the retirement age, and changing the inflation indexing of retirement benefits are tempting targets for "productivity improvement"; they involve big numbers in relatively short time frames. But what are the long-term effects of pension reform? Across-the-board pension reductions may make career government service less attractive at precisely the time that government requires its most sophisticated workforce. Extending retirement age also increases the training costs needed to update the skills of an aging workforce whose every incentive is to remain bound by golden handcuffs in the form of generous pensions. The point is that the relationship between public productivity and workforce management is complex and requires a logic more sophisticated than a "volume-up, costs down" mentality allows.

Nevertheless, a sustained drive to improve government personnel operations is justified for many reasons. Without a management-based system of personnel administration, the public workforce remains vulnerable to any faction that alleges overpayment, overstaffing, and a lack of excellence. Self-protection is one reason a prudent manager (public or private) will want to submit to a careful, productivity-based scrutiny. With an external review, either analyses will discover opportunities for cost savings, or they will not. If they do, less effective practices can be exchanged for more effective ones without compromising productivity goals. If analysis finds no opportunity for cost savings, then executives can defend personnel practices based on proven rather than unproven operating requirements.

Another advantage of rigorous oversight is that public policymakers are entitled to know how many workers are needed to run government programs under alternative strategies. No administration, Republican or Democratic, will long finance a large bureaucratic mystery whose practices and products remain obscure to those who pay for them. The current evidence suggests that fiscally constrained policymakers are willing to boil public bureaucracies down until convinced of the need to finance personnel, programs, and offices. In such an environment, government executives and managers will find a continuous managerial review of personnel practice in their self-interest. Periodic external reviews could convince an unappreciative public that putative management excellence is legitimate. External review can do no damage and is potentially useful in documenting improvements.

The Workforce Management Agenda

The question of workforce management, first raised by the Grace Commission, did not die with a filing of the commission's report. Subsequent examinations by central management agencies have found that improvements were needed in the way the government workforce was managed (U.S. General Accounting Office, 1989). While the reception of recent findings has been as chilly as we might expect, the essential significance of these reports is not blame finding. The key point is the repeated acknowledgment by all central government management agencies that strategic management of human resources is now one of the new management games on which public productivity depends. Public personnel offices, like their private-sector counterparts, no longer preside over a low-stakes exercise in bureaucracy. Whatever their previous incarnations, offices of personnel management have become significant management players who have much to say about government performance and accomplishment. Moreover, general managers bear added responsibilities for workforce management that were not of concern in an earlier era.

The real value of the Grace critique of federal personnel administration goes far beyond its review of a single office. In effect, the commission simply uncovered a transformation of the operating administrative environment in which the rising significance of human resources fundamentally transforms management practice. It also recognized a critical management problem (even if it did misread the data) and, by inventing a new function—workforce management—left personnel managers to struggle with a difficult set of issues. Fortunately, at this writing organizational learning is underway: the Office of Personnel Management (OPM), as well as other government personnel offices, recognizes the magnitude of the problems it faces and appears determined to meet the challenge (U.S. Office of Personnel Management, 1989).

It is also true, however, that the Grace Commission, and other similar oversight bodies, simply begged an important question. They identified a management problem, but presented few concrete hints to explain how the challenges should be addressed. What, after all, is workforce management? Can it be done? How? The answers are not self-evident. Hortatory urgings unaccompanied by clear guidance make only a limited contribution. Indeed, one can appreciate OPM's impatience with well-meaning suggestions that lack specific guidelines for action (U.S. General Accounting Office, 1989, pp. 132–159).

What can be done? One beginning is to compile a list of goals describing what workforce management seeks to achieve. The list would have two parts: goals to be pursued and activities to be avoided. Something like the following list, adapted from a recent federal report (U.S. General Accounting Office, 1989), could represent the goals:

1. Managerially minded offices shall provide overall leadership and future oriented direction.
2. Delegate, where possible, operating personnel decision-making authority in order to let program and mission requirements drive human resource decision making.
3. Workforce management offices shall design performance management systems that link pay, performance, and performance appraisal systems such that the improved performance and productivity of the individual worker are encouraged.
4. Management offices shall engage in planning for future workforce needs and develop strategies for meeting those needs.

Workforce management also implies a list of things *not* to do:

1. Good human resource management does *not* engage in fruitless attempts to gain control over individual personnel decisions since such micro manipulations undermine effective general management aims.
2. Management avoids short-term workforce convulsions designed only to save money in the short term by applying such draconian workforce measures as reductions in force, arbitrary hiring freezes, and downgrades that undermine the morale and effectiveness of the workforce.

Few would disagree with such a standard textbook list. The problem, of course, is to understand what these aims and responsibilities really mean for public-sector managers. How do we provide central and strategic leadership and planning when the basis for decision making has already been delegated to operational organization levels? Specifically, how can leadership, delegation, workforce enhancement, and innovative planning be simultaneously accomplished? How can the impact of budget shifts be absorbed by labor-intensive agencies, other than by workforce cutbacks and other painful convulsions? The challenge is to understand the thinking and work that are required to make true workforce management a possibility. To begin, we must explore the fundamental changes that have affected human resource management and try to understand what those changes mean for managers, both public and private.

Chapter Two

The Rise of
Human Capital Issues in
Public and Private Organizations

The discovery that people are, in their knowledge, skills, and abilities, a source of present and future productivity means that people are more than current charges against productivity, more than simply operational costs to be minimized. It means that people are assets. They are, in their persons, a kind of capital. As a general and theoretical matter, the significance of human capital in explaining differential rates of national economic development has long been noted (Schultz, 1971; Denison, 1967). The most recent evidence is the decline of traditional industries—textiles, paper making, leather goods, wood products— where productivity depends on some combination of natural resources and trained skill of workers with experience manipulating the tools of a particular craft. Evidence is also implied in the rise of research-based industries—petrochemicals, electronics, information processing—where products are derived from organized research, new product invention, and industrial process improvement (Lawrence, 1985).

However, while data tracking the rise and fall of firms, industries, and societies tell us that human capital (HC) exists, it is a difficult commodity to grasp because it is a subtle asset and takes many forms. At its core, HC defines the human capacity to be productive. By definition, an asset locked inside people is distinguished in several ways. First, investments in the stock of HC are invisible but variable. Investments can take many forms: improved selection methodologies, smart recruitment systems, supportive compensation systems, education, on-the-job training, manpower migration, health maintenance, and research and development (R&D) activity (Schultz, 1971). Casual evidence suggests enormous significance of such investments. As just one example, consider training. In private corporations, training and development divisions run corporate education programs that, by one estimate, total $40 billion annually (Carnevale, 1983).

In 1985 IBM made an after-tax profit of $6 billion and spent $2 billion on training; the same year Bell companies reported after-tax profits of $6 billion and spent $2.8 billion on training. Additional illustrations would also include the $79 million Xerox corporate learning center in Leesburg, Virginia, and the $60 million Kodak center in Rochester, New York (Odiorne, 1986).

Second, HC is defined not by the number of available workers, but by what the workers are capable of doing (Schultz, 1971). Worker capability, however, is itself a multifaceted and extremely slippery notion. Theoretical formulations (Becker, 1964; Schultz, 1971; Thurow, 1970) suggest that human capital can be divided into general and specific categories. *General* human capital consists of the knowledge, skills, and abilities (KSAs) that are common to many jobs and employers. *Specific* human capital are the KSAs uniquely preferred and valued by a single employer. In general, the task is to manage the portfolio of KSAs against the changing requirements of jobs designed to fulfill the missions of agencies and corporations. Thus, managers will need to be evaluated not only on the extent to which they meet nominal productivity goals but also on "their stewardship regarding the enhancement of the human capital assigned to them" (Fossum et al., 1986, p. 372).

Third, unlike nonhuman capital, such as land, buildings, and financial assets, human capital is *embodied in people*. It is not a commodity for which property rights are exchanged for payment (Lamberton, 1971; Becker, 1964). It is more correct to say that knowledge and skill are assets distributed under a variety of mechanisms in which the receipt or purchase of an asset in no way reduces the asset for the donor or the seller (Schultz, 1971, p. 48). Knowledge and skill may be destroyed or allowed to deteriorate, but the losses and gains of HC often do not depend on property rights; they depend on flows of information and knowledge. Even the sale of proprietary knowledge (such as trade secrets and patents) involves the reproduction of knowledge and information rather than a transfer of title (Boulding, 1966).

These HC characteristics lead us to several conclusions. For one thing, pricing is difficult (Boulding, 1966). Notwithstanding fees paid for lectures, hot tips, news magazines, and information services, a standard economic unit of knowledge does not yet exist. Except for mechanical systems of intelligence marketed as computer hardware and software, there is no available "bit" or "chunk" to which prices can be attached. Second, it is therefore difficult to give financial meaning to the stocks and flows of human capital, although the accounting profession is beginning to dig into the subject (Flamholtz, 1985). However, the real value of human capital lies not simply in the numbers of information "bits" processed, but in the human capacities and insights enabled by knowledge and information. Thus, human capital definitions must include the human capacity for generating more knowledge and capacity. This is the R&D process, through which old knowledge is constantly being supplanted by new knowledge and new capacities. New capital is internalized and becomes the exclusive property of the individual possessing the understanding, insight, and knowhow (Boulding, 1966).

We thus encounter a third tentative conclusion. Since human capital depends on information exchange, HC is not instantly transferrable; it cannot be conveyed from a seller to a buyer at the precise moment of transaction. It can be acquired only by vesting knowledge and skill in a person *over time* (Sharp, 1981). People cannot be separated from the HC they possess; there can only be a reproduction or sharing of capital (Schultz, 1971). Knowledge codified and stored in a magnetic disk, for example, remains a valueless asset until a human being accesses and stockpiles the value potential locked there. The obvious conclusion from this rule of delayed transfer is that in postindustrial systems, information transfer mechanisms—conferences, publications, communications between personnel—are strategically important. Personnel mobility, for example, facilitates *knowledge* transfers, as distinct from merely transmitting and receiving *information*, simply because the people who know something and the people who need to know that same something can be brought together. Enhanced personnel mobility is therefore one of the fastest ways to grow human capital.

Unlike nonhuman capital stocks, human capital does not become consumed or depreciate with use. Quite to the contrary, it often grows with use—the right kind of use. Human capital can, however, depreciate in two ways: first, idleness and lack of practice time cause human capital to degenerate; second, human capital can become obsolete relative to other knowledge. In the first case, skills deteriorate; that is why SWAT teams, musicians, surgical teams, and aerospace workers require constant practice to keep skills sharp. In the second case, discovery and invention continually redefine knowledge boundaries (Fossum, Arvey, Paradise, and Robbins, 1986). The constant threat of workforce obsolescence and deterioration stands at the core of the current human resource management problem.

Management of Human Capital

Precisely how human capital affects management has never been systematically addressed. Private-sector management analysts are still developing the concepts and frameworks within which the significance of HC can be assessed. One particularly comprehensive attempt to create a map of the human resource management (HRM) territory views HRM decision making as influenced by a series of stakeholder interests and situational factors such as workforce characteristics, business strategy and conditions, management philosophy, labor market, unions, task technology, laws, and societal values. The policy choices of HRM are the pivotal activity in which managers "manage" human resource flows, reward systems, and work systems in order to create desirable short-term and long-term consequences. The short-term consequences consist of the "four Cs": employee *commitment* to work and organization, *competence, cost effectiveness* of policies and HRM practices, and *congruence* between the goals of employees and the goals of organization (Beer and others, 1984). Even though very general, such a map serves as a useful organizing rubric for general managers and scholars. By contrast this book represents an attempt to identify the concrete HRM issues that arise when one focuses on the pivotal activity of HRM decision making. Regardless of the book's ultimate impact, serious private-sector work on the management of "human assets" antedates by several years comparable efforts in the public sector.

The strategic role of HC in *public*-sector HRM has entered active public affairs debate and discussion (Levine, 1985; Grace, 1984) only slowly and in small steps. The public discussion is quiet and confused and is not self-consciously a debate about human capital management. Part of the confusion is that the role of government in the postindustrial order is not well understood. Part derives from the difficulties of workforce management itself. And part has to do with how the link is made between government productivity and the workforce.

On the productivity side, government clearly plays a variety of roles in the emerging "new political economy" (Smith, 1975). Government is a direct service producer: health and welfare services, statistics and information products, research and development, education, parks management, law enforcement, and so forth. It is also an indirect provider when it serves as a regulator, arranger, and supporter of services produced by nongovernmental instrumentalities of public policy. In the first case, government workers produce final services. In the indirect case, government produces intermediate products that make service provision possible; for example, public workforces are often the pillars around which are built elaborate public–private contracting systems, third-party payment for services, and banking mechanisms (Weidenbaum, 1969; Savas, 1987; Seidman and Gilmour, 1986; Kettl, 1988).

If the general productivity role of government is obscure, the specific functions of government personnel can be even more mysterious. One of the complexities is that multiple standards exist for describing the relationship between human resources and productivity. Human resources are typically assessed in terms of three primary dimensions: (1) the final product (sometimes referred to in terms of function or industry); (2) the occupational position, irrespective of the product; or (3) the qualities of knowledge, skill, and ability that reside *within the person* regardless of the product and the position.

Different data are collected, depending on what managers want to know about the workforce. For example, the product view concentrates on the output side of human effort. At an aggregate level of analysis, product data are collected and reported by several government agencies. To illustrate, the Office of Management and Budget's standard industrial classifications (SIC) group the final products produced in the general economy. In the SIC reports, government is treated as a single division—"Public Administration"—that incorporates seven major groups. A more refined description of government products is found in the Bureau of Census reports, which record government employment by function. An examination of those data would show that more than half of the 13 million full-time and part-time state and local government employees work in education. Another 14 percent deliver human services. Roughly 10 percent are employed by police, fire, and highway patrol divisions and in jails and prisons. The remaining 25 percent is spread across a broad array of functions including transportation, environment and housing, local utilities, and other small pockets of employment.

Curiously, less than 7 percent of the state and local government workforce is engaged in central administrative functions (budget, procurement, personnel, planning, finance, auditing). This finding is important because it establishes that government workforces are not bureaucratic in the sense of being staffed by a large layer of administrators who produce only intermediate products; the data show there are not enough of them. Government workforces—teachers, welfare workers, doctors, nurses, transit workers, police, fire fighters, prison guards, sanitation workers, and utility workers—are still, in the main, associated with the production and delivery of final products and services. Measuring the extent to which government arranges for as well as directly produces specific public goods requires an array of employment data (such as a product-by-occupation matrix) that is not now available. Such a data base would have to explore how work is done.

A second primary human resource dimension is occupational, based on positions. Even though no universal definition of "occupation" yet exists, the underlying notion of a standard occupational classification (SOC) incorporates the idea of tasks, duties, and responsibilities inherent in the work processes of the position rather than either the resulting product or the personal characteristics of the occupant. Thus, occupational classification focuses on the work processes of three main categories: labor, trades, and crafts; the administrative, professional, and technical (APT) occupations; and executive, scientific, and managerial occupations.

The third dimension reflects the (KSAs) in *people,* apart from the products produced and tasks performed. It is in this third dimension that the most profound changes have occurred in both government and industry. The rise of knowledge-based industries mandates new skill requirements and a new compensation perspective: people are employed and paid based on professional knowledge and competence that come from trained intelligence. Thus, the real "products" of knowledge-based occupations (the professions) are either the knowledge embedded in "smart" products or services that derive from the knowledge and skill acquired by the worker: physician, lawyer, accountant, scientist, engineer, social worker, or teacher. Productivity does not occur simply because the professional processes fifty cases a day (a task), or files reports (a duty), or directs a staff of some determined size (a responsibility).

Clearly, there are complex blends of product, position,

and person elements in real organizations and a large number of ways to describe what people do. The management task, however, is to establish the relevance of human resources to strategies and organizational goals. For example, in education and training programs, a teaching "position" can be described in terms of tasks and responsibilities associated with managing classes of a given size, writing lesson plans, dispersing curriculum packages, and keeping order. Productivity, defined as the growth of student knowledge, results from "time on task." In effect, teachers so classified administer a process by which students teach themselves.

An alternative conception of productivity might define a teaching position in terms of elements that have nothing to do with those "position" attributes. For example, a teaching position defined in terms of transmitting a knowledge of differential and integral calculus makes the "position" requirements of teaching coterminous with the knowledge and skill contained in the intellect of a formally trained *person*. In this case, productivity results when the minds of the trained teacher and the student interact over time and knowledge is transmitted from one brain to another. In effect, the performance of bureaucratically prescribed "position" attributes—managing, writing, dispersing, keeping—may be important but not strategic to the core business of instruction. A third alternative—the most difficult one to identify precisely—is to define the work system as a blend of product, position, and personal elements; clearly, there are many ways to connect the work of people to the productivity of enterprise.

All examples are classified as an educational "function" by U.S. statistical agencies. Yet they represent alternative means of producing the final product and establish different human resource requirements. In the second example, personnel operations focus on the personal expertise and skill of the math teacher. In the first, personnel operations focus on the performance of tasks. In the third, a combination of elements defines the work system. In any case, determining whether the position-based definition, the person-based definition, or some combination is most appropriate is a policy decision that drives the rest of human resource management. Many government white-collar jobs and some blue-collar jobs—engineers, mathematicians, accountants, foresters, computer hardware technicians, and so forth—are subject to this kind of policy decision. The final determination depends on whether the end product is defined as a knowledge product produced by government personnel, a performance of tasks associated with teaching, managing the work of others, or some combination of elements.

In postindustrial societies, however, much of this mystery is removed. The production of knowledge-intensive products and the use of automated production processes expand dramatically the employment based on knowledge, skill, and abilities of *persons*. This is implied in the rise of a service-based economy. It is particularly implied in the production of knowledge and information products that, by definition, can be derived only from intellectually trained personnel. Indeed, in the case of R&D products, knowledge *is* the product. Another way to reinforce this key point is to note that without relevant human capital, productivity does not and cannot occur, even though people may be fully employed in an energetic performance of tasks, duties, and responsibilities.

Government as Postindustrial Workforce

The extent to which government service delivery is representative of postindustrial production systems has never been examined. As we have seen, to measure accurately the product–position–person mix requires statistical reporting not now available for any level of government. Some clues can be gleaned from available sources. For example, the Bureau of Census collects data that relate the 13 million state and local employees to the "product mix" of more than 82,000 units of local government. The clear majority of state and local employment is potentially knowledge-based work, depending on work system design. For example, over 65 percent of employment is classified as producing education, health, and welfare "products." These areas are dominated by human service professionals whose basis for service is what they know and are capable of doing based on mastery of a knowledge base.

Federal employment data are more accessible, but only partially digestible. For example, the data are not organized according to major product lines. Nor is the federal personnel classification system of "series" and "groups" amenable to an occupational ordering of employment data (McGregor, 1985). One clue about the knowledge-intensive nature of federal employment is found by recording the employment that produces knowledge products. This can be done by counting employment in R&D agencies, where new knowledge and knowhow are the products, and agencies whose chief products include statistics, analysis, and information services.

One study scanned the distribution of federal employment across all bureaus and agencies whose basic product could be easily defined as a pure "knowledge product" (McGregor, 1988). The scan yielded a count of ten departments other than State and Defense where significant employment was claimed by operating "civilian bureaus" producing knowledge products. For example, over 61 percent of the Department of Commerce falls in this category in such bureaus as Bureau of Census, National Oceanographic and Atmospheric Administration, Patent and Trademark Office, National Bureau of Standards (the title at the time of the study), and the National Telecommunications and Information Administration. In addition, at least six independent civilian agencies (for example, National Aeronautics and Space Administration) could be characterized as knowledge agencies. When the total employment leveraged by knowledge products in the non–national security agencies was added up, it came to over 120,000 people, or more than 11 percent of the total 1986 federal civilian workforce not employed by national security and diplomacy agencies. The point is that significant portions of the federal workforce produce *only* knowledge.

The scan both underestimated and overestimated the extent to which knowledge work characterizes federal productivity. The underestimation occurs because many line production agencies *not* included in the scan provide "smart" products and services: engineers in the civilian corps of the Army Corps of Engineers, lawyers and accountants in the Federal Bureau of Investigation, linguists and computer programmers in the National Security Agency, historians in the National Park Service, foresters in the Forestry Service, and so forth. The overestimation occurs because not all employees employed in the identified ten departments and six independent agencies work in knowledge *occupations*. Many employees at even the most sophisticated R&D facilities must provide security, clean the buildings, cut the grass, perform routine support tasks and duties. While it is true that many support functions can be contracted out, it is a safe bet that many of the employees in the federal departments and agencies covered in the scan were performing less than high-tech work. This conclusion, however, is an *occupational* speculation about the skill mix of persons required to produce final *products*. Only a personnel information system that accurately distinguishes among classes of products, positions, and persons can establish the extent to which knowledge-intensive *products* also employ people in "low-tech" *positions* and the extent to which low-tech *products* require high-tech skills (a characteristic of *persons*), such as might be required to design and maintain sophisticated production and distribution systems.

Notwithstanding these estimation problems, the scan clearly reveals that knowledge production consumes a measurable share of federal civilian employment—by simple count, well over 11 percent of the federal workforce. In some cases, such as the departments of Commerce and Energy, the vast majority of the workforce produces *only* knowledge products. The quality of the products derives directly from the human capital stored in a largely professional workforce. In other words, the management of human capital and the management of the final product are one and the same.

The government employment pattern is not static, although government workforces have traditionally employed large numbers of knowledge workers. For example, as early as 1960, federal, state, and local government employed 16 percent of the national labor force. Approximately two-fifths of the government workforce (including teachers) were employed in administrative, professional, and technical (APT) occupations—twice the ratio of the total labor force. The rich occupational mix has meant that government could employ only a much smaller portion of labor, trades and crafts, machine operatives, farmers, and miners than the rest of the economy (National Manpower Council, 1964).

The federal workforce appears to be the most knowledge intensive of the government workforces and has become increasingly sophisticated. For example, white-collar employment—APT and clerical occupations—covered over 40 percent of a federal labor force of 2.4 million civilians in 1957 and 50 percent of a labor force of 2.8 million employees in 1977 (Couturier and others, 1979, chap. 10). Within this broad transition, however, even more dramatic changes have occurred. For instance, during a time when total federal employment rose only 17 percent, the employment of clerical personnel declined while dramatic increases occurred in the following areas (Rosen, 1985, pp. 24–28):

Lawyers: up 54.9 percent from 1968 to 1980
Social service, psychology, and welfare: up 78.9 percent from 1968 to 1980
Medical, hospital, dental and public health: up 40.3 percent from 1968 to 1980
Computer specialists: up more than 60 percent from 1960 to 1980
Engineers: up 60 percent from 1960 to 1980

The federal workforce is highly professionalized by comparison to the national distribution of occupations. For example, in 1980 100,000 federal engineers accounted for nearly 4 percent of total federal employment, while 257,000 engineers employed in the private service (nonmanufacturing) sector accounted for less than .5 percent of total national employment (Rosen, 1985, p. 27).

In briefest terms, the rise of human capital in public production systems establishes that public workforces are strategic assets rather than mere operational inputs with costs to be managed by the administrative routines of budgeting and personnel. A corollary is that human resources belong on the balance sheet of enterprise, where assets and liabilities are compared, as well on the current income and expenses accounts where people are traditionally classified as an operating cost (Odiorne, 1984; Flamholtz, 1985). Public and private enterprises have been slow to convert human capital into acceptable standards of human resources accounting (Odiorne, 1984, p. 8; Flamholtz, 1985), but that does not destroy the power of the human capital insight.

Strategic Management of a Strategic Resource

A significant puzzle remains, however. In discussions of resource management, the term "strategic" has multiple uses. One interpretation refers to the *strategic management* of an important resource. Another refers to the management of a *strategic* resource. A third interpretation refers to the *strategic management* of a *strategic* resource—S^2 in our terminology. Each interpretation introduces a different range of problems, but the "double strategic" forms the essence of workforce management.

Strategic Management of the Workforce. Strategic management has a literature too vast to track here. What is interesting is that the appearance of a literature on strategic human resource management (Odiorne, 1984; Fombrun, Tichy, and Devanna, 1984; Douglas, Klein, and Hunt, 1985) roughly parallels the realization that management in turbulent environments requires a reexamination of the basic purposes and missions underlying modern organizations. Both public and private American managers have been confronting the vulnerabilities of global recession and economic turbulence, competitive threats, shifting client demands, and uncertainty about the premises of organizational existence. The strategic management of human resources has ridden in on the discovery that human resources are a critical piece of the strategic thinking required to revive the competitiveness of public and private organizations (Fombrun, Tichy, and Devanna, 1984, chaps. 1–3; Douglas, Klein, and Hunt, 1985, chap. 4).

How does the strategic management approach help us think about workforce management? There is not a single strategic model. On the contrary, there are several. One approach, for example, leads to a strategic view of "the human resource cycle" (Devanna, Fombrun, and Tichy, 1984, pp. 33–51). Strategic managers are exhorted to take a long-term, design-oriented view of corporate and agency selection, appraisal, rewards, and development systems. The result is an attempt to integrate personnel operations with overall strategic planning and management.

A second perspective treats the problem as the management of a capital asset portfolio (Odiorne, 1984). In this analysis the critical task is to make strategic investment decisions that maximize the growth of human capital. High-performing "stars" and "workhorses" must be identified and given proper investments of training and development. By contrast, "problem employees" and "dead wood" must be weeded out, although the how and where of the weeding are left to the reader's imagination.

Yet a third approach (Douglas, Klein, and Hunt, 1985) takes as a point of departure the multiple-role perspective. This multifaceted examination of human resources is required when managers attempt to achieve a strategic fit between the external environment and internal deployments of resources. The ability to view human resources from the competing perspectives of the chief executive, the personnel director, the employee, the shop steward, the first line supervisor, and the financial manager enables managers to establish links between strategic, tactical, and operational levels of management.

Regardless of the approach adopted, the strategic workforce management agenda (see Figure 2.1) clearly goes far beyond the bounds of traditional personnel operations, defined by the details of what one author calls the "human resource cycle" (Devanna, Fombrun, and Tichy, 1984). It also ties the management of people directly to strategic planning (Nkomo, 1988; Walker, 1980) and the cultivation of workforces that can somehow be harnessed to productivity goals. At a more operational level, this means managing the *availability* of people (the supply side) by managing the human resource cycle—selection, performance appraisal, compensation and rewards, and training and development—in ways that meet the operating *requirements* (the demand side) of enterprise programs, productivity goals, and resource constraints.

There is a short way to summarize the discussion: The essence of strategic workforce management is to make the right people available in the right place at the right time. This is a simple statement with a powerful set of implications, to be explored in subsequent chapters. First, the strategic view envisions the continuous experimentation and redesign of whole parts of operating personnel systems in the interest of achieving productive balances of personnel requirements and availability. This involves multiple roles associated with line man-

Figure 2.1. Strategic Human Resource Management.

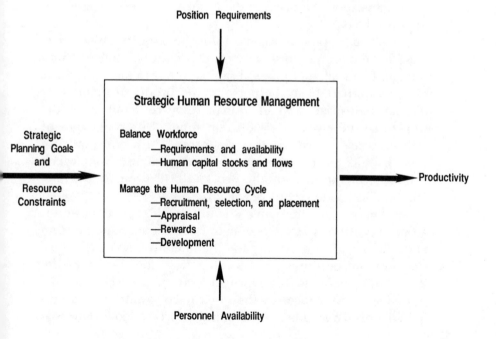

agement, resource allocation (budgeting), position design and management, and personnel management. It also involves the guardianship of both stocks and flows of human capital. In short, the strategic management problem is to manage a whole workforce by managing the interactions among goals and resource constraints, position requirements, personnel availability, and final products.

Management of a Strategic Resource. Strategic workforce management is very different, however, from the management of a *strategic* resource. In the former case, the concern is with discerning the effects of environmental change (the strategic environment) on human resource policies and programs; no presumption exists about the relative importance of human resources to strategy except agreement that human resources are a nontrivial, complex resource that must be managed over the long haul to achieve desired productivity. In the latter case, however, people become *the* resource without which productivity becomes impossible. Put another way, the strategic goals of the organization are fused to the human capital that generates final products.

When do people become a *strategic* resource? When they cease to be mere production inputs that must be combined with human, financial, and physical capital inputs to make products that stand apart from the persons who produced them. Traditional industrial views of human resources would view the workforce merely as a production input. Different types of personnel are joined to other resources in a production process that fits people to preestablished positions from which products, or outputs, result (Brock, 1984; *Scientific American,* 1982). This is one way to view Figure 2.1.

There is an alternative way to view the figure, however. In postindustrial systems people can become inseparable from both the production process and the final product itself. Thus, the position, personnel, and productivity domains of Figure 2.1 become increasingly congruent. This occurs when *knowing something* is simultaneously the input (labor available to do required work), *and* either the production process (knowhow that understands how to produce the product) or the final product itself (a "smart" output), or both. Precisely when do workforces become strategically important resources? To repeat, the second strategic meaning exists whenever humans cease to be production inputs only and become inseparable from either the production process or the final product. This occurs in two ways: any time the "product" is a knowledge-based product, and any time production depends on a "smart" production process. Examples abound and are summarized in Table 2.1.

In this meaning of "strategic," human capital cannot be separated from the output because people *are the product*. This obviously occurs in research and development organizations where new knowledge and invention exist as understanding and knowhow possessed by the researcher or by those to whom the researcher passes knowledge and information. Another example of the fusion of final product to human capital is found in the many capacity-building programs achieved through workforce training and development. In effect, the product is a readiness condition in which people know how to deal with a threat or problem; in the public sector, much of national security, emergency preparedness, and economic recession safety-net activity depends on trained readiness. A third example of the congruence of human capital and final product is found in knowledge-intensive human services; public health, education, and social service are all instances of a final product being defined by, respectively, a health professional's diagnostic skill, the teacher's subject-matter competence, or the social worker's knowledge of community support networks.

In a second set of cases, human resources are strategic because people are used to develop "smart" production processes. People are strategic in instances where the speed of learning provides a significant advantage in meeting competitive threats and capturing markets (Belkaoui, 1986; Comfort, 1985). People are strategic to production processes when they are used to develop mechanized production systems, such as applying artificial intelligence to public services (Karna, 1985; Hadden, 1986). Finally, people can be strategic to operations processes when interruptions in production are required to accommodate the product to client need; examples are found in job-shop services where, for instance, social services might be tailored to meet individual client needs and requirements. Smart job-shop production stands in contrast to line operations production, where cases are processed only with regard to categorical formulas that can often be automated (Rosenthal, 1982), as in the case of formula-disbursed employment security checks.

The organizational effects of these two meanings of "strategic" are not well understood. In both cases, human resources are strategic to goal attainment. However, the financial flows, balance sheets, and ratios of payrolls to total operating costs are different. In the first case (labeled "HR as both input and output" in Table 2.1), it would appear that salary costs will be high both by comparison to the general labor force and as a proportion of total operating costs. Yet, were a balance sheet to be constructed, extraordinarily rich assets would be revealed. For example, board-certified health professionals producing billable treatments generate many times their salaries in income earned by the institution that employs them. Or, to take another example, scientists and engineers whose creative R&D abilities generate grants and contracts that not only pay for themselves, but justify the existence of whole facilities founded on discovery and invention. And if their work leads to new product development, then the value of the human asset becomes the value of whatever spinoffs occur discounted by the probability that they will succeed. One conclusion, therefore, is that the value of human assets in the first category is many times the salary expenditure, no matter how high.

In the public sector, there is another accounting problem, for in many cases the *public* value of the human asset vastly exceeds normal private-sector accounting methods of valuation. Indeed, current financial management methods vastly underestimate the real value of the public workforce. The results can be bizarre. For example, readiness is a productive potential stored within trained personnel who know what to do when a given emergency arises. The value of that resource is seen by comparing the trained asset to the obverse—*not* knowing what to do, or even worse, not knowing how to find out

Table 2.1. Human Resources as Strategic Resource.

Production Stage	Examples	Illustrations
Human resources as both input and output	Research (for example, new knowledge)	National Institutes of Health, space and earth sciences labs
	Development (for example, prototypes)	New satellites; new serums
	Training and development	Readiness, preparedness
	Knowledge-intensive services	Health, education, social services
Human resources as "smart" production process	Learning curve	Aircraft procurement
	Automated production	
	Intelligent job-shop production	Permit issuance
		Human services

what to do. The specter of a human asset that erroneously launches nuclear-tipped missiles, cannot predict weather accurately, cannot respond to natural disaster emergencies, and so forth, helps establish the strategic value of human resources. Thus, in some cases such as readiness and security, the value of a public workforce can equal the total value of the entity being protected. Indeed, in theory there is nothing that society would not invest to train people to make the correct decisions on society's most severe challenges.

A different picture emerges where people run "smart" production processes (see the "HR as smart process" category in Table 2.1). The ability of people to learn, automate production systems, and develop intelligent and increasingly fast reactions to case management in a job-shop production situation are all examples. In many cases, smart production systems produce a declining claim on the aggregate share of operations costs assigned to personnel services. This is because the wage bill leverages ever-increasing levels of productivity. Thus, pay levels for personnel can be dramatically increased—the case of highly automated production systems is a classic illustration—

because the productivity value of a comparatively small and smart workforce is high relative to current cost (The Roosevelt Center, 1987).

The value of the production process asset is different from the first case, where the value of the final outcome (discovery, new products, readiness, and the like) derives directly from human capital that is *both* input and output. In the case of smart production processes, the value of the human asset is fixed by the extent to which the process adds value to final products. If marginal process improvements leverage large productivity increases, the value of human resources as a process asset increases enormously. Attempts to change the slopes of learning curves or produce "smart" production systems have large potential payoffs. Indeed, in the expert systems applications, the payoffs that can accrue to intelligent knowledge engineering are huge.

The Case of the Double Strategic

There is logically a third meaning of strategic human resource management: strategic management of a strategic resource (S^2). The S^2 condition obtains whenever public managers attempt to manage strategically a workforce in which human capital is *both* a strategic input to production and *either* a strategic component in the production process, *or* an output, *or* both. In the first case, people design automated systems of production, including intelligent systems that can respond to general environmental turbulence and the demand for product variety. In the second case, a workforce can be employed in situations where intelligence is built into products. Finally, there is the merged situation, where the same human capital is at once all three dimensions; for example, in research the human capacity for original insight and discovery (input) leads to research discovery (process) from which new knowledge is produced (the output). In the last case, the product either exists in the human mind or is written down to be understood only by people who *know* the significance of what they are looking at.

When and how can managers engage in S^2 management? The simple answer is that whenever the strategic aims of a public agency or corporation depend on the human capital requirements enumerated above, S^2 management is a requirement. When do such conditions obtain? More often than managers traditionally recognize! Consider the following illustrations:

- When the "product" shifts from time-on-task to a knowledge-based service, such as health, education, social service, and research and development (Drucker, 1968).
- When prisons, mental illness, and mental retardation facilities shift from custodial, chronic-care service to acute-care provision or "active treatments" required by courts and third-party reimbursement systems.
- When knowledge-intensive scientific and technical excellence must be maintained as a means of controlling programs developed by a contractual workforce (Trento, 1987).
- When managing personnel transitions in high-technology enterprises is the key to the retention and development of high skill levels in human resources (Niehaus, 1985).
- When a combination of digital communications skills and computing is a requirement of agency strategy (Keen, 1986), either for using telecommunications for competitive advantage or for implementing large-scale public programs in which dense streams of data are generated among public service arrangers, providers, payers, and clients.
- When the slope of a learning curve is essential to program success, for example in the ability to react to special circumstances, design and routinize new production technologies, or acquire products and services from contractors (Belkaoui, 1986).

There is, in short, no shortage of opportunities for an S^2 approach to human resources. How public managers might begin to address the problem is discussed in the next three sections of the book.

Summary

The challenge facing those who would be strategic human resource managers—workforce managers, in our terminology—is substantial. The task of making the right people available at the right time to do the right things appears simple, but it poses a number of seemingly insurmountable obstacles, of which one is the sheer complexity of the problem. It becomes clear that the key to meeting the challenge is to understand the four basic subproblems that affect human resource management, as implied in Figure 2.1. One set consists of the demand-side requirements for human resources posed by public policy. The second set consists of the supply-side identification and management of those human attributes strategic to productivity. The third set consists of managing the strategic planning goals and resource constraints that limit the choices available to public managers. Finally, there must be a way to convert strategic choices into the level of operational detail required by personnel systems such that human resource management targets and goals can be met. Chapter Three shows what a strategic workforce management logic entails.

PART TWO

THE WORKFORCE MANAGEMENT LOGIC: BALANCING SUPPLY AND DEMAND FOR HUMAN KNOWLEDGE, SKILLS, AND ABILITIES

The challenge of the "double strategic" is met by developing a logic that connects general management strategy to operations decision making on both the requirements and availability sides of the workforce management problem. Availability is the supply side of the logic and is generally governed by the employment system created to manage human resources. Requirements—the demand side of the equation—are developed through policy decisions and operational strategy. Workforce management involves the purposeful reconciliation of requirements and availability.

Chapter Three

Connecting
Strategic Decision Making
to Operations

Understanding the productivity demands of strategy and policy as they affect the workforce forms the heart of workforce management. The S^2 agenda, particularly, means that all human resource managers must learn to think systematically about the many connections between strategy and people. Governmental strategy imposes a further complexity, however, because public policy also requires democratic accountability and control. The democratic policy process is particularly demanding in requiring public managers to accept the constitutional and political constraints placed on decision making and to respond to public inquiry about the uses to which employees are put, their costs, and their personal characteristics.

Accountability patterns vary with the constitutional and political structures of federal, state, and local governments, but the general U.S. pattern involves a fragmented executive structure caused by checks and balances systems. Fragmentation also characterizes a political process that works against convenient centralization of human resource information. Thus, even if it were desirable to impose a corporate structure on government operations, the political process would make it impossible in all but the most unusual circumstances. The realities of politics and public management, in short, pose enormous challenges for those who would be workforce managers, in addition to the normal "managerial" and organizational challenges that are already difficult enough. Indeed, in the minds of many a case-hardened public practitioner, the idea of strategic public-sector human resource management may well be an oxymoron.

What We Know About the Subject

Where does one turn to learn how to perform workforce management, let alone public-sector workforce management? The obvious source is the personnel management literature that details how people in large organizations are managed. Personnel texts are legion. Collectively they cover personnel administration in both the public and private sectors in great detail. They embrace a diversity of approaches and perspectives grounded in a seemingly endless array of specialized knowledge, techniques, and approaches.

For all the seeming diversity, however, there is a remarkable underlying constancy in the personnel administration literature. Regardless of founding definitions, all texts and related personnel office practices are concerned with the policies, procedures, techniques, and theories that describe actions taken by organizations *on individuals*. Thus, virtually all texts devote whole chapters to the problems of recruitment, selection, performance appraisal, compensation, training and development, employee discipline, supervision, job design, and labor relations. Since the dominant unit of analysis in the personnel literature is the individual worker and groups of individuals organizationally bound for some productive purpose, personnel administration has been traditionally preoccupied with the *supply* of human resources and the actions that affect the availability of supply.

A second pattern, notable by the rare exceptions, is that personnel management refers to the repetitive procedures through which "personnelists" recruit, select, train, appraise, compensate, develop, and discipline a labor force. Figure 3.1 groups the myriad personnel functions and actions in terms of four categories: staffing and employment, appraising and com-

Figure 3.1. Personnel Operations and Functions.

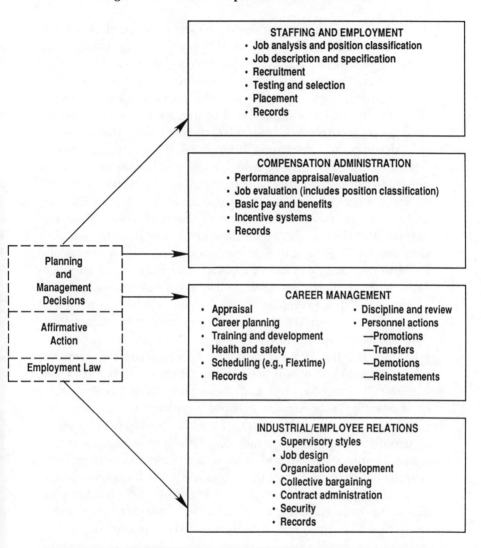

Source: Adapted from Peterson, R. B., Tracy, L., and Cabelly, A., 1979.

pensating performance, career management, and employee relations.

In short, the vast majority of the personnel literature centers on descriptions and prescriptions for the conduct of what we shall refer to here as "personnel operations." Yet, what is managerial about personnel operations? Administration of a staff function is clearly very different from line management of an enterprise. The latter exists to oversee the production of final goods and services desired by customers and clients *outside* the organization. Personnel operations, by contrast, are designed to satisfy an *internal* constituency and consist of the myriad transactions and practices that define the relationship between an organization and its individual employees. Public and private organizations are identical in this distinction. What remains unfinished is the establishment of how it is that the design and management of internal operations affects the capacity of organizations to satisfy external constituencies—and vice versa—whose purchases and sponsorships sustain the organization in the first instance.

We begin with a basic axiom: managers are most fundamentally concerned with solving problems that stand in the way of achieving organizational purposes. Problems acquire strategic, tactical, or operational significance depending on whether they involve matters of organizational purpose or survival (strategy), the design of operating systems and the deployment of resources (tactics), or the day-to-day management of production systems (operations). Thus, the *managerial* interest in people goes beyond traditional personnel actions—recruitment, selection, training, and so forth. Such actions merely affect the *supply* of personnel by determining the availability of people to do work and their motivation to perform. The more fundamental managerial issue is to establish the human *requirements* of organizations and finding ways to bring personnel requirements and supplies into balance. This is the goal of workforce management: to establish the most fundamental strategic and tactical design constraints within which personnel operations are conducted. These are general management choices. Thus, *workforce management decisions* are made about organizational goals and objectives, the instruments of production, the allocation of resources, organizational and personnel system design, and the organizational processes through which workforce decisions are made. Such decisions establish the choices available to personnel operations. Indeed, they make the vast majority of personnel operations decisions.

Differences Between the Public and Private Sector

The discussion cannot proceed far without an acknowledgment of the similarities and differences that characterize public and private human resource management. At a theoretical level, the workforce management logic and the administrative division of labor are similar for the two sectors. The general workforce management task is to engineer a balance of workforce requirements with the availability of personnel, in effect to balance supply and demand, although the use of formal economic terms is not precisely descriptive of the management problem. In one sense, the balancing act is axiomatic: requirements and availability are an identity and, over the long term, *will* equate just as certainly as supply, one way or another, *will* equal demand. The management problem, however, is to achieve the equation on terms compatible with strategic organizational goals. George Bernard Shaw's wry comment that "we either get what we like or like what we get" suggests the problem confronting all management decision makers.

A second similarity is that the issue of balancing requirements and availability goes beyond simply managing human resource flows. Supportive cultures, employee commitment, multidisciplinary teams, high levels of motivation, and strategically designed reward systems are all potential parts of the package. For example, if the statistically correct number of unmotivated people, incapable of working on a team, shows up on the availability side of the ledger when the strategic requirement is for a more highly committed and cooperative workforce, then the workforce equation is out of balance. Workforce management will have to contend with all the variables to deliver acceptable final results (Beer and others, 1984).

A third similarity is that in the general management logic, operating personnel systems are the *dependent* variable. Personnel systems that cannot meet the strategic requirements of the organization are candidates for overhaul, regardless of how operationally smooth they might otherwise be. Both public and private management are confronting the need to move away from overweaning management systems that do not enhance productivity. There has been slow, but growing, recognition of this problem in the public sector. For example, explicit recognition was given in the formulation of the Civil Service Reform Act of 1978 (Campbell, 1978) and in the general management reviews of federal personnel management (U.S. General Accounting Office, 1989). James E. Colvard, former deputy director of the Office of Personnel Management, put the problem this way (1987, p. 3): "In the past, the personnel system became the staff function tail that wagged the dog in terms of decision making about the work force in the federal sector. The line manager, while accountable for the work output, de facto has the administrative process, as interpreted by personnelists, make the management decisions for him or her. This was not an insidious plot of any kind and in fact worked amazingly well considering the obtuse process, which is a very positive commentary on the dedication of the personnelists of the federal government, and the persistence of federal line managers. But much greater productivity and efficiency could be achieved if so much energy were not required to deal with the administrative system but rather could be focused on work accomplishment."

There is also some evidence that both government and industry are moving away from the heavy-handed "paper entrepreneurialism" that characterizes rigid bureaucratic operations (Reich, 1983). Aggressive managers, particularly those managing technologically advanced firms and agencies, have moved to break up monolithic organizational and personnel systems that stifle innovation. In the private sector, for example, many corporations maintain only skeletal staffs that preside over conglomerate activities. Small central staffs are charged with external finance, corporate relations, information processing, and a nominal amount of corporate planning. Real management power and responsibility reside with managers of subsidiary divisions, who are given great latitude in designing and operating independent profit and cost centers. The test of management excellence is in productivity and performance and not in the elegance and uniformity of large operating systems. In effect, management and administrative operations are driven by corporate goals and performance objectives. Personnel systems are designed to suit the productive needs of operating line managers, who do not waste time and resources sustaining unwieldy and unproductive administrative operations.

Less well recognized is that much of government has been managed in a stylistically similar manner. For one thing, line departments are really nothing more than holding companies presiding over a diverse portfolio of missions, agencies, and bureaus (Seidman and Gilmour, 1986). The centers of management decision making and productive action are the bureaus, regulatory boards, and public authorities and corporations and their constituent field centers and institutes. Second, as in the private sector, public-sector firms operate against goals and objectives. That public-service goals do not include making a profit on invested capital is not a denial of purposeful activity. It simply means that other goals and strategies inform decision making (Bragaw, 1980). It means, too, that line public managers possess an increasingly strong hand in establishing the operating systems that meet their productivity needs.

Despite these similar logics and organizational generalities, there are important differences between the two sectors, and they affect how the workforce management problem can be approached. The literature codifying possible differences and similarities is extensive both in general terms (Murray, 1975; Rainey, Backoff, and Levine, 1976; Allison, 1979; Perry and Kraemer, 1983) and in terms of human resource management (Brock, 1984, chap. 1; Meyer, 1983, chap. 1). Three particular distinctions emerge in nearly every discussion.

First, the "public culture" of democratic politics exposes management practice to a level of scrutiny unknown in the private sector. The "fishbowl" effect is particularly burdensome because of the demands for information about the workforce and all other aspects of public management that may be posed by the press, interest groups, courts, regulatory bodies, and legislative investigation and inquiry. Serious requests for information cannot be ignored. The structure of politics in the United States encourages visibility, and laws, such as the federal Freedom of Information Act and state and local "sunshine" laws, exist in plentiful array through which public information can be pulled from public bureaucracies.

Second, "management" in the public sector is not subject to a corporate definition that coheres in the office of the chief executive. The task of public management is constitutionally divided among multiple actors, each of whom holds a key to the human resource management puzzle and each of whom constrains the choices that may be made. The practical result is that public managers are required to manage agencies and programs under circumstances where budget and accounting systems, organizational structures, procurement requirements, and civil service operations are not under their full control. Furthermore, often legislatures and central control agencies are dealt a very strong hand in the design and operation of public management systems. The result is a deliberate diffusion of authority based on principles of political design rather than management choice. The fragmented executive and managerial structure stands as a permanent institutional feature of the public landscape.

The third distinction lies in the different meanings of policy. "Strategy" in the private sector refers to business policy and the pattern of choices that promote basic goals of the firm. Private-sector strategic management involves aligning the internal structures and processes of the firm with the challenges, threats, and opportunities in the environment. Should a fast-food franchise looking for new markets develop a new product line? Should a department store chain develop a customer service orientation as a way of increasing market share? In public management, however, strategy is directly tied to public policy. Strategic public management involves the collective welfare of whole populations. This is a high-stakes exercise. Public management mistakes are reckoned not in failed firms and disappointed stockholders, but in the failure of services that whole publics do not receive and in the collective threats or lost opportunities endured by all.

The Meaning of Strategy

Notwithstanding public complexities, what is interesting about public management is that complex goal determinations are, in fact, made (Bragaw, 1980; Webb, 1969; Held, 1982). Strategic planning, often of a very high order, does go on at all levels of government. Most of it occurs at the bureau and agency level, however, not at a governmentwide management level. Furthermore, the connection between strategic planning and the public workforce is most often forged from the requirements side of workforce management rather than the availability side. Only rarely does supply create its own demand. Present-day U.S. health care, where the mere availability of new specialists and procedures creates a demand for treatment, stands as perhaps one example of the exceptional case that proves the rule.

The workforce management problem, then, is to give operational meaning to the idea that it involves making the right people available in the right place at the right time. This leads, in turn, to several more questions. In the first place, what is right? People currently employed in a given organization at a particular time do not necessarily constitute "rightness." For example, public schools, universities, research centers, and businesses are forever discovering that their employee skill mix does not match the changing requirements of the competitive marketplace (Butterfield, 1989). If goals, missions, and final products producing desired outcomes constitute rightness, where do people fit in? This is "the rightness problem."

A second implication occurs in defining what about "people" is important—"the people problem." There are, after all, many possibilities. One is that it is the skills, abilities, and intellectual capacities inside the human being that are important; people are needed for themselves. Another possibility is that it is not really *individuals* who are critical but the tasks, duties, and responsibilities they perform. A third possibility is that what is needed are technologies by which work is done, in which case people are functionally necessary as the operators of an automated process. A fourth is that people are needed not as individuals, but as participants in a collective entity that forms a productive system; what is needed, in other words, is a team.

Rightness is also constrained by the resources available. Do adequate resources exist? Can public managers afford the preferred strategy by which the right people are made available at the right time? Are there cheaper alternatives? The third problem consists of coping with the resource constraints, which is "the budget problem."

Fourth, if the people required by policy goals are not already available, what actions are required? Personnel managers must somehow devise ways to manage individual people in ways that bring demand and supply for human resources into balance. As noted, the tendency to balance is axiomatic; in the long run, effective supply *will* equal effective demand. The problem is to engineer the correct balance. This is "the personnel management problem."

Fifth, we confront the problem of timing. People must be available at the right time. In stable and unthreatening environments, missed timing is awkward but generally not catastrophic; things simply get done a little late. In turbulent situations, however, the strategic environment changes, and the corresponding definition of productivity is also affected. Firms and agencies either hit or miss markets and opportunities for productivity. Early and late arrivals are not merely awkward, they are strategic blunders. When the productivity windows are open and missed, nothing is produced. This is referred to as "the timing problem."

The final problem is the most daunting. Suppose there is agreement in principle about goals, constraints, timing, and the role of people, how does the job get done? The mechanism by which right people, right place, and right time are joined still remains a mystery. Is it an automatic mechanism managed by some invisible hand, by which people simply know when to show up and work? Or is "rightness" brought about by an overt act of management and, if so, what instruments and methods are used? This is "the implementation problem." Because it is such a complex subject, the implementation discussion is deferred until the last section of the book. The first five issues are discussed in greater detail.

The Rightness Problem. What do people produce? Connecting productivity to people is tricky business. People are important because they are the vehicle for human achievement. As we saw in Chapter Two, sometimes people are mere inputs to the production process, and sometimes they *are* the final product itself. In all cases, however, the significance of people to production is determined by the goals and purposes that justify concerted effort. The implication of this question is that a formal connection does exist between purpose and people, but it normally occurs on the demand side rather than the supply side—the opposite side from the focus of traditional personnel administration. In the public sector, for example, the link between public policy and human resource management is simple and direct: public policy commitments create missions and activities that *require,* in turn, the skills and faithful efforts of people.

A few simple illustrations of the demand-side nature of "rightness" will suffice to show the direct link between public policy goals and the human resource management agenda. When government decides that a competitive push must be made to advance the state of the art in aerospace, an array of sophisticated scientific and technical skills comes into sharp demand; when the space effort is cut back, human resource managers must deal with adjustments in the demand for the same skills. When government accepts the challenge of stimulating economic growth in depressed parts of the country, entrepreneurial and marketing skills are required. If public policy moves in the direction of pumping capital through various banking mechanisms into the construction of homes, offices, and central city rehabilitation, then investment, insurance, and real estate skills are required. Finally, if public policy expands entitlement programs, then skills associated with computerized check-disbursement systems are in demand. Note that the existence of a clearly defined goal and mission simply establishes that some kind of work must be done by someone in order to reach a desired end. How people become involved is answered only when one arrays the availability side of the challenge (the people side) against the tasks, activities, and skills required to make the products that represent productivity.

The People Problem. Why are people important to the implementation of policy? There are many possibilities. One is that people are valued for the products they produce. The work of guarding prisoners, coining money, meeting social work clients, treating patients, and building satellites are all examples of one definition of why people are highly prized: because of their functional role in producing some final product. Another possible answer is that people are important because of what they do. In other words, people are prized in terms of how they spend their time, which might be defined in terms of patients treated, streets patrolled, goods produced, and services provided. In this case, people are hired for the things they do to occupy their time as found, for example, in the positions that they hold, the tasks they perform, and the responsibilities they discharge. The repetitive performance of tasks enables the production of desired outcomes.

Yet a third dimension by which people become important is the knowledge, skill, and abilities they possess. This is particularly important where knowledge-intensive technology is strategic to the final outcome. For example, if government regulates the release of effluents into streams, then technically trained inspectors are required to detect illegal releases; environmental protection depends on *knowing* when illegal releases have occurred. If the public guarantee of pension plans against default remains a government goal (as in the case of Earned Retirement Income Security Act), then successful management of a pension benefit guarantee corporation requires employees who understand actuarial mathematics and are able to measure accurately the risks and costs involved in public assump-

tion of pension plans in danger of default. If, in a third example, public policy seeks to monitor world crop production
by remote sensing instruments mounted on planes and satellites, program success depends on skills involving satellite engineering, remote sensing design and production, computer
programming to convert spacial distributions of digitized
telemetry into maps, and a knowledge of agronomy sufficient
to convert spacial distributions of crop signatures into intelligible crop estimates. In all these examples, what is important
and "right" about people are the attributes of intelligence,
training, and ability in the individual worker.

In essence, then, there are many things about people that
make them potentially productive and useful. They can be
functionally useful because of the products they produce. They
can be necessary for the performance of tasks, duties, and responsibilities. They can be useful because of what they know.
Or they can be useful for some combination of all three dimensions. Determining which of these factors is strategic for
productivity, however, is a function of a policy implementation
design that determines precisely how public goals and people
are to be linked. We will return to this problem.

The Budget Problem. Can government afford to pay the people
needed to achieve public policy goals? The link between budgeting and human resource management is important, and
poorly understood. Casual inspection suggests, for example, that
"budgets" are concerned only with money and "personnel
management" is concerned only with people. Certainly, the
American public budgeting literature reflects this view. For example, one of the best-known definitions (Schick, 1966, p. 243)
posits that "budgeting has always been conceived as a process
for systematically relating the expenditure of funds to the accomplishment of planned objectives." Another equally famous
view begins with the notion that "budgeting is concerned with
the translation of financial resources into human purposes"
(Wildavsky, 1964, p. 1). Such views reinforce the point that the
expenditure of funds, not the management of people, is the
consuming budget issue.

Such definitions can lead to the misapprehension that the management of funds and the management of people are two functionally distinct enterprises protected, respectively, by budgeting and personnel offices. In fact, the management of people and the management of money are linked. Budgeting, in its financial dimension at least, simply involves placing monetary constraints on public management; it does no work and does not implement programs. Moreover, separation of financial and personnel disciplines obscures the resource linkages between money and employment (and, for that matter, capital equipment, technology, and information) on which program achievement depends. What is often ignored in the literature is that in its broadest meaning, budgeting is a political and administrative function that allocates resources—money, personnel, equipment—to the goals of public enterprise. Budgeting is a way of reconciling the competing demands of top-down pressures seeking to limit resource expenditures and bottom-up demands for increases.

Historically, budgets have been used to constrain human resource management in many ways. One technique is to use authorized permanent and temporary employment ceilings, such as end-of-the-year employment totals or a total number of full-time equivalent (FTE) workers, as a means of controlling the total employment allocated. Second, budgets can constrain the use of salary dollars as a way to control either the size of the workforce or the distribution of salaries paid; managing to payroll programs is one way to decentralize workforce decision making about the number and types of employees in favor of adherence to a payroll total (U.S. General Accounting Office, 1990). Finally, budgeting offices can occasionally constrain the skill mix and grade distribution through ceilings on average grade, which, in turn, control pay. In short, in the public sector there are many very powerful budget instruments that can be used to *control* a public workforce.

Control of a public workforce is obviously very different from workforce management. Budgeting offices rarely understand the workforce implications of using these three controls. For instance, when an agency employment ceiling is reduced, management is faced with several choices. It can try to squeeze more work from a smaller workforce. It can cut its labor force and reduce services. It can maintain or even increase its services by contracting out for services, if financial allocations permit. Indeed, one of the ironies is that an agency might even shift its in-house work force to a richer skill mix simply by contracting out janitorial, clerical, and other manual work, retaining the higher-level professional and administrative responsibilities on the government payroll. This possibility was not considered by the Grace Commission report, discussed in Chapter One.

However, budget offices also often attempt to control public employment through ceilings on average grade, in essence a kind of pay and grade inflation control. This is a different kind of control, because the choices often facing management are personnel actions that will lower the average grade of an agency. One option is painful: management can reduce the number of expensive, highly graded personnel through retirement, downgrading, reductions in force, and absorbing attrition. Another option is to lower the average grade of the agency by hiring more people at the lower end of the grade structure. This can be done by shifting the skill mix of the agency in the direction of hiring more secretaries, clerks, and entry-level professionals. The pressure mounts to hire more new employees classified in low grades.

At this point, however, the interactive dilemma appears. Interactive effects of workforce controls create complications. For example, in order to reduce the average grade, a higher employment ceiling is often needed. This is because more low-level new hires must be brought on board to reduce the average grade; thus, there is pressure for workforce growth. When an agency is constrained on *both* employment ceiling *and* the average grade, management must then respond with a complicated mix of hiring, reductions in force, and contracting actions.

One general conclusion is that sloppy and uninformed budgetary constraints can bring about unforeseen and undesirable shifts in the skill mix, perhaps undermining agency productivity. For instance, if severe constraints on both the employment ceiling and average grade result in substantial reductions in force, then prior investments in human capital are wiped out. If this double constraint produces a decision to contract out all highly graded and high-priced talent, then the agency risks losing control of its mission, since the people left will not be able to do the substantive work assigned to the agency or perhaps even to oversee the work done on contract.

The point is that budgetary controls of the workforce are very powerful levers with which to produce massive changes in public employment size, pay levels, and skill mixes. Yet, effective human resource management requires that workforce changes occur by design and not by accident. Ironically, however, the key to achieving a proper workforce design, size, and skill mix lies outside the budget discipline. Budgeting is simply a resource constraint placed on management decision making. The core function of budgeting is to establish the resource ceilings under which management must operate; it remains for managers to establish the workforce requirements of public productivity and translate those requirements into claims on resources.

The Personnel Management Problem. To this point, we can imagine a system in which the connection between mission and people is known (the rightness problem), the human resource requirements of policy are known (the people problem), the implementation strategy has been set (to be discussed in Chapter Twelve), and resources are allocated (the budget problem). Still, nothing is produced. Individual people have not been acted upon in a way that causes work to be done. This is the job of personnel management. More will be said about the personnel management puzzle in later chapters, but the strategic significance of personnel offices lies with the highly specialized service they provide.

Whatever else the personnel discipline accomplishes, it operates on the individuals of a workforce. Thus, once an organizational mission is known (policy), personnel requirements are defined, the implementing machinery is in place, and the resources have been allocated (budget function), the human resource problem becomes one of enabling the right individuals to work in timely fashion on the right problems. To accomplish this objective, the manager has available an enormous range of tools associated with staffing and employment, appraising and compensating performance, career management, and motivation and employee relations depicted in Figure 3.1. In effect, many actions for individual workers are often implied in the form of actions affecting recruitment, selection, placement, training, compensation, appraisal, development, promotion, discipline, and so on.

Two conclusions are relevant to understanding the personnel function. The first is that it should now be clear why, strictly defined, personnel administration is a supply-side, operational discipline rather than a demand-side, strategic discipline. Some entrepreneurial personnel offices have taken on a more strategic portfolio by reconfiguring their roles to include a strategic approach, but the nuts and bolts of personnel management operations are still concerned with the day-to-day, people-based actions that achieve results and goals within resource constraints and time lines already imposed by other disciplines.

The second point is that like all operations, the personnel discipline tends to establish standard operating procedures that govern decision making. But which operating rules and procedures? As Chapter Four will show, there is an infinity of designs by which the personnel function can be managed. Futhermore, once design is set, a series of operational assumptions are put in place that govern all other personnel routines. These routines, as we will see, determine how people are treated in organizations. Lack of clarity about the basis of personnel system design can do much to undermine the strategic purposes and goals that form the basis for workforce management. It deserves separate and extensive treatment in another chapter.

The Timing Problem. As if human resource management were not complex enough, time is increasingly a problem. The problem takes several forms. It appears most generally in attempts to meet the managerial need for human resources at the right time, a task that is not monumentally difficult when environments are stable and lead times between management decision and human resource action are long. When the definition of "right time and right place" is subject to change from environmental turbulence, the techniques and systems for managing people will come under pressure to change as well. In dynamic environments, static human resource management systems lock the public manager into last year's news. Adaptable systems permit timely adjustments.

So far so good. When time itself is the basis for competitive survival, however, the game changes abruptly. Time becomes a strategic variable, and personnel operations become a strategic tool of productivity. Indeed, sluggish personnel operations can destroy an organization's ability to meet the strategic challenges on which survival and productivity depend. For example, in the private sector, increasing the speed with which products can be developed, produced, and distributed has increasingly become a strategic aim of corporations (Gupta and Wilemon, 1990; Spencer, 1990). For example, two to five years is the current estimate of time required to move microelectronics discoveries and inventions from the laboratory to the production line (Mensch, 1979). Large corporations such as General Motors and General Electric have radically restructured their organizations, simultaneously reducing their workforces by 25 percent over a ten-year period running roughly from 1976 to 1986 and upgrading their workforce skill mix in the process. In time-based competition, the winner is the team that responds to a market need or develops a new product first. The best competitors, in the words of George Stalk, Jr., (1989, p. 28), "know how to keep moving and always stay on the cutting edge."

The extent to which time-based competition characterizes the public workforce is not clear. Despite popular myths that nothing ever changes in public management, there is persuasive evidence that public-sector change and competition do exist (Bragaw, 1980). Currently, the pace of strategic events in the external environment appears to be quickening for both the public and private sectors (Kooiman and Eliassen, 1987; Walton, 1987; McGregor, 1988; Perry, 1989). There lurks a great paradox in dealing with the time dimension of human resource management, however. Time-based competitiveness implies a rapid learning process that accelerates the speed at which people learn the tasks and routines involved in new product development and improved production processes (Belkaoui, 1986). In this respect, U.S. employment systems appear to be flexible. For example, massive retraining efforts are now underway to facilitate the timely adaptation of the national workforce; one text on the subject of retraining the American workforce claims that "nearly half of the jobs in the U.S. economy are transformed or replaced every five to eight years" (Miller, 1989, p. ix). Moreover, government appears not to be immune to the forces of change that blow across the entire U.S. economy. The strategic, demand-side requirement that people innovate and adapt to rapidly changing conditions to remain competitive has never been more clear, for both the public and private sectors.

On the other hand, there are apparent limits to human adaptability and the capacity to learn and absorb change (Coleman and others, 1966). Research simply does not know what the possibilities for learning are. This is a sobering reminder that the route to producing flexible, smart, fast, and adaptable production systems may be severely limited. The United States has particular reason to be concerned. For years our nation has been producing a bumper crop of marginally educated adults whose intellectual skills are below fifth-grade math and seventh-grade English, yet the competitive requirements for corporate survival in a global economy include the equivalent of a two-year technical college mastery of mathematics, science, and English. The failure to acquire basic skills early in life makes clear the challenge faced by a large proportion of an aging American workforce (Butterfield, 1989). Moreover, the problem is not unique to the United States. The entire world very well understands the connection between human development and marketplace response time and is developing programs to deal with perceived human capital shortfalls (Rajan, 1990). The answer to the question "How much time is required to create specific forms of human capital?" holds the key to making human resource management systems adaptable and capable of coping with the time problem.

The Logic of Strategic Workforce Management

It should be clear by now that there is an enormous difference between traditional personnel operations and strategic decision making. Personnel management offices and managers who concentrate on the *individual people* of a bureau or agency focus on only one small piece of the puzzle. More strategically positioned personnel offices work with the issues associated with the human resources required to achieve goals. They start the workforce management discussion on the requirements side and make a deliberate connection with workforce availability. Figure 3.2 provides a graphic representation of the overall workforce management logic; compare it to the domain of traditional operations shown in Figure 3.1.

Strategy. The logic of Figure 3.2 summarizes the discussion thus far and links together the many components of workforce management. In brief, operating personnel requirements derive from strategic definitions of productivity. The requirements problem decomposes into three sets of problems Each problem set represents the strategic, tactical, and operational requirements choices confronting management decision makers. The first and most significant set of choices involves policy decisions about organizational purposes and instruments. In private enterprise, for example, decisions to create new product lines, increase market shares, cut production costs through automation, and advance the state of a particular technology are all examples of strategic decisions that affect workforce requirements (Tichy, Fombrun, and Devanna, 1982). Those decisions are strategic because they fix the results to be achieved and establish the size and skill mix of the labor pool *required* to achieve goals and objectives.

Figure 3.2. The Strategic Approach to Public-Sector Human Resource Management.

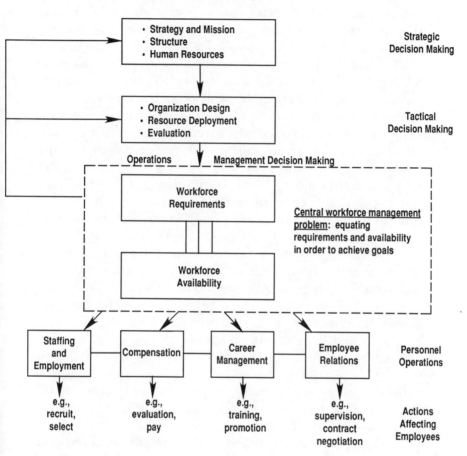

Obviously, government is disciplined by the same logic. For example, when governments fight wars, conduct research and development programs, stimulate economic development, or care for the indigent, human resource requirements result. Mission requirements do not, by themselves, directly determine personnel operations in either public or private enterprise. For one thing, decision makers still confront the question of choosing a basic instrument through which strategies and missions can be realized. For example, the "make or buy" decision—whether to implement programs and produce products in house or to contract out—is a strategic choice. A decision to make products and services means that the enterprise must acquire production knowledge and skill. A decision to buy services and products means that the enterprise must either manage a procurement process or oversee projects and production processes operated by some other workforce.

In reality, however, public-sector managers possess a full range of options through which public policy can be implemented. The choices are much more complex than a simple "make-or-buy" decision (Weidenbaum, 1969; Savas, 1987; Seidman and Gilmour, 1986). In the first place, public managers—especially at federal and state levels—can charter and fund the delivery of services through lower-level government agencies that can actually produce the services.

Another implementing device used frequently by the aerospace and defense sectors is negotiating contracts for goods and services with private corporations. Indeed, many private vendors have over time become government-oriented organizations. Corporations such as Lockheed, General Dynamics, Raytheon, and Pratt Whitney augment the real size of the government workforce as a result of complex procurement actions (Weidenbaum, 1969). Indeed, at many government installations, it is sometimes not possible from casual inspection to tell the difference between civil servants and private contractor personnel working for the same agency.

A third pattern is found in the complex relations now established between government agencies and "third-sector" organizations that supply workforce talents needed by government (McGill and Wooten, 1975). Included in the third-sector list would be voluntary organizations (such as churches and civic groups), nonprofit organizations such as universities and foundations, independent public authorities, and public corporations. Also included are privatized corporations created for specialized purposes; indeed, the growth of private, government-sponsored corporations has been a recent phenomenon in the United States (Seidman, 1975).

In short, public managers now have available the full array of implementing instruments that a modern economy can provide. The result is that they are heavily involved in managing both public and private workforces. A further conclusion is that government "make-or-buy" decisions force nearly continuous competition between government workforces and other, nongovernmental workforces that could be used to implement public policy. City sanitation workers must compete against private contractors. State mental health facilities must compete with community-based, nonprofit corporations and private hospitals. Federal aerospace researchers must compete with private vendors. It appears, in short, that the growing demand for a sophisticated array of public services will continue to impel public managers to search for those workforces whose skills match the missions required by public policy and whose costs are competitive.

Tactics. The link between strategic decision making (policy making) and personnel operations is still not complete, however. A series of middle-level, or tactical, decisions confront the manager. These implementing decisions include: the design of an organizational system within which work can be accomplished; the allocation and obligation of funds and other resources that constrain operational human resource requirements; and the evaluation of resource deployments against objectives. Tactical decision making deals with how something is to be done. In the workforce, it deals with the implementation of policies and strategies that must somehow bring workforce requirements and availability together. But precisely how are goals and people joined? The middle-managerial dilemma is extraordinarily complex; our space does not allow detailed examination of all of the many organizational designs that might be developed. One critical resource that has been insufficiently appreciated in management designs is technology (Tushman and Nelson, 1990).

Management decisions about technology involve at least three dimensions (Perrow, 1973). First, technology can refer to the technological sophistication and complexity of the production process itself; for instance, complex programs executed on a computer rather than slide rule, abacus, or desk calculator. Second, technology can refer to a reliance on capital equipment; thus, there are capital-intensive production methods and labor-intensive methods. The third definition refers to the production process itself, briefly defined as the package of production techniques and tasks that constitute production operations (Perrow, 1967; Woodward, 1965; Lawrence and Lorsch, 1967). There are small-batch, nonroutine operations in uncertain environments (R&D organizations, for instance). There are large-batch, mass-produced processes in stable environments (entitlement check disbursement). A third option is the mixed mode, represented in newer, flexible production systems that can be easily switched from large to small batch and from routine to nonroutine; these are the "smart" systems.

Determining the basic technology design is a major implementation challenge. Use of high technology typical of capital-intensive production processes is obviously very different from a reliance on low technology typical of labor-intensive production systems. For example, in the implementation of government entitlement programs, Medicaid checks can be issued by an army of clerks assigned the specialized tasks—mail, claims processing, examination, payment authorization, payment, auditing—required to process individual claims (Brock, 1984). An alternative process of technology might use computers to issue checks along with a series of summary statistics about the characteristics of recipients. Clearly, the first process creates enormous demand for large numbers of caseworkers and clerks, while the second generates enormous demand for computer technicians, systems analysts, and policy analysts.

Choices of production technology have profound effects on the demand and supply of labor. What is not always clear is which choice of technology is correct, or how to move production systems from one technology type to another. Nor is it clear what happens to people who undergo major transformations of technology (Zuboff, 1988). Part of the confusion lies in the fact that choices of technology can be both a strategic and a tactical decision. Technology acquires strategic significance when it defines the mission or goal of an agency or corporation. For example, when the mission of an organization is either to advance the state of knowledge or to develop prototypes and new products such as satellites, social service delivery models, or new construction methods, then strategy is largely congruent with choices of technology. Technology, in this instance, adds strategic value to the firm or agency. Obviously, strategic choices of technology affect workforce requirements.

The tactical issue, by contrast, involves organizational and managerial arrangements through which human resources are deployed. Use of computers to reduce operating costs would be one example. Or, to take another example, if the goal is to advance the state of a given technology, then the resulting requirement is to organize people into teams attached to small-batch, nonroutine projects. By contrast, if the strategic aim is merely to produce as efficiently as possible those products and services for which the production requirements and markets are already known, then an organization's personnel can be deployed differently. Often, a labor force possessing routinized skills geared to the repetitive operations of large-batch, mass-produced production processes will be required.

Operations. Ultimately, no work is done until strategic and tactical choices are converted into operations decision making. This conversion, in turn, does not occur until operational requirements and operational availability are compared, as shown in Figure 3.2, and personnel actions taken to produce a balance between the two sides of the workforce management equation. Clearly, however, once both strategic and tactical decisions are made, operations decisions are severely constrained. Furthermore, once the operational requirements are known, the vast majority of personnel management decisions are made. Regrettably, many requirements-side decisions are made without consulting personnel specialists, who often arrive on the management scene to preside over damage control rather than to contribute to general management excellence.

Part of the problem is surely the fault of the personnel management community that has not bothered to think strategically about the connection between public policy and personnel. Part of the reason for the chasm that separates personnel management from line management, however, lies with the difficulty of the problem. In essence, strategic workforce management requires getting down to details. Workforce managers must think strategically about the employment system that governs availability (Chapter Four) and also about the precise connection between public policy and workforce requirements (Chapter Five).

Chapter Four

Linking
Employment System Design
to Human Resource Availability

Contrary to popular belief, public service bureaucracies are enormously flexible instruments. Flexibility is due to the many different ways to design employment systems. Clarity about the strategic choices available to human resource managers is essential because once those choices are made, the basis for managing (or mismanaging) people is set.

At issue are three sets of design choices that make up the heart of any human resource management system. The first deals with the choice of labor market. The second deals with the choice of employment system in the likely event that the "internal labor market" option is chosen. The third choice sets the design of the human resource management system. While in theory public and private managers have identical design choices, I believe that in practice the complexities confronting the public manager are greater.

Labor Market

The most basic human resource management choice occurs when managers decide whether to use external or internal markets (Doeringer and Piore, 1971). The point appears self-evident, but important: managers do not have to use administered bureaucratic systems to get work done. Many managers, in fact, rely to some extent on self-service, voluntary labor, and contract personnel drawn from external labor markets (Savas, 1987). In the internal case, the "pricing and allocation of labor is governed by a set of administrative rules and procedures." In the external case, however, "pricing, allocating, and training decisions are controlled directly by economic variables" such as prices, laws of supply and demand, and competitive markets (Doeringer and Piore, 1971, pp. 1–2). Alternatively, an external market can consist of volunteer workers. Thus, managers must choose between designing an employment system governed by internal rules of formal organization versus a relatively unmanaged labor market where the supply and demand preferences of employee and employer jointly establish the prices and rewards of employment in exchange for work.

While it is certainly true that the majority of the U.S. workforce is employed in large organizations operating according to internal rules of administration, reliance on external labor markets is not unheard of and may be increasing slightly. Voluntary labor is one example; enormous productivity has been achieved from voluntary booster organizations, service clubs, cooperative arrangements, and citizen volunteers in legislatures, boards, and commissions. Furthermore, outsourcing labor by employing individual contract laborers—consultants, contractors, and migrant labor are a few examples—can be a significant form of staffing. Indeed, the use of independent consultants and networks of consultants is a well-established and growing practice around the world (Golzen, 1990). In such situations, workers contract as individual jobbers and labor markets are governed by the "employment at will" doctrine, where employment may be terminated by the employer at any time without cause, subject, of course, to the requirements of binding contracts. Thus, there are many ways to avoid using bureaucratic arrangements as the basis for productivity.

The advantages of relying on external markets are obvious. In the voluntary case, work is done without a labor cost. In the contract case, employees may be hired and fired as needed. Compensation levels can be set and reset as productivity levels permit. Employers may use competitive pressures to bid down wages and bid up work levels. Employees are free to organize and use labor scarcity and collective job action to counter proposals and manipulations by employers. The external market is a potent force in the competitive search for efficiency. Who needs internal labor markets and bureaucratic red tape?

External markets have several limitations. First, short-term relationships create uncertainty. To be sure, migrant workers can be hired to pick crops. Band boosters can staff the concession stands from which income is earned to buy uniforms and instruments. Self-help groups and families can look after each other's children in diverse child-care arrangements. Volunteer fire fighters and vigilantes are used to protect public safety. Personal services contracts can be used to supply security guards at the gate and data entry at remote job sites. In all these examples, however, the employment relationship is short term. Workers are free to quit and relocate on short notice, leaving to the employer the task of finding replacements.

A second constraint on freewheeling manipulations in external marketplaces is a legal one. The current reality is that people are a regulated resource. Personnel may not be treated simply as a free good, available for exploitation, to be employed, used, and discarded at the whim of an employer. The conditions under which people may be recruited, selected, compensated, promoted, disciplined, and protected from occupational hazards are now bounded by public law and court decision (see Table 4.1). Public policy has clearly stepped into the marketplace to ensure that fairness, equity, and nonexploitation of labor apply to human resource management practices, especially recruitment and selection, compensation administration, and occupational health and safety. Also increasingly regulated are the processes by which employers and employees jointly decide which employment practices shall be governed by explicit agreement codified in contracts and memoranda of understanding. One of the casualties of human resource regulation is the "employment at will" doctrine. Courts now hold employers accountable to a fairness standard under which a breach either of fair treatment procedures or "good faith" is grounds for litigation. Employers who fail to exercise care in the design of systems of employment do so at the risk of litigation and the expense of extensive punitive damages (Lubin, 1983).

A third limitation is that external markets worked well under conditions that are fast disappearing. So long as a surfeit of labor existed with people competing for work and productivity depended on relatively simple and repetitive tasks, a dependence on external markets could probably be defended as a strategy, subject to appropriate social norms about fair and equitable treatment of workers. When labor scarcity is more often the case and final products require sustained and coordinated effort involving large teams of people, however, reliance on external markets can be disastrous. In effect, external

Table 4.1. Common Sources of Human Resource Regulation.

1. *Hiring: rules and procedures for appointment*
   Civil Rights Act of 1964: Title VII
   EEO Act of 1972
   Age Discrimination Act of 1967, 1978
   Rehabilitation Act of 1973
   Civil Service Reform Act of 1978 (federal government)
   State and local civil service statutes and ordinances
2. *Wages and hours plus benefits*
   Davis-Bacon Act of 1931: prevailing wage
   Fair Labor Standards Act of 1983 . . . 1977: minimum wage; exemptions are salaried employees
   Equal Pay Act of 1963, amended by the Education Act of 1972: prohibits sex discrimination in pay policy
   Social Security Act of 1935, 1937 (and amended): payroll tax
   Civil Service Reform Act of 1978 (federal government)
   State and local civil service statutes and ordinances
3. Working conditions
   Occupational Safety and Health Act of 1970
4. Placement—covered by collective agreement
5. Discipline and discharge—grievance policy
6. Job design—unregulated by law
7. Employee-employer relations—subject to collective negotiation and collective bargaining law
   NLRA (Wagner Act) of 1935: private sector
   LMRA (Taft-Hartley) of 1947: private sector
   LMRDA (Landrum-Griffin) of 1959: private sector
   Civil Service Reform Act of 1978 (Title VI): federal sector
   State and local statutes and ordinances

markets do not work well in cases where productivity requires any combination of three conditions: special skills not found in external labor markets, teams of people working together over long periods of time, or advanced knowledge and expertise. Under any combination of those conditions, labor must be trained to be productive and the costs of turnover are high, both in recruitment and selection and in lost human capital that accompanies personnel turnover. Only internal labor markets create the conditions of continuity and security that can attract teams of people trained to produce highly complex products requiring a mastery of intricate production processes. Thus, when productivity depends on teams of trained personnel working together over long periods of time, reliance only on potentially unstable external markets can produce great uncertainty. Employers cannot justify the costs of employment and training if their investments can be summarily wiped out by departing workers. Employees can be reluctant to commit themselves to long-term relationships that are inherently unstable and depend on managerial whim. Only internal markets and rules establish the certainties that justify the extended employment relationships required for many modern systems of productivity.

Here the problems begin, however. While external labor markets operate according to laws of supply and demand, the rules that govern internal markets are based on administrative design. Yet those rules have received only the most sketchy treatment (Doeringer and Piore, 1971; Stahl, 1976; Sayre, 1964). The basis for internal labor market organization depends on decisions about two levels of design strategy: the first establishes the employment system within which the employment relationship is defined; the second establishes the strategic constraints within which human resources management and personnel operations are conducted. Let us look further at both.

Employment System

Public and private organizations differ in several important respects. Perhaps the most important is that public organizations have been forced to deal with political partisanship in human resource management matters. Another difference is the democratic requirement for visibility and accountability that is imposed on management decision makers. A third difference is found in the way public policy defines workforce requirements, for in the end it is public policy that creates the missions of government and authorizes the delivery of goods and services to citizens. Thus, the link between public policy and human resource management is simple and direct: public policy commitments produce missions that require, in turn, the skills and faithful efforts of employees.

But which employees? Employed under what rules? Private-sector organizations face the same questions, of course, but the requirements of democratic politics and public policy raise the stakes of the answers. The public workforce is the transmission belt through which political and social consensus and disagreement are converted into public outcomes. Patterns of partisan politics directly affect public employment system design and are potentially affected by those designs. Indeed, one special concern derives from the potential electoral influence of the public workforce itself. Government, especially at state and local levels, is a labor-intensive business that in the aggregate employs roughly 15 percent of the total nonagricultural labor force. But employed public servants are also voters, and the electoral impact of over 44,000 employees in Los Angeles, 41,000 in Chicago, 21,000 in Houston, 33,000 in Philadelphia, 21,000 in Detroit, 24,000 in San Francisco (U.S. Bureau of the Census, 1989, p. 289) is kept constantly in mind by mayors and county executives, city and county councils, and state officials. (The figures define 1986 noneducational employment for cities ranked in descending order of central city population.)

The second source of political influence comes from the fact that public employees use employee associations and labor unions to protect their interests. While both the size and organization of the public workforce suggest that public unions have great potential influence on the content of public policy, the effects of a unionized workforce on policy must be considered unclear. As of this writing, there are no unambiguous generalizations about what substantive public policies are affected (Public Service Research Council, 1982; Osigweh, 1985), except for the obvious financial pressures created by employee demands for higher pay, benefits, and working conditions (Stanley, 1971) and unions' ability to create pressure on management by withholding public services from aggrieved citizens.

Finally, elected public officials feel enormous pressure to gain control of the administrative routines governing the public workforce in order to render public employees accountable to electoral majorities. In blunt language, the problem arises in public service that elected officials must assure themselves that the policies on which their electoral fortunes depend receive sympathetic and responsive treatment from the public agencies assigned to implement public policy. How is this policy responsiveness achieved? In the United States, one option—still attractive to many—is the use of patronage employment (Tolchin and Tolchin, 1971) to acquire control over the working lives of public employees. Spoils or patronage systems can be used to govern the lives of public employees in matters such as recruitment, selection, promotion, adverse action, and pay. In such systems, public employees who implement public policy are fully aware of what the future holds should the policies of their political masters be contravened.

How else can the workforce be disciplined to serve the public policy objectives of government? The answer to this practical question reveals one of the most basic confrontations of the simultaneous demand for merit employment and public policy responsiveness (Mosher, 1968). "Merit" implies a public service that is recruited, selected, placed, promoted, disciplined, and paid based on principles that do not vary with partisan political faction. Merit principles compete with traditional patronage and collective bargaining principles. Indeed, merit employment systems presume that public policy is best served by administrative machinery and procedures that filter political influence from human resource decisions. Moreover, merit machinery is designed to break the grip of political factions on government workforces (Sayer, 1948). Competitive principles of employment systems design are summarized in Table 4.2.

What is traded away when, in the name of "merit," a regulatory buffer is placed between partisan politicians and the career public employee? One obvious answer is that mastery of bureaucracy by elected officials is lost. The loss of control occurs because merit systems work to prevent direct exposure of career officials to the will of a political person whose tenure, even if appointed, depends in some way on electoral outcomes. Merit systems are not universally acclaimed. They require an extensive investment in administrative overhead and have been accused of stunting public productivity. For example, both merit and collective systems lack, as Martin and Susan Tolchin point out (1971, p. 304), the advantage of a system of "clear-cut rewards in return for good service and unquestioned loyalty." Ironically, one of the great managerial virtues of a patronage system is the extent to which the will of the political person can be brought to bear directly on individual careerists (Tolchin and Tolchin, 1971). By contrast, one of the great limitations of a merit system lies in the corollary requirement that impersonal rules, regulations, and regulatory machinery are needed to guard the "merit" relationship between public employer and employee.

Clearly, then, the competing ideas of patronage, merit, and collective employment are complex and go far beyond simplistic assumptions that patronage causes corruption, that collective employment breeds labor unrest and inefficiency, and that merit produces competitive excellence (Backoff and Rainey, 1977). The stakes involve more than simply productivity and control of corruption; they also involve the control of the public policy machinery itself.

Notwithstanding lively debate, the merit idea has prevailed in public employment. Both patronage and collective systems have fatal flaws that have been increasingly exposed as public-sector work requires knowledge-intensive capabilities that characterize an increasingly sophisticated public sector. Merit systems have survived since the federal civil service charter was

Table 4.2. Employment System Design Principles.

System Variable	Collective System	Merit System (Civil Service)	Patronage System
Recruitment and selection	Entry positions of bargaining unit	Open competitive examination of candidate's fitness for position	Political clearance
Promotion	Based on seniority	Competitive based on evaluations of individual merit	Connection to sucesssful candidates
Classification	Collectively negotiated classification plan subject to grievance procedures	Based on job analysis covering work requirements, candidate knowledge, skill, and ability	Nonmerit schedules ("policy making and confidential" positions)
Pay	Negotiable and subject to bargaining power of union	Based on job evaluation and pay plan; subject to prevailing local rates in some fields	Fixed by organization level minus party contribution
Hours, leaves	Negotiable	Based on management requirements	Fixed by political party and general labor practice
Separation	Seniority ("last hired, first fired")	Protected career; rules of separation for those with "status, or standing"	Election loss or at will of sponsor
Basis for employee relations	Contract administration	Equal treatment for individuals	Determined by electoral outcomes
Grievances	Appealed with union representation to impartial arbitrators	Appealed through management with recourse to merit protection agency	Subject to partisan appeal through political party

Source: Adapted from Mosher, F. C. (1968), pp. 197–198.

first locked in place by the Pendleton Act of 1883. In general, all merit principles affirm the need for fair and equal treatment of employees without regard to politics. They protect public employees from politically motivated meddling. They establish, at least in principle, the need to compensate public employees on scales comparable to the private sector.

Merit principles can also change. For example, the latest modifications of U.S. federal principles are found in the Civil Service Reform Act of 1978 (see Table 4.3). Not surprisingly, the 1978 reform act affirms traditional principles, but there are some anomalies. First, the principle of variable reward tied to individual performance supports the establishment of incentive-based compensation systems rather than flat-rate, across-the-board systems. Second, the liberal use of training and education for employees who have made a career out of government service suggests support for programs to keep government workers competitive with the private labor force. Third, the 1978 principles affirm the need of career government services to filter the effects of partisan politics from the employment process; at the same time, those protected accept the need to limit their participation in overtly political arenas. Fourth, "whistle blowers" who reveal, based on reasonable evidence, administrative practices that constitute a violation of rule or regulation are protected from reprisal.

Merit principles serve as the most general guide to employment system operation. They are extremely limited, however, because they are incomplete as either a strategic or an operational guide. Only by specifying the managerial choices by which a system of employment must operate can there be knowledge about relevant practices. Merely positing the need for fair and equal treatment for all employees leaves too much to be explained. What, after all, constitutes "fair and equal opportunity" in employment, compensation, appraisal, and career development decisions?

Human Resource Management Designs

While merit principles provide a broad framework for human resource management, their main function is to constrain po-

Table 4.3. Federal Merit System Principles.

Federal personnel management should be implemented consistent with the following merit system principles:

1. Recruitment should be from qualified individuals from appropriate sources in an endeavor to achieve a work force from all segments of society, and selection and advancement should be determined solely on the basis of relative ability, knowledge, and skills, after fair and open competition which assures that all receive equal oportunity.
2. All employees and applicants for employment should receive fair and equitable treatment in all aspects of personnel management without regard to political affiliation, race, color, religion, national origin, sex, marital status, age, or handicapping condition, and with proper regard for their privacy and constitutional rights.
3. Equal pay should be provided for work of equal value, with appropriate consideration of both national and local rates paid by employers in the private sector, and appropriate incentives and recognition should be provided for excellence in performance.
4. All employees should maintain high standards of integrity, conduct, and concern for the public interest.
5. The federal work force should be used efficiently and effectively.
6. Employees should be retained on the basis of the adequacy of their performance, inadequate performance should be corrected, and employees should be separated who cannot or will not improve their performance to meet required standards.
7. Employees should be provided effective education and training in cases in which such education and training would result in better organizational and individual performance.
8. Employees should be:
   a. protected against arbitrary action, personal favoritism, or coercion for partisan political purposes, and
   b. prohibited from using their official authority or influence for the purpose of interfering with or affecting the result of an election or a nomination for election.
9. Employees should be protected against reprisal for the lawful disclosure of information which the employees reasonably believe evidences:
   a. a violation of law, rule, or regulation, or
   b. mismanagement, a gross waste of funds, or an abuse of authority, or a substantial and special danger to public health or safety.

Exact wording of merit system principles taken from U.S. House of Representatives, *Civil Service Reform Act of 1978, Conference Report,* 1978, pp. 4, 5.

litical manipulation rather than to define the strategic principles on which operational practice would rest. Yet all human resource management systems are guided either de jure or de facto by assumptions and design choices about such matters as hiring, paying, appraising, and developing human resources. These founding assumptions combine to establish the strategic design of a human resource management system.

Design assumptions may be codified by statute or regulation. They may exist in the form of explicit assumptions built into the actual operation of a personnel system. Indeed, they may also represent unconscious choices that result from the combined weight of tradition and deeply held beliefs. Regardless of origin, they are strategic and they drive the rest of personnel operations. Table 4.4 shows the basic choices, outlined in terms of four strategic dimensions of human resource management. Each is discussed in turn.

Employment—Job Design. Job design refers to work system structure where a specialist or generalist design is the main choice. Loosely defined (Mintzberg, 1979, pp. 69–80), the label "specialist" may be applied to positions that require *either* substantial repetition of tasks involving mastery of a comparatively narrow field characterized by little depth ("horizontal speciali-

Table 4.4. Strategic Dimensions of Human Resource Management Design.

Human Resource Management System	*Design Choice*
1. Employment system	
a. Job design	Specialist versus generalist
b. Recruitment	Open versus closed
c. Selection	Program versus career
2. Compensation system	
a. Job evaluation	Rank-in-job versus rank-in-person
b. Compensation	Time-based versus contribution-based pay
3. Career management system	Elitist versus nonelitist training and development
4. Staffing structure	Personnel system layering: Vertical separation Horizontal separation Bipartisanship Horizontal overlap

zation") or *little* administrative control over the direction and content of the job ("vertical specialization"). The objective in "specialist" systems is maximum mastery of the substantive details of a single job that, by itself, performs only a few of the routines required to produce a final product or service.

Generalist positions, by contrast, embrace *either* task variety ("horizontal enlargement") or a degree of depth defined in terms of enriched perspective and control ("vertical enlargement"), or both. The knowledge, skills, and abilities required to perform the generalist job are either many, self-controlling, or comparatively broad in nature. The definition of "broad" places the analyst on dangerous ground, but a useful definition might be to say that broad or general positions are ones where the worker confronts relatively comprehensive questions that must be answered in order to produce some final product or outcome. Thus, generalist designs more directly link employment to final products and outcomes—one person performs all the tasks associated with providing a service to a client, building a car, or completing a program, or sees to it that such tasks are effectively performed.

A concrete illustration of the design options can be found in the human resource field itself. One way to design the human resource management function is to staff according to the major specialties: recruitment, selection, and placement; job analysis and classification; wage and salary administration; employee/employer relations; training and development; health and safety; benefits and employee services. An employee hired under a specialist design would concentrate on one of those seven fields. The specialist design enhances mastery in a single functional area.

The generalist design envisions a very different arrangement. People employed as general human resource managers would offer to line operating divisions—engineering, sciences, quality assurance, and so forth—the full array of personnel services listed above. Thus, one generalist design might seek personnel who can perform all the functions. In another, even more strategically positioned design, the incumbent knows all the personnel functions and the general strategies on which the enterprise is based. Which is better? Knowledge and skill requirements limit the prospects for wide-scale application of the generalist design; people simply cannot know everything about everything. Yet, it has been a standard presumption that a generalist design has beneficial effects on employee satisfaction and productivity. The presumption has deep roots in organizational psychology, which, at a theoretical level, finds that people derive great internal satisfaction from continuously expanding work and achievement opportunities. A corollary is that people can also be alienated by dull and overspecialized work that prevents their making a full contribution to a productive organization.

The basis for the debate lies in an important distinction between two different dimensions (Mintzberg, 1979) along which all jobs can be converted from specialist to generalist designs. One is horizontal enlargement, which increases the number or variety of tasks a worker performs. The second is job enrichment, which expands vertically the level of responsibility by which a worker participates in planning and controlling the work. In job enlargement the work repertoire is expanded. Under job enrichment, workers take responsibility for organization productivity demands and the constraints that affect the pace and quality of their work. In a typical job enrichment scheme, workers also participate in managing the organization itself.

Since the mid 1970s, testimonials have accumulated extolling the virtues of job enlargement and enrichment both in this country and abroad (O'Toole, 1974). However, studies suggest contradictory results. One summary review concludes that vertical job enrichment or vertical plus horizontal job enlargement produces desirable gains in productivity and morale, but that horizontal job enlargement by itself does not (French, 1978). There is simply no final resolution to the debate about whether job enrichment and enlargement are desirable. Furthermore, it is important to bear in mind the impact that a shift from one system to another will have on other areas of human resource management. For example, moving from a specialist to a generalist design creates pressure for the compensation system when "generalist" employees expect to be paid more than "specialized" employees. Training and development strategies also require adaptation.

In the end, however, the debate may simply become increasingly academic, for reasons tied to the emerging postindustrial world in which modern managers must now operate. If the public sector in any way emulates the direction and pace of trends in private business, then it is likely that public managers will be forced to pursue *both* job enlargement and enrichment strategies simultaneously. Furthermore, jobs will not be static, but instead will be placed in constant motion by management decision makers (Schneider and Konz, 1989). Strong evidence of job change is found in corporate trends (begun in the 1970s and accelerated during the 1980s) involving a wholesale redesign of the way work was done and work systems were engineered (Kanter, 1986). Among the innovations (Wallace, 1989; Kanter, 1986), have been the following:

- Massive workforce reductions through cutbacks, load shedding, and automation.
- Reductions of corporate level staffs.
- Simplified organization designs resulting in flatter organizations with fewer middle managers.
- Extensive employee involvement in organizational governance and decision making, including information sharing.
- Organization design overlays consisting of matrix organizations and the use of ad hoc project teams for product development.
- Stimulation of internal entrepreneurship and innovation through internal venture funds.
- Development of flexible work systems to provide more employee choice about schedules, hours, and nonwork responsibilities.

These innovations occurred because the strategic environment of public and private enterprise changed. Factors such as massive changes in workforce characteristics (Kanter, 1986), computer and telecommunications technology (van Gunsteren, 1987), and the competitive nature of the strategic environment have combined to force a continuous restructuring. In short, the requirements of corporate survival have dictated continuous innovation.

Employment—Recruitment. There are two competing recruitment strategies based on different relationships between external and internal labor markets (Sayre, 1964). One is an "open system," where recruitment occurs from the pools of talent found in external labor markets and in feeder pools available within the organization. In open systems, people already employed continuously compete with people potentially available from outside the organization. External and internal labor markets are continuously compared and competed at all levels of organization.

A second choice is "closed recruitment," where recruitment from outside the organization occurs only at the entry level. Thereafter, only internal recruitment governs the ascent into journeymen and managerial positions. In closed systems, lateral entry at midcareer and senior career levels from external labor markets is virtually nonexistent.

Which strategy is best? Closed systems are probably best for growing a sense of cohesion and sophisticated culture. Closed systems "grow their own" talent by taking in at entry levels promising raw material and, through training, development, and career management, raise a succession of people who speak a common language and hold in common a set of core values. Under the rules of a closed system, what would otherwise be a mechanistic bureaucracy becomes a kind of unified team or clan (Ouchi, 1980) striving to achieve a common purpose. It would seem that closed systems are also useful instruments for guarding proprietary information and secrets and hence are most frequently found in the public sector in areas of diplomacy, defense, military systems, and national security.

Open systems of recruitment, on the other hand, are particularly well adapted to turbulent external environments and changing technologies where an organization's strategy is built on its ability to keep up with rapid change. Where organizations lack the capacity to "grow their own" or their strategies require buying advanced technical skill on the open market, open recruitment systems can be enormously useful in tapping new labor markets and forcing competitive comparisons between in-house careerists and external sources of talent. In addition, closed systems of recruitment can form cozy, but deadly, impediments to modernization and competitiveness simply by protecting unproductive cultures and bureaucratic inertia. Open systems, by contrast, open up organizations to the forces of change and innovation and the new ideas that lateral entries from the outside bring with them; yet these same forces generate their own sources of uncertainty and are potentially destabilizing.

Employment—Selection. The act of employment presumes the existence of a criterion or standard by which people can be appraised and selected. One selection strategy is to staff organizations on a program basis. The aim is to select employees whose knowledges and skills match the knowledges and skills required to run a specific program. Thus, government program staffing might recruit, retain, and promote people based on job-ready skills useful in banking, insurance, insurance regulation, highway construction, medical research, or welfare casework. A second strategy is to staff an agency or company on a career basis. Here the objective is to recruit and retain people for a lifetime career of continuous employment with one agency or corporation. Because career-based systems assume that employees will be employed over the long haul, career-based selection seeks to measure an applicant's long-term potential rather than specific skills; programs and product lines will come and go, but people remain.

Clearly, selection methods are affected by each strategy. In program-based selection, practical experience, qualifying professional degrees from recognized institutions, internships and residencies, board certifications, and samples of work products are all indicators of marketable skill and job readiness. In career-based selection, selection criteria focus on surrogate measures of learning potential and fundamental skills and abilities that indicate the existence of trainability and adaptability. In career systems, the capacity to learn and acquire new skills is the critical variable.

Compensation Systems. A second basic design category is the strategy that governs job evaluation and compensation. Job evaluation fixes the base value of a position or person to an organization. Compensation refers to the contents of the pay envelope: basic pay, benefits, incentives, bonuses, compensatory time. Job evaluation refers to the process by which basic pay is fixed and vested; compensation refers to the size and composition of the total payout, the end point of the job evaluation process.

On the surface, both job evaluation and compensation strategies involve choices from among a seemingly finite list. In fact, the combined list of choices under each heading is very large, the combinations of possibilities even larger. Furthermore, job evaluation and compensation systems are in motion, in the sense that substantial experimentation is underway in both. Even so seemingly simple, bureaucratic, and static a labor force as that found in the People's Republic of China has been found to be highly complex and quietly dynamic (Shenkar and Chow, 1989). Given the multiplicity of strategies available to design both process and outcome, it becomes immediately apparent that there is no "one best way" to design compensation systems. Both dimensions are most productively assessed from the perspective of the strategic "fit" of the compensation plan to the overall strategic planning (Hufnagel, 1987). Also, regardless of the initial choices made, they will need to be continuously modified in light of new challenges.

In the interest of simplifying what can be mind-numbing complexity, one can mark the polarities of compensation system choices and thus better envision the full range of options. Traditionally, the dominant job-evaluation strategy has aimed at preserving a bureaucratic ordering of positions where compensation is organized by a hierarchic chain of command

(Kanter, 1986). In essence, what is traditionally paid has been the position. Payout has occurred under the implicit assumption that incumbents of positions are entitled to the compensation vested in those positions. Position incumbency captures the compensation package attached to the position. Moreover, rank-in-the-job evaluation systems rest on the additional assumption that only a detailed description and analysis of the duties and responsibilities of a position can be the basis for fixing compensation. Job analysis becomes the foundation of job evaluation, and position classification schemes, factor benchmark comparisons, and point rating systems, too numerous to name or discuss here, become the basis for converting position information into judgments of employee worth. Traditionally, most of the U.S. white-collar governmental workforce has been based on the rank-in-the-job strategy in which people are paid for assigned activities, duties, and responsibilities—characteristics of positions—rather than for some personal characteristic, rank, or contribution they bring *to* or cause to be done *in* the position.

There is a second compensation strategy, however, one that vests rank and pay in a person rather than a position. Person-based reward systems fasten compensation to the rank held by an employee regardless of the variety of tasks, duties, and responsibilities that may be assigned. Thus, the rank-in-person employee carries an organizational rank and title—professor, general, consul, ranger—that permits task variety without classification. He or she can move among different positions in different organizations without changes in pay. In other words compensation is packaged according to distinct levels of prestige, privilege, pay, and skill held by a person, for whom compensation is portable. There are many examples of rank-in-person systems in U.S. government; the foreign service and military officer corps are two examples.

While both systems of job evaluation conduct job analyses that collect, organize, and compile critical job facts, each system is supported by its own information system. Rank-in-job systems must develop elaborate sources of information about job content through job analysis and auditing. Job analysis pro-

vides the position data against which can be arrayed the qualifications of those whose employment eligibility and placement
must be determined. In rank-in-person systems, human resource managers are more concerned with maintaining accurate inventories of human skills that can be matched against
knowledge, skill, and ability requirements of specific jobs (Prien,
1977; Leich, 1960).

Each job evaluation system has its own mix of advantages and disadvantages. The advantage of position-based evaluation lies in the relative ease and precision with which the
principle of "equal pay for equal work" can be established across
a highly diverse workforce. Furthermore, managers acquire a
rich amount of data on the structure of work being done and
the packages of work that carry standard position titles and
ranks. Position-based systems obviate the need for overly refined assessments of individuals and their contributions. Compensation inheres in the position itself.

Several difficulties are also incurred in rank-in-job systems. The most obvious one involves the costs involved in collecting, organizing, and analyzing position-based data. In addition to administrative overhead, one must consider the
disruption of line operations. Rank-in-job systems, even "strategic" systems (Schneider and Konz, 1989), require a vast paper and computerized data management empire that is expensive to set up and maintain.

By contrast, rank-in-person systems seem to enjoy far
greater flexibility in workforce assignment as well as minimal
disruption of line operations required to collect information.
Rank-in-person systems encourage organizational and occupational mobility of persons without reclassification and flexibility
of work assignment. Personal rank (senior executive, distinguished professor, general of the army), together with a brief
résumé of experience and achievements, serves as the summary of what a person knows and can do, on the basis of which
assignments to positions can be made without invoking an
enormous bureaucratic exercise.

Rank-in-person systems are not without difficulties. The
same flexibility of assignment that is a source of strength in
turbulent times and environments, generates little data about

the uses to which the workforce has been put. Task-related data are captured in the minds of people rather than in detailed position descriptions. In person-dominated systems (universities, orchestras, hospitals, research labs), therefore, human resource managers lack a precise set of data on which staffing standards and planning can be undertaken, since people may be variously assigned to a changing mix of tasks, duties, and responsibilities. (However, it should be noted that task and activity data are often implied in the final *results* that person-based systems achieve rather than in the performance of intermediate processes.)

Regardless of job evaluation strategy, however, people must be compensated. This brings the manager face to face with the problem of assembling compensation packages. Once again, many choices exist. Nearly all public and private compensation plans have been founded on a "status basis." A "status basis" derives from the preservation of bureaucratic forms of industrial organization in which the traditional pay system is "based largely on the cost of hiring (market forces), later rationalized into grading systems based on levels of responsibility (internal equity)" (Kanter, 1986, p. 519). It is important to note that a status basis for compensation can exist regardless of whether rank-in-job or rank-in-person job evaluation principles are used. In pure form, status-based compensation systems are also closely tied to time-based pay; people are paid based on the time spent in a particular position or personal rank.

Status-based pay systems are under enormous pressure, however, from alternative systems that reward *contributions* rather than time spent in a designated status. There are several of these alternatives, and they appear to be enjoying increasing popularity (Kanter, 1986; Wallace, 1989; Ost, 1990). Detailed discussion of a truly strategic approach to compensation must be left to another volume, but some of the contribution-based systems include:

- *Pay-for-performance:* This is the least radical departure from status-based pay; "merit pay" is allocated to individual behaviors and achievements.

- *Performance bonuses:* Pay is allocated to a special incentives pool for rewarding unusual contributions on an episodic basis.
- *Entrepreneurial pay:* Pay is allocated to those who create something new: new ventures, milestones reached, spinoffs achieved, inventions developed.
- *Gain sharing:* Pay is allocated to collective accomplishments of groups, teams, and organizational units that share in cost efficiencies, output achievements, and profits generated.
- *Skill-based pay:* Pay is allocated for knowledge, skills, and abilities.

All contribution-based systems challenge assumptions of traditional hierarchy in many ways (Kanter, 1986). First, none of these schemes, with the exception of base rates anchoring merit pay increases, depends in any way on attaining a particular organization status or position; instead, pay is allocated to those behaviors, achievements, and skills that are *not* based on organizational status. Second, the organizational processes by which pay is determined require levels of employee input that potentially undermine traditional hierarchic processes where subordinates perform work and are evaluated by superiors who manipulate reward systems. In a true contribution-based system, the superior is called upon to discuss with the employee what constitutes a contribution and what its value is. Even the comparatively conservative assumptions of merit pay, or pay for performance, require at least some two-way discussion about what constitutes "merit" or "performance." The catch is that once a determination is made in advance of performance, hierarchical control of the paycheck is destroyed; employees who deliver "performance" collect the compensation. Third, when the portion of the paycheck that is determined by a compensation-based scheme grows large enough, the chain-of-command assumptions that superiors earn more than their subordinates can be turned upside down. In true contribution-based systems, subordinates can theoretically earn more than their superiors; this pay inversion can occur particularly in cases where performance bonuses, entrepreneurship, and skill are the basis for reward.

Clearly, there is an endless array of compensation plan designs and strategies for developing them. The need for a strategic approach to compensation plan development is implied in the rich variety of alternatives available (Hufnagel, 1987). Furthermore, research is just beginning to identify the new compensation possibilities and their likely organizational impacts.

Career Management System. The third strategic dimension of human resource management design is the career management system. This is governed largely by choices of training and development systems and the rules of access to human capital investment. All career management systems are driven by two facts of organizational life. First, new employees rarely arrive job-ready and able to work at a full performance level. They must be trained and oriented to the work systems in which they are expected to perform. Second, even if employees are initially skilled, an employment relationship of any duration must struggle with the need to grow skills and human resource capacity that meet the changing strategic needs of organization. Training and development systems are especially important in career-based selection designs, where job-ready skill is not a dominant selection criterion.

Because training and development represent a substantial investment of resources and are tied to other aspects of human resource management, the criteria by which the investment is made deserve careful assessment. Much training and development activity revolves around identifying and developing those who will rise in rank within the organization as opposed to those who will not. The promotion pattern, in turn, establishes the way future managers and executives, as well as other key scientific and technical personnel, must be trained and developed.

At polar extremes, there are two basic training and development strategies available; both refer to the career stage at which a person's chances to rise to a top position is determined. In the first, human resource management systems are "elitist" when, at an early career stage, a candidate is told, in effect, that his or her future prospects are assured. Systems are "nonelitist" when the decision about the ultimate level of career achievement is deferred until late in a person's career (Armstrong, 1973). Deferring the decision preserves an incentive system that allows and makes it rational for all persons in the organization to compete. Elitist systems remove that incentive, but they offer other advantages; for example, they can be useful as recruitment devices for ambitious people who wish to discover early in their careers what the prospects for a top job are.

Whether the elitist option has desirable or undesirable organizational effects in terms of motivation, productivity, equity, and organizational climate has never been systematically researched, although partial evidence suggests that motivation and morale are sometimes suppressed. The public services of many European countries—most notably France, Germany, and Great Britain—have traditionally maintained elitist traditions. A good example of the morale problem is found in the civil service system of France. Candidates for public management positions in France are sorted at graduation either into the Grands Corps or the *Administrateurs civils* based on a highly structured and competitive system of graduate school education. Members of the Grands Corps are recruited from the top-scoring students from the top technical and nontechnical schools. Students from lesser schools with lower scores are admitted only as lower-level *administrateurs civils*. Once admitted, the course of career development is set. Members of the Grands Corps have a license to compete for the highest positions in business and government. Those excluded from the Grands Corps spend the rest of their lives knowing that they must work in second-level positions (Armstrong, 1973).

The public services of the United States, by contrast, traditionally have been based on nonelitist training and developing principles. There are significant exceptions, however. For example, the foreign service officer corps and the military officer corps maintain elitist traditions. In both cases, attendance at certain schools or selection for special midcareer education programs (McGregor, 1974) are ways by which top candidates can be tapped early and separated from the herd.

Staffing Structures

The discussion of strategic designs for human resource management applies equally to public- and private-sector organizations. The public sector, however, presents special complexities. Public organizations are rarely staffed with a single personnel system in which all employees are bound by a common set of design assumptions. Police departments combine sworn uniformed personnel with nonsworn white-collar civil servants. The armed services mingle military and civilian white- and blue-collar workers. At professional levels, the U.S. State Department interlaces several personnel systems including the foreign service officer corps, the foreign service staff, the foreign service reserve, and the white-collar general schedule. In addition, most public systems employ large numbers of contract and volunteer workers who work alongside full-time government employees. Finally, virtually all *public* systems mix "classified" personnel—people hired for protected, or merit, positions—and patronage personnel for whom employment is subject to political review. The result is a confusion of multiple systems thrown together in a jumble. In short, public service systems are heavily layered.

How can the several public personnel systems be layered to form an effective working unit? Merely naming the various percentages (20 percent patronage and 80 percent merit) does not establish a design. In general, there are four basic strategies for personnel system layering.

One option is to separate the different systems vertically, or hierarchically, and designate one system as the elite group. This constitutes a system of vertical separation. European countries traditionally make such hierarchic distinctions in which politically appointed decision makers form the top group and in turn are served by elite careerists in the administrative classes. In France, the administrative class is vertically subdivided into elite and nonelite personnel systems—the Grands Corps and the *administrateurs civils*. Members of the administrative class preside, in turn, over other vertically arranged systems involving executive, clerical, and blue-collar personnel. Even in this design, vertically separated personnel systems often overlap, and members of different systems perform similar work with rules of access that often permit people to move from a lower to a higher system (Brown, 1971; Suleiman, 1974). For example, there are recently expanded opportunities for "executive class" *administrateurs civils* to compete for places in the Grands Corps.

A second layering option is horizontal separation; two separate systems exist in parallel, with duplicate skills in each. Employees of the two separate but horizontally layered systems will often occupy the same installation, and yet perform parallel tasks. For example, the coexistence of uniformed military and civilian personnel systems at the same military installation where both systems contain a full range of managers, engineers, technicians, and clerical personnel. Another example can be found in the use of contract personnel who share installations with government employees (or vice versa). In each example, separate zones of work responsibility are carved out and operate in tandem.

A third option is bipartisanship layering (or multipartisanship), which involves parceling a single set of jobs between two or more personnel systems using an established formula. Bipartisanship is most used by U.S. state governments, where patronage-dominated personnel systems must deal with the administrative instability caused by electoral competition. In pure patronage systems operating without a partisanship agreement, losing-party loyalists holding nonmerit positions are wiped out. The frequent result is complete chaos. One way to blunt the administrative instabilities of electoral swings is through a bipartisanship arrangement, such as Indiana's 1971 "60–40" law, which regulated the losses of jobs party members suffer when defeated. Similar ideas are at work in international public services, such as the United Nations, where jobs are allocated by worker nationality, with fixed formulas defining the share of employment going to each nation.

The fourth design option is the horizontal overlap of separate systems of employment. Unlike a system of horizontal separation, horizontal *overlap* involves a merger at the working levels of administration of people who, even though performing similar kinds of functions in proximity to one another, belong to separate systems of employment. Numerous examples of horizontal overlap are found in the federal government in overlaps of patronage (that is, Schedule C) and merit schedules of employment (Heclo, 1977). Thus, under horizontal overlap, people occupying policy-making and confidential positions are interlayered with those in classified (merit) positions. Horizontal overlap can occur at every level of U.S. public service, ranging from clerical to executive levels. High-level administrative change will involve many people ranging from chefs and chauffeurs to administrative assistants and private secretaries whose basis for appointment is with patronage rather than with merit. Yet the political retinue will work side by side with career civil servants carrying the same job titles whose appointment is protected by civil service.

Can complex systems of public personnel layering be made to work? In spite of the potential for confusion, there is no reason why complexity cannot be made productive, at least in principle. The main culprit would appear to be confusion derived not so much from the fact that people from different personnel systems work together at the same locations, but from the flux and uncertainty generated by the often shifting boundary between politics and administration (Rosen, 1975).

Obviously, layering needs to be approached with great care. The realities of politics and public policy suggest that people who play separate and distinct roles in government are probably best protected by distinct personnel schedules and employment procedures. Indeed, uncertainty and confusion are the problems, not complexity. Scant evidence drawn from private-sector research suggests that clarity in the division in labor among multiple systems and, paradoxically, integrative links among them can result in a highly effective workforce. On the other hand, sloppy distinctions, unclear assignments, and few lateral linkages can produce an administrative nightmare (Lawrence and Lorsch, 1967).

Summary

All of public-sector human resource management depends on a complex series of designs that determine most of the operational details. Once the basic, or strategic, choices are made about labor markets, employment system types, and human resource management designs, the vast majority of decisions are made. Even within the rubric of what is commonly referred to as a "merit" system, many design choices are available. For the most part, American public services have been based on specialist job designs, open recruitment systems, and selection systems geared toward program-based staffing. These designs have been accompanied by rank-in-job compensation systems and nonelitist training and development systems. Such a system has been based on an industrial model of personnel administration and has served reasonably well as a human resource management template. Whether such a design can survive in the postindustrial era is deferred to a later chapter.

Our most significant conclusion is that, contrary to popular belief, public service is an enormously flexible instrument. Moreover, the world of strategic human resource management appears likely to change as technology progresses and new methods of work organization are found. For example, the rise of team-centered production units made up of cross-skilled personnel is one innovation that will challenge traditional ways of organizing work. The result of such challenge is likely to be a reliance on person-centered systems of production as public productivity derives from knowledge-intensive products and applications of information technology and work automation. How this can occur will be developed in subsequent chapters.

Chapter Five

Determining
Human Resource Requirements
from Strategic Goals

The design of an employment system, discussed in Chapter Four, addresses the problem of workforce availability. Nothing concrete has yet been said about the problem of workforce requirements. Both private and public managers struggle with the requirements problem, but in the nonprofit world of government and third-sector corporations, there are special problems. How many people does it take to run the public railroad when there is no competitive market test of efficiency? What staffing levels are actually required to provide adequate public health care? How many uniformed police are required to ensure public safety? How to join the world of workforce management to the world of substantive public problem solving is the core of the requirements-side issue. In essence, what is needed is an understanding of how policymaking (strategic planning) and management decision making interact and how specific workforce requirements result from the policy formulation process.

Recasting the Workforce Management Logic

As noted in Chapter Three, the workforce management logic revolves around a deliberate comparison of workforce "demand" and "supply" and deciding how the two sides can be equated. In reality, however, the terms "demand" and "supply" are misnomers. Real managers are less concerned with plotting abstract demand and supply curves and are more concerned with managing, respectively, levels of workforce *requirements* and *availability* as defined by goals, resource availability, and operating work systems.

The lure of rational workforce management beckons. If it were possible to *know* what the requirements and availability for a given service are, we could engage in precise and knowledgeable management. Explicit strategies could be developed by which requirements and availability could be brought into balance. As we will see, however, the barriers to precise calculation are enormous. The key to "knowing" lies less with the availability side than with developing a strategy by which requirements can be established. Availability measurement is not a trivial exercise, but the basic methods of accounting for personnel "supplies" are known and well developed (Bennison and Casson, 1984; Bartholomew and Forbes, 1979). Less well understood is the requirements side of workforce management.

There is no easy answer to the earlier rhetorical questions about public workforce requirements, but we can describe a basic logic by which the problem can at least be approached. Figure 5.1 graphically displays the requirements-side logic in greater detail than was explained in Chapter Three. At policymaking levels of management, decisions in three areas form the strategic basis for defining workforce requirements: missions and goals; selection of implementing machinery; and the technological design that forms the basis of a work system. Collectively, these three decision sets fix the basis for the rest of the workforce requirements exercise.

The most fundamental, or strategic, level of workforce management involves developing a strategic sense of the final outcomes that must somehow be engineered within the constraints of finite resources, threats, and competition. At least three choices are made at the level of workforce strategy, or policymaking. The first is to determine the missions, objectives,

Figure 5.1. Workforce Management Functions and Decisions:
Requirements Side.

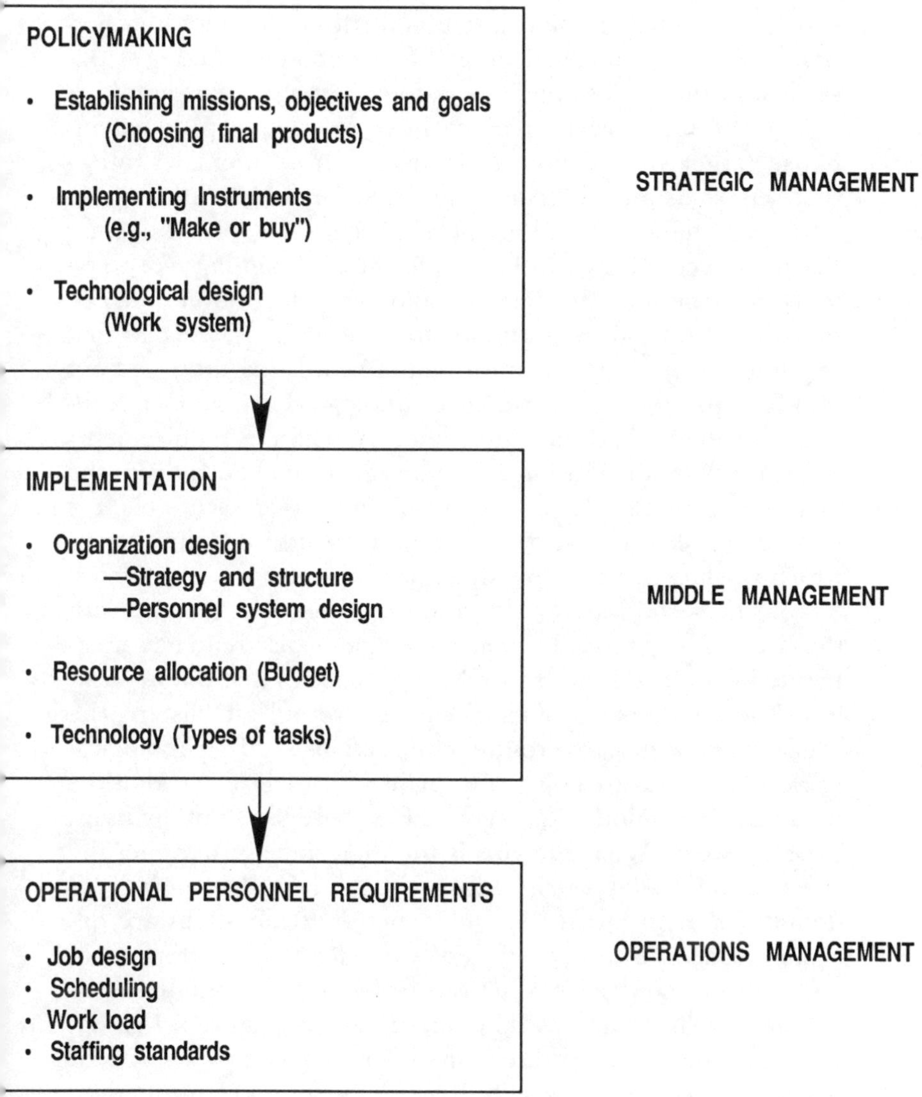

POLICYMAKING

- Establishing missions, objectives and goals
  (Choosing final products)

- Implementing Instruments
  (e.g., "Make or buy")

- Technological design
  (Work system)

STRATEGIC MANAGEMENT

IMPLEMENTATION

- Organization design
  —Strategy and structure
  —Personnel system design

- Resource allocation (Budget)

- Technology (Types of tasks)

MIDDLE MANAGEMENT

OPERATIONAL PERSONNEL REQUIREMENTS

- Job design
- Scheduling
- Work load
- Staffing standards

OPERATIONS MANAGEMENT

and goals that define the essence of productivity; defining the mix of final products establishes the bottom line of agency and bureau activity. The second element of strategy is the basic choice of implementation instrument through which the bottom line will be reached. This implementation strategy constrains all the tactical and operational details; for example, a decision to build workforce capability by making products in-house rather than contracting out is a fundamental strategy that sets goals and directions, in turn, for middle and operations management. The third strategic choice involves selecting the basic technologies to be employed in designing work systems; for example, the determination that the bottom line can be reached only through automation of work systems or that applications of electronic information processing must be built into final products is a strategic technological decision. In summary, strategic determinations about workforce requirements affect every other decision a firm or agency makes. Indeed, the fact that certain decisions are "prime mover" choices—choices that affect all other choices—becomes a useful definition of which workforce issues are strategic and which ones are not.

The second level of decision making must grapple with the issue of how missions, objectives, and goals are to be implemented. These are the "second-move" choices that follow strategy. Tactical decision making revolves around establishing the organizational designs, resource allocations, and technological choices that convert policy and plans into reality. It should be noted that the middle management exercise does not, by itself, produce work. What remains is the final stage of defining the specific, day-to-day work assignments that fix the operational definitions of productivity. Only when individual jobs are designed, schedules are produced, work loads are determined, and staffing standards are set can real workforce requirements be known. Thus, the central point implied by Figure 5.1 is that defining workforce requirements involves a complex series of decisions and calculations. The problem-solving chain holding up productivity is a long one. Figure 5.1 also indicates where to start start solving the puzzle, for the anchor of the entire requirements calculus is policymaking and the process by which strategic choices are made.

Two Approaches to Policy Formulation

Policy formulation involves developing policy options that are effective, efficient, and feasible. There are many approaches. The many possibilities are perhaps best seen by considering two contrasting alternatives—synoptic and strategic approaches—which frame a continuum (Lindblom, 1977). The synoptic formulation is the more ambitious approach, in the sense that synoptic managers are confident of their ability to treat problems comprehensively and analytically. Indeed, they have great faith in synoptic planning as well as management. Their confidence lies partially with the latent assumption that there is one individual—the decision maker—whose role is to provide central direction and guidance for an entire system of activity. In workforce management, synoptic policy formulation produces an analytically "correct" number of workers required to perform a task or accomplish a goal—for example, the number of professionals required by an analytically projected demand for health care service, or the maximum health service levels a given level of employment could sustain. The synoptic analyst would gather all data showing both employment levels and patient service demands and attempt to derive a correct relationship between input and output variables. We will return later to the types of calculations that might be done.

The second approach to policy formulation is strategic planning. This approach depends on different assumptions, the most fundamental of which is that the intellectual ability of central planners, policymakers, and managers to master the substance of complex problems is severely limited. The implication is that there is no single decision maker whose views can be supreme because no one knows enough. Strategic planners and managers adopt a view of policy formulation in which analysis *derives from,* rather than preempts, the interactions and decisions of the multiple decision makers in a complex service delivery system. As a result, the strategic approach depends on social interactions to reach planning outcomes that planners are either unwilling or unable to reach analytically. Policy analysis is always partial, incomplete, and limited to the solution of strategically important problems.

An analogy taken from highway policymaking illustrates the two different approaches (Lindblom, 1977, p. 314): "Consider two methods of policy making or planning for a twenty-year program of vastly expanded highway building. Synoptic theory requires that all the proposed highways be seen as part of an integrated grid and that no one highway be justified except in relation to the others. Strategic policy makers or planners will, however, operate on the assumption that they cannot see clearly twenty years ahead. They will also believe themselves incapable of grasping all the inter-connections of traffic that make the case for one route dependent on the design of other routes. They will therefore decide now on some of the required highways, then analyze the results before scheduling others."

A more concrete way to envision the competing claims of two obviously different approaches to strategy formulation and workforce requirements is to apply both hypothetically to a state-level mental health system.

Synoptic Planning. A good illustration of the rational-comprehensive aspirations of synoptic planning is found in input-output analysis, which can be simply described as an accounting technique that relates labor inputs and service outputs. Indeed, the formal aim of the input-output exercise is to show the interdependencies among *all* labor inputs and service outputs in a given domain. If we imagine an illustrative domain consisting of a statewide mental health system, how could the goal of rational workforce requirements policymaking be achieved?

In practical terms, synoptic policy formulation means that there must be a reporting system whereby every service provider gives to a single decision maker or planner a stream of data about labor inputs and service outputs. The data must be fully comparable across all reporting units, meaning that the same definitions, measurement methods, and reporting formats must be used by all service providers. Such a reporting system means, if actually implemented, that some central planning office must be in a position to receive and process a stream of data required for input-output data manipulation. An adaptation of Wassily Leontief's classic matrix (1966) to mental health workforce analysis is shown in Figure 5.2 to illustrate the synoptic logic.

Suppose further, for the sake of illustration, that a decision maker feels that some action must be taken to ensure that a sufficient number of nurses is available. Now can input-output analysis be applied to this very practical problem? The table matrix outlined in Figure 5.2 frames the synoptic answer.

We depart from Leontief's original illustration in two stylistic respects. First, the illustrated table does *not* depict transactions among industries defined in terms of sales (outputs) and purchases (inputs), in which the sales outputs are shown in rows and the purchased inputs are depicted in the columns of a square matrix showing all exchanges among all industries of an economic system (Leontief, 1966). Second, the "transactions" in our table are not measured in terms of the money values of interindustry sales; public managers are not really interested in calculating the *sales impact* of the rise in demand for services. We assume that the system of mental health delivery to which we apply synoptic planning is predominately a public system for which the "sales test" is not a sufficient measure of either input or output.

Our concern is with a state's mental health workforce, more particularly, specific categories of labor such as professionally trained nurses. We are interested in the relationship between the units of mental health labor needed to provide specific services, which can be defined by such measures as the number of patient-days of treatment provided by the facilities included in the mental health domain. To facilitate the organization and presentation of the matrix, we reverse the customary input-output matrix, the labor inputs are summed *along the rows* and the mental health outputs are summed *down the*

Figure 5.2. Sample Input-Output Table for Mental Health Patient Services.

PATIENT OUTPUTS BY PROVIDER

OUTPUTS \ PERSONNEL INPUTS	(1) State Hospitals 1, 2 .... N	(2) CMHCs 1, 2 .... N	(3) Other Providers 1, 2 .... N	(4) Training Schools 1, 2 .... N	INPUT TOTAL
1. Psychiatrists, physicians, and dentists					
2. Psychologists					
3. Social Workers					
4. Nurses					
5. Pharmacy personnel					
6. Therapists					
7. Counselors, teachers, and associates					
8. Dietary personnel					
9. Attendants, aides, and technicians					
TOTAL PATIENT CARE STAFF					
10. Support staff: administrative clerical, and maintenance personnel					
GRAND TOTAL—ALL INPUTS					
OUTPUT — PATIENT SERVICE TOTAL				**	
INPUT/OUTPUT RATIOS				**	

The figures used would depend on whether one were attempting to show the teaching staff required to serve the patients treated at a teaching facility or the teaching of future practitioners. If the former, then the number of patients or patient-days would be the output measure; if the latter, then students in training would be the measure.

columns. Note that the table consists, in effect, of two columns in each service provider column, one for patient output summaries to be summed *down* each column and the other for staffing levels of personnel inputs to be summed *across* the columns.

A real input-output table can, in theory, be tailored to a specific mental health system. On the input side of Figure 5.2 for instance, there is no special classification for paraprofessionals, an omission that will trouble decision makers attempting to plan such programs. Furthermore, different input measures may be used: "person-hours," "person-days," "person-weeks," and so forth. These input measures must be operationally tied to comparable output measures such as patient-days, patient-episodes, or patient-weeks. For purposes of illustration, in Figure 5.2 we allow for the existence of private practices, clinics, and private hospitals under column 3 and teaching institutions under column 4. State institutions and publicly funded community mental health centers (CMHCs) are listed in columns 1 and 2. Clearly, there is room for connoisseurship in the development of real-world input-output analysis. Furthermore, the data demands made of providers are enormous.

The matrix in Figure 5.2 suggests two different applications of potential interest to policy formulators and workforce managers. First, one can derive labor input requirements from forecasts of service output levels by multiplying a projected patient load by staffing coefficients. Projections of work load can be derived in several ways, including extrapolation of work-load trends, educated guesses, and use of models. (The annotated bibliography in Appendix C provides more detail about analytic planning techniques.) To the forecast patient load are applied *staffing standards coefficients* that describe the skill mix needed—required numbers of psychiatrists, nurses, psychologists, attendants, and so forth. Coefficients are perhaps best thought of as rules of thumb that show the resource requirements of productivity, in this case the number of people required to service the needs of some number of patients. Coefficients can be simply expressed in terms of a personnel-to-patient ratio, for example.

Once a staffing standards decision is promulgated, however, the arithmetic of the input-output table is technically simple and straightforward. The workforce input total is the product of patient load and staffing standards coefficients, as shown below.

$$\begin{matrix} \text{Total} \\ \text{workforce} \\ \text{requirements} \\ \text{(Inputs)} \end{matrix} = \begin{matrix} \text{Patient} \\ \text{load} \\ \text{(output)} \end{matrix} \times \begin{matrix} \text{Staffing} \\ \text{standards} \\ \text{(Coefficient)} \end{matrix}$$

In effect, the labor requirement has been derived from guesses about work load. Synoptic workforce planners can begin to compare labor input requirements with the known availability of labor and contemplate the actions necessary to equate the two. The calculation mechanics are illustrated in Appendix D.

The second application of the input-output logic can be found by reversing the procedure described above. Instead of deriving the labor inputs required by the output demands of a mental health system, analysts can derive the outputs a system can produce given a fixed level of labor input. This is arithmetically accomplished through the simple manipulation,

$$\begin{matrix} \text{Patient load} \\ \text{(Output)} \end{matrix} = \frac{\begin{matrix} \text{Total workforce} \\ \text{requirements} \\ \text{(Inputs)} \end{matrix}}{\begin{matrix} \text{Staffing standards} \\ \text{(Coefficient)} \end{matrix}}$$

The result is a set of planning projections describing the output capacity of a state's mental health system. In effect, if we take the availability of a state workforce as predetermined, a derived estimate of the system's service level can be established.

Input-output analysis is flexible. Where planners are not convinced of the validity of staffing standards, one can try out the results of different staffing assumptions. For example, the derivation of real-world coefficients is not simple. Indeed, the derivation of staffing standards coefficients is one of the most difficult pieces of the planning puzzle. In the mental health example, one source of staffing standards can be found in the hospital accreditation process (Joint Commission on Accreditation for Hospitals, 1979). Another source of standards can be found in the staffing requirements of insurance providers that administer Blue Cross/Blue Shield programs and such third-party payment programs as Medicaid, Medicare, and Title XX. Even the courts have prescribed staffing standards for institutional confinement of the mentally ill. Court cases such as *Wyatt v. Stickney* (M.D. Ala. 1972) have even promulgated specific patient-staffing ratios. It is not the purpose of this discussion to establish the "correct" staffing standards. Such standards are the result of professional judgment about what constitutes acceptable care. The implications of staffing according to a "medical model," or a "Wyatt v. Stickney model," or a "social service model" can be compared and assessed. Furthermore, both outputs and inputs can be derived depending on the planning problem at hand. The analysis is both comprehensive and analytically rational.

How useful is such analysis for statewide mental health planning? There are several possibilities. Decision makers can forecast the staffing implications of forecast changes in *demand* for mental health service caused either by funding shifts, by greater public acceptance and use of mental health services, or by changes in the occurrence of mental disability. Alternatively, they can use input-output analysis to explore the implications of supply constraints on the delivery of services. For instance, one can discover the extent of a shortfall in the supply of psychiatrists, nurses, therapists, and other skilled personnel. Mental health administrators can then discover the extent to which workforce supply shortages might endanger the accreditation of mental health facilities and lead to the curtailment of funding and service capacity. Decision makers can presumably contemplate actions that will lead to increasing the supply of trained personnel, including an expansion in training programs, expanding workforce development programs, and improving compensation schedules. In short, input-output tables allow planners to show comprehensively and analytically the relationship between the supply and demand for labor.

There are problems with applying synoptic tools to complex realities, such as mental health systems. One set of problems arises because of the assumptions built into the classification and measurement of mental health inputs and outputs. The most obvious assumption is uniformity and completeness of information. To be useful, input-output analysis requires a workforce classification system common to all providers of mental health service. There must also be a comparable set of categories into which mental health outputs can be subdivided. Both input and output classifications must be mutually exclusive and mutually exhaustive so that analysts can aggregate the inputs and the outputs to obtain statewide totals and disaggregate the totals to break out the components of mental health care such as mental illness, mental retardation, inpatient treatment, outpatient treatment, and so forth.

This is hard work. In many states, for example, standard output classifications—the patient treatments—and the input classifications—the workforce classifications—do not exist. Government workforce classification systems are particularly awkward. In the state of Indiana, for example, the state personnel system uses more than 338 different position titles for the 7,100 positions authorized by the state's mental health institutional manning table, and no one institution uses more than 130 position titles. The community mental health centers, by contrast, report their workforce totals in 26 classifications (including the category "other") for a total workforce that exceeds 4,000 persons. There are no official crosswalks that connect the two systems.

Even if problems of classification and common data collection were to be solved, there is a second major problem with using input-output analysis on a statewide basis. The static technological assumptions of staffing coefficients are not necessarily applicable. To carry out the mathematical manipulations of input-output analysis, one makes several technological assumptions, including:

- Cost–output relationships are unchanging (constant return to scale)

- There are no jointly produced services.
- There is an absence of input substitution because of shifts in the price of labor.
- No technological change (new drugs, new treatments) occurs.
- Production coefficient constancy is an appropriate assumption for all providers of mental health service.

Once again, the practical realities are that substantial experimentation is now occurring and will continue as mental health financing changes, new modes of community service delivery are developed, and new forms of medication and therapy are discovered and used. Furthermore, professional personnel particularly feel the effects of change; people trained as psychiatrists, nurses, psychologists, and social workers are encountering curricula designed to accommodate new technologies, treatment methods, and modes of service delivery. The evolution of community-care modes of service delivery has also spawned substantial experimentation with the use of paraprofessionals.

Problems with input-output classifications and calculating the effects of technological change are *not fatal* to input-output analysis. Analysts can develop tables based on alternative classification schemes and reasonable estimates. In effect, multiple comprehensive analyses can be developed that depict the relationships between inputs and outputs *assuming* a given set of classifications and staffing coefficients. For instance, the workforce effects of staffing according to a "modern medical model" can be compared with the workforce effects of staffing according to a "social service" or a "natural helping network" model, each of which posits different technological relationships between labor inputs and service outputs.

The fatal flaw of input-output analysis derives from yet a third problem. Input-output analysis for a complex domain, such as statewide planning, can be developed only by adopting a political structure in which a central decision body—a planning intellect—commands the collection of data, the analysis of results, and the application of findings. (Otherwise, why do the work?) Yet planners ordinarily do not and should not make operational staffing decisions. Only a perverse application of input-output analysis would attempt to bind operating and professional mental health managers and providers to the constraints and knowledge gaps of a crude input-output table. For example, the structure of community-based mental health treatment means that a large number of community-based service providers determine the kinds of people they will hire, the salaries to be paid, the mix of disabilities they will treat, and the design and location of service delivery, all tailored to meet the needs of specific clients in specific locations.

To develop an input-output matrix that does *not* arise from the realities of an increasingly diffuse service-delivery and decision structure is to divorce planning from real decision making. When that happens, analysis no longer serves the purposes for which planning was initially justified: *to improve the quality of workforce decisions*. For example, if one were to attempt to use synoptic analysis to forecast the mental health labor inputs required by service demands, the resulting demand forecast would bear no *necessary* relationship to real labor requirements. In short, analysis unalloyed by real operating requirements obscures the effective demand for mental health workers. Without operational information, the labor demand calculated from an input-output table would be simply an analytically derived demand, not necessarily a correct derivation of a real requirement. Such requirements are known only to operations-level managers and decision makers.

Strategic Planning. An alternative to synoptic policy formulation is to approach decisions strategically. That is, decision makers recognize from the outset the complex nature of the enterprise they seek to manage and look for strategic opportunities to intervene. The strategic approach is distinguished by several characteristics. First, planning should integrate the interactions and decisions of operating mental health systems with the analytic requirements of planning. Second, strategic planning can arise only from discrete, strategically selected, practical problems. Third, such integration of operations and planning can proceed on a case-by-case basis, as decisions must be made in areas such as training, finance, skill shortages, organizational and service delivery design, program investment, evaluation, and so forth.

To conclude that strategic problem solving is a more sensible course than synoptic planning does not mean that a modern investment in input-output analysis is inappropriate. Public service planners might well profit from the attempt to fill in the matrix shown in Figure 5.2. That would permit mental health planners to see a complete system modeled *as if the numbers were true*. Much of planning analysis revolves around responding to the "what if" inquiries of planners and managers. The point, however, is to realize that such synoptic modeling derives from analytic assumptions rather than operating realities.

The reasons strategic policy formulation is frequently preferred to the synoptic formulation bears repetition. One is the absence of uniformity among the units for which planning is being attempted. A second is the lack of adequate information tools that would support synoptic analysis. A third is the existence of political weakness at the center of a social system that is unable to command and control data gathering and classification efforts and the decision making that bind the many affected enterprises. A fourth is the existence of rapid change that renders plans obsolete as soon as they are promulgated.

Operational Requirements

In the end, how can operational workforce requirements be derived? The logic is simple, even if the actual derivation is difficult. Regardless of the method of policy formulation, requirements logically depend on two factors: work load and staffing standards. Work load can be thought of as the volume of work carried by a workforce in a fixed period of time. Staffing standards define the numbers and types of people needed to service a given work load. Each factor, in turn, is conceptually derived as a function of many independent variables.

In the mental health case, work load, for instance, is affected by the following variables:

- Population characteristics (c).
- Economic (e) factors such as state and federal budgets, disposable income, cost and price of service.
- The supply (s) of specialized facilities and skills (a common pattern in mental health fields, where the case load demand for service is fixed by the *supply* of personnel and facilities); in essence, supply can create its own demand.

In a similar fashion, staffing standards, or coefficients are affected by several variables:

- Productivity (p), the case load mental health workers can carry.
- Technology (t), the kinds of treatments provided.
- Delivery system (d), the kind of facility and organization structure for dispensing service.

What is envisioned, in effect, is that staffing requirements will be made increasingly precise and defensible by means of data and analytic models that remove, over time, larger and larger pieces of guesswork from forecasting and planning. The analytic relationship of work load and staffing standards to workforce requirements is shown in the following simple equation:

$$\text{Requirements} = \text{Work Load} \times \text{Staffing Standards,}$$

where

$$\text{Work Load} = f(c,e,s)$$

and

$$\text{Staffing Standards} = f(p,t,d).$$

Whether the functional relationships should be established as a result of axioms and mathematical formulae or as a result of regression coefficients needs no resolution here. Future research will help resolve some of these issues. The point for this discussion is that analytically defensible estimates for fixing workforce requirements can be derived easily in support of workforce planning.

Several different methods of establishing staffing standards are available. Staffing can be done on an hourly full-time equivalent (FTE) basis, where the work requirement is defined on the basis of time. It can be done on a shift coverage basis, where "filling stations"—staffing physical locations at fixed times—becomes the standard work definition. Third, staffing can be done simply on the basis of whole positions or slots filled, as distinct from shifts worked. Fourth, staffing can be viewed in terms of particular productive activities completed, where case loads, numbers of consultations, or numbers of procedures define the work requirement.

No single standard is universally appropriate. For example, in hospitals, prisons, state parks, and police, days of coverage and the filling of stations, or beats, might predominate; in institutional settings, attendants on wards, security personnel, and switchboard operators would be covered by the "station-fill" concept. The hourly standard, by contrast, would apply to administrators, most maintenance personnel, and many professional personnel whose work is defined as a time-based contribution to productivity and who may or may not remain on call during the off hours.

These two methods of fixing staffing requirements are joined by others. For example, staffing by slot, or position, would be most applicable to organizations where people work however long they must to accomplish goals and objectives. Universities, research institutes, and many businesses with salaried professional employees are leading examples of work systems not adequately defined either by hours worked or number of stations filled. Community-based social services delivery, to take still another example, has a staffing requirement based on the provision of outpatient treatment. Service is therefore provided on a work-load basis where the work load is, with the exception of inpatient care (a surrogate measure of acute care), organized on the basis of number of visits and hours of consultation. In work-load case, staffing standards are perhaps best organized either on a case-load basis or in terms of FTE coverage. The FTE standard is a flexible one that can accommodate the diverse staffing arrangements typical of community-based service delivery systems that require small and constantly changing staffs employed both full-time and part-time and including both direct employment and contract employees.

A Technical Illustration

For all of the conceptualizing and policy formulation, the manager still does not possess an operational definition of the precise number of specific people needed by a particular work system. Two concrete illustrations will help show the level of complexity involved in converting staffing standards and work-load demands into operational requirements. (The reader more interested in strategic issues may wish to skip this section, with the warning that major policy issues still lurk beneath the surface of a seemingly technical illustration.) One example concerns the application of an FTE approach to derive an hourly requirement. The other involves an application of the "station-fill" approach.

The general method illustrated here and in Figure 5.3 is broadly adaptable to other methods of operationalizing human resource requirements. In essence, one must estimate the work load, convert the work load to a personnel requirement, inflate the actual work load by the extent to which a loss rate (vacation, sick time, training time, official holidays) involves legitimate time away from the job, thereby increasing the coverage that must be planned, and convert the estimate of paid coverage (either hours, shifts, slots, or case load) into the number of employees required. The notion of a leave or loss rate is pivotal, because it acknowledges the extent to which employers are paying for work that is *not being done;* this is not all unproductive time, for its definition can include the replenishment of the labor force through rest, training, or personal wellbeing, so that actual time spent on the job is fully productive. Indeed, the loss rate can be deliberately engineered in a strategy where human capital is created through classes or workshops that are not part of work system coverage. Enormous potential exists for modernizing and upgrading workforces through a creative use of loss rates in organizations.

When total paid person hours is the operational definition of a personnel requirement, the strategy is to estimate the total required hours (TRH) of work to be accomplished, inflate the required hours by the extent to which extra hours must be contracted in order to recognize a legitimate "leave rate"—often collectively bargained—by which official time off the job reduces the coverage one person can provide and thereby increases the total paid manhours (TPM) that must be planned by the manager. The FTE conversion simply divides the total paid manhours by the operating definition of the number of hours that constitute one FTE person. The final result is the number of FTE persons who must be employed to cover the estimated work load.

For example, suppose a work-load analyst for social services in a county welfare system discovers a work requirement of 3,000 person hours of coverage necessary to provide a set of consultation services. The human resource planning problem is to calculate the requirement for people employed in occupation X that provides the coverage. Parenthetically, the total required hours can be derived in several ways. One way is job analysis, where the time required to complete specified tasks is estimated from collecting and assessing job facts. Another technique is to determine time requirements through industrial or clinical engineering where analysts attempt to estimate the time needed to complete a procedure or set of procedures. Regardless of the technique employed, the total required hours (TRH) is generally stated as the product of the work-load units (WLU) and the hours required per WLU. Thus, if a standard patient consultation is thirty minutes and an estimated annual number of consultations (WLU) is 6,000, then the total number of required hours (TRH) is 3,000 hours. The logic of calculating the FTE requirement is abstracted in Figure 5.3.

Given that the work-load problem is solved, how many FTE welfare workers in occupation X are required to cover the TRH? Two further steps provide the answer. The first is to convert the TRH to total paid manhours (TPM). This is computed as:

$$\frac{\text{Total Required Hours (TRH)}}{1 - [\text{leave rate proportion}]} = \text{Total Paid Manhours (TPM)}.$$

The second step is to convert TPM to the FTE employment requirement by dividing the TPM by the number of hours one FTE person is paid to work. Thus, if the leave rate is ten percent, from sick leave, vacation days, and other days off, then:

$$\text{TPM} = \frac{3000}{1 - .10} = 3333.33 \text{ hours of salaried work must be contracted.}$$

It is assumed in this example that the basis for work is salary rather than an hourly wage rate. If one assumes that in one year one FTE is paid for 2,080 hours of work (50 weeks times 40 hours per week and 2 weeks of paid vacation), then 3333/2080 = 1.6 FTE persons, the number of on-board personnel required to provide the hourly coverage.

A second illustration is found in the calculation of shift coverage requirements. The logical problem in the "station fill" case is to determine the number of individuals (NI) required for filling shifts or stations. In this case, the object is to establish the number of shifts covered per year (SCPY) and to compute the NI by dividing SCPY by the number of shifts an individual can do per year, adjusted for the leave factors that reduce the actual availability of personnel: paid vacation, holidays, sick leave, and personal leave days. The number of shifts one individual can do per year (SIPY) is found by multiplying the number of shifts one person is assigned per week times the

Figure 5.3. Derivation of Staffing Requirements.

A. Full Time Equivalent (FTE) Requirements*

1. Derive total required hours:

| Work Load Units (WLU) | X | Hours Required Per WLU | = | Total Required Hours (TRH) |

2. Convert TRH to paid manhours:

$$\frac{TRH}{\text{One minus the leave rate (\%)}} = \boxed{\text{Total Paid Manhours (TPM)}}$$

3. Convert TPM to required FTE:

$$\frac{TPM}{\text{Hours one FTE is paid per year (e.g., 2080 = 52 weeks x 40 hours/week)}} = \boxed{\text{Required FTEs}}$$

B. Number of Individuals (NI) Required for Shift Coverage**

1. Compute number of shifts covered per year (SCPY):

| Number of shifts/week | X | Weeks covered/year | = | SCPY |

2. Compute number of shifts an individual can do per year (SIPY):

| Number of individual shifts/week | X | Weeks covered/year | = | SIPY |

3. Remove vacation, holiday, sick leave, and personal leave shifts from SIPY = Available shifts per individual (ASPI):

| SIPY | - | Number of Vacation Shifts | - | Number of Holiday Shifts | - | Number of Sick Leave Shifts | - | Number of Personal Leave Shifts | = | ASPI |

4. Derive number of individuals (NI) required to fill all stations per time period:

$$\frac{SCPY}{ASPI} = \boxed{\text{NI (caution: the time period may be years, months, weeks or 24-hour periods)}}$$

*Source: Adapted from Avellar, J. W., 1982.
**Adapted from Taylor, E., 1981.

number of weeks of coverage, but the available shifts per individual (ASPI) is less than the SIPY because of the loss factor.

One way to envision the number of individuals required to fill all stations per time period (one year in this example) is to work the logic shown in Figure 5.3 with one station that must be staffed 24 hours per day for 365 days of the year—police coverage, for example. To staff a single post around the clock for one year, the number of shifts to be covered per year (SCPY) is 1,092, (21 weekly shifts multiplied by 52 weeks). However, the number of shifts one individual can do per year (SIPY) is normally limited to 5 eight-hour shifts per week for no more than 52 weeks; in this example, we could fix SIPY at 260. But SIPY is itself a bogus number, since the value of ASPI, the available shifts per individual, is fixed by the value of SIPY minus the leave rate. As an example, we will use the following definition of leave to illustrate:

> Paid vacation: 12 days, or shifts
> Holidays: 13 national holidays, or shifts
> Paid sick leave: 6 days, or shifts
> Personal days: 3 days, or shifts

The total leave is 34 leave shifts, not counting possible training and development and personal leave days. So, in this conservative example, the value of ASPI is 226 actual days of shift coverage that may be provided by one person per year. The loss factor, in effect, is 13 percent.

How many workers must be employed to staff one station on a 24-hour basis? Where an annualized number is required, the answer is clearly 1,092 divided by 226, or 4.83 person years of work. The 4.83 staffing standard also holds for shorter periods of time if one is willing to prorate the loss factor over time. If the loss factor is distributed over time, in lumps, then adjustments must be made in the ASPI calculation.

The above calculations are easily made on spreadsheets and hand calculators and can be modified to suit the personnel policies of any particular setting. For example, the staffing standard of 4.83 persons employed for each 24-hour station fill can also be converted to find the number of individuals required to fill only one eight-hour shift on a seven-day basis. In the example above, the eight-hour coverage factor is 4.83/3 = 1.61 individuals per eight-hour period. Thus, if 20 individual stations must be filled in a single eight-hour period, then

32.2 persons (20 × 1.61) will have to be employed to cover the stations seven days a week.

Balancing Requirements and Availability

It is useful to conclude this chapter by recalling that requirements are only one part of the workforce management puzzle. Availability is the other side. However, availability is as difficult to define and measure as requirements. The following have at various times been considered as definitions of labor availability:

- The number of persons qualified to practice in an occupational area, whether actively practicing or not.
- The number of persons available to practice an occupation at a given time, including those employed, self-employed, and available for work but currently unemployed.
- The number of *unemployed* persons qualified to practice in an occupational area.
- The number of entrants, including newly qualified practitioners reentering the market after a period of nonavailability.
- The number of persons in an occupational area who would be in the market if the pay (or other compensation) were raised by specified amounts above prevailing levels.

At any given time, any of those might be relevant definitions of the effective availability or "supply" of personnel.

How does the workforce manager cope with the potential confusion inherent in so many complex meanings? The basic answer for a practicing manager is to ignore for now the theoretical notion of "supply" as being too imprecise for managerial use and to substitute a term that acknowledges the nature of the supply-side ambiguity. In effect, the five definitions really indicate the conditions under which supplies of labor might actually become available for use by management. So the concept of "availability" appears to define the general notion that at different times and conditions, people of varying capabilities can be made available to do work in any organization.

At least three dimensions characterize the notion of workforce availability. The first pertains to the stocks and flows of people in a labor market. A "stock" of labor is the number of people who belong to an occupation at any one time, and a "flow" is the movement of labor from one category to another. A second dimension refers to the extent to which the stocks and flows of labor are *actual* or *potential* availability: actual availability refers to the stocks and flows of people either newly arrived or currently practicing an occupation, whereas potential availability includes the stock and flows of people who, whether currently practicing or not, are *capable* of practicing an occupation. A third dimension is the extent to which personnel stocks and flows are *controllable* by administrative action (such as hiring), or may remain uncontrollable because the timing and magnitude of personnel movement is a function of factors beyond administrative manipulation (such as death or retirement). Ultimately, then, stocks of personnel are controllable only to the extent that flows of personnel are controllable.

An illustration of several of these concepts is shown in Figure 5.4. Personnel stocks and flows are depicted by boxes and arrows, respectively. Both controllable and uncontrollable accessions to occupational positions and separations from positions are included. The movement from a stock of apprentice and probationary positions to "protected," full-performance positions is depicted as an added classification refinement. It does not take great imagination to envision how Figure 5.4 could be adapted to the terminology and structure of a variety of management uses. Indeed, technology exists by which managers can report their estimates of personnel stocks and flows for each year of operation in terms of columns, or vectors, of data representing the various classes of personnel. A supply-side report should logically be organized as:

$$\begin{array}{c} \text{End of year} \\ \text{(stocks)} \end{array} = \begin{array}{c} \text{Beginning of year} \\ \text{(stocks)} \end{array} + \begin{array}{c} \text{Accessions} \\ \text{(flows)} \end{array} - \begin{array}{c} \text{Separations} \\ \text{(flows)} \end{array}$$

Figure 5.4. Model of Personnel Stocks and Flows.

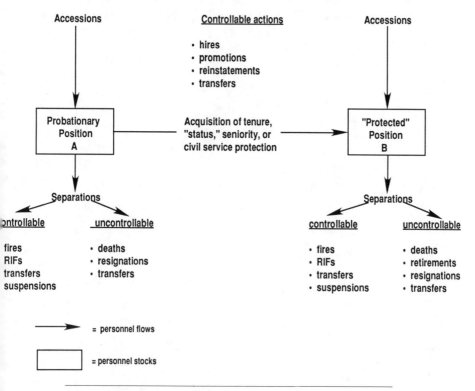

Source: Adapted from Gringold, R. C., and Marshall, K. T., 1977, p. xxi.

Thus, reporting workforce availability can easily be compared with operational workforce requirements. The comparison frames the workforce management dilemma. Hidden in this discussion is that none of this analysis can be undertaken without a workforce classification scheme that allows quantitative comparisons of requirements and availability. This is a critical problem deserving separate treatment, for without proper information that sorts the workforce into managerially meaningful classifications, the implementation of any kind of workforce planning and management system remains problematic. Indeed, a poor structure for capturing strategic workforce distinctions can make even the most analytically clever system utterly useless. Workforce classification is the foundation on which the development of a managerially useful information system rests.

PART THREE

WORKFORCE INFORMATION SYSTEMS AS A STRATEGIC TOOL

The workforce management logic entails managing massive amounts of information about the workforce and presents managers with an extraordinary intellectual challenge. Multiple stakeholders control different pieces of information about the workforce and require different information for decision-making purposes. Multiple schemes exist for characterizing the nature of the workforce in terms of position, person, and product characteristics. Furthermore, modern workforce management envisions experimentation with a number of different strategies. Only a successful management of information adequately supports multilevel workforce decision making. Fortunately, user-oriented applications software is available to assist with workforce data-base management.

Chapter Six

Information Needs
of Decision Makers

There is a sonorous ring to the phrase "management information systems." However, behind the seeming coherence and sophistication lies a potential confusion that often escapes discussion. Workforce management, particularly public-sector management, adds to the confusion because it involves a large number of politically significant actors, each with a specific stake in directing, regulating, constraining, deciding, or otherwise knowing about workforce management decisions. These are the "stakeholders," and public and private managers both need to deal with them effectively.

Both sectors must deal with employees and their representatives, general management, and the larger community (Beer and others, 1984). While it can be argued that public managers confront no stakeholders who own private shares of the enterprise, there are public-sector analogies associated with the financing and direction of public enterprise. Furthermore, the stakes tended by each actor include multiple values, goals, and concerns that are partly economic, partly psychological, and partly political. Thus, in both sectors there are bound to be clashes between management, employees, and the general public over costs and reward structures, allocation of status and intrinsic workplace satisfactions, the definition of rights and privileges, and the exercise of influence over decision making.

In the public sector, however, the openness of a management process that calls for public accountability has an enormous impact on the way stakes and stakeholders are defined. This is implied in a political context that contains substantial checks and balances between competing branches of government and political institutions. It seems that "publicness," by definition, authorizes both multiple stakes and stakeholders, and, in addition, supplies the political leverage by which stakeholder interests can be articulated and defended. By contrast, private systems are distinguished by being relatively closed to external supervision and regulation. The existence of multiple, authoritative actors who impinge on workforce management is merely one reason why the public-sector management job is so difficult. The net result is that while both public and private managers employ the same basic logic in thinking about workforce management, public-sector realities make the problems more complex and the solutions more difficult to develop.

All stakeholders seek information about workforce decision making. They want to know whether their interests are being defended or threatened and to gauge the effects of prospective decisions on their domains. Public managers, in particular, need to pay attention to stakeholder need for information—or, put differently, the user need for information—for public-sector stakeholders denied adequate information are in strategic positions to impede management accomplishment. Conversely, adequately informed "information users" are often in a position to be of enormous assistance in workforce decisions. Thus, understanding the information needs of specific end users, or stakeholders, is a fundamental step. Moreover, because of the complexity and size of the stakes, it is imperative that the public manager understand both the number of workforce information users and the stakes that define their interests. In effect, the user information requirement is also a public management information requirement.

Public-Sector Stakeholders

A public sector "user requirement" is defined here as an occupational information need essential to the successful performance of authorized duty by a public actor that may be an agency, an office, a recognized group, or a person. Occupational information may also be useful, desirable, informative, or important. But for occupational information to be *required,* it must be directly tied to questions a public user must address and decisions that must be made as a result of the user's charter or mission. The list of potential users of public workforce information is long and, for purposes of simplification, is reduced to five categories. Each category is ranked in terms of the extent to which the user is *removed from* internal personnel operations and the generation and handling of raw data that flow from personnel transactions.

The first category includes all users directly involved with the continuing operation of a personnel system. Users in this category are involved in public personnel management and define and generate the raw data used in workforce classification and analysis. Users include:

Agency personnel offices
Central personnel agencies
Merit systems protection boards
Labor relations authorities

The second category is information users who confront workforce budgeting and management decisions. Whereas personnel operations involve taking actions (hiring, firing) to fill personnel supply needs, workforce budgeting involves placing constraints on resource availability, which limits the effective demand for labor. Budget and management decisions derive from the conversion of public policy goals into implementation choices from which decisions are made about whether to expand or contract specific programs, whether to use government workforces or contract workforces, and whether to change the constraints, or ceilings, under which personnel needs are determined. These users include:

Offices of personnel *management*
Offices of management and budget
Legislative budget agencies and committees (U.S. congressional budget office and state legislative service agencies)

The third category is program planners and managers. These users are planners engaged in establishing future goals for departments and agencies or operating programs. This user is concerned with the production of final goods and services within the resource constraints of money and people. Workforce information is of value to them only insofar as data bear on the productivity of public operations.

The fourth users are the oversight bodies charged with ensuring public agency accountability, compliance with law, and program efficiency and effectiveness. The techniques of oversight include pre- and post-auditing, program evaluations, and the use of special hearings and studies. Oversight agencies exist in both the legislative and executive branches and include the following:

Equal Employment Opportunity Commission
Departmental and agency inspectors general
Ombudsmans
Human rights commissions
Legislative oversight bodies (U.S. General Accounting Office and state legislative services agencies)

The fifth category is organized public interest—the general public and organizations that articulate public information needs (news media) as well as interest groups with specialized information requirements. Examples include:

Students and trainees
Schools and education commissions

Unions
Employers
Minority groups
Professional associations

In sum, at the root of all user quests for workforce information is a set of descriptors about who people are and what they do for work. An accurate description of how people are occupied can only be achieved by developing an occupational classification system that classifies people in terms of their work and the relationship of that work to an organization. A classification system revolves around seven core data elements. Taken together, these data elements define the essential basis of an occupation.*

1. *Title:* the name given an occupation and people holding a position classified as belonging to a given occupation.
2. *Description:* a summary definition of the distinctive features of any given occupation.
3. *Duties:* an enumeration of the tasks and responsibilities associated with a given occupational *position.*
4. *Qualifications:* an enumeration of knowledges, skills, and abilities that must be possessed by *people* classified as belonging to a given occupation.
5. *Level:* the degree of organizational responsibility (supervisor, nonsupervisor, manager) associated with a given occupation.
6. *Career:* the sequence of positions (apprentice, senior practitioner, master, instructor) a practitioner might be expected to hold during a single career.
7. *Function:* the industry, mission, or purpose that describes the result, or the *product,* associated with a given occupation.

The information needs of the five user categories are not confined to the seven dimensions of an occupation, how-

---

*I am indebted to George S. Maharay of the National Academy of Public Administration for his many insights about the basis for occupational classification.

ever. Users also typically require information related to an occupation, such as:

1. *Personnel actions:* the personnel decisions that result in a change in the status of an employee, such as hire, transfer, promotion, forcible separation.
2. *Size:* the number of people and proportion of the workforce found in any given occupation.
3. *Compensation:* the pay, benefits, and other remuneration associated with a given occupation.
4. *Location:* the geographic placement of people in given occupations and the distribution of occupations or groups of occupations across space.
5. *Enterprise type:* the organizational structure in which members of an occupation find employment. Examples include government agency; private, profit-making corporation; not-for-profit corporation.
6. *Population characteristics:* age, sex, race, education, background attributes.
7. *Comparative labor market indicators:* pay and benefits, terms of employment.

Information Consumption

The result is that classification data must be combined with occupationally related data to produce useful information. Operating personnel agencies need to know the effects of personnel actions, such as hires and separations, on the size of an occupation in a given government agency. The Equal Employment Opportunity Commission needs to know the extent to which there are race or sex differences in the distribution of the workforce across selected occupations. Obviously, the possible combinations of variables are very large. Indeed, focusing on the many combinations of data elements means losing sight of the fundamental data issue for information system design: whatever the combination, users require precise distinctions about occupational status and occupationally related data elements. Thus, it is the proper recording of occupational distinctions that constitutes the raw data problem for workforce information systems. For public-sector users, each of the distinctions derives from the unique problems faced by the five types of users.

Operating Personnel System Users. Operating personnel system users consist of all offices which administer the rules and regulations promulgated by offices of personnel management (OPMs), merit system protection boards (MSPBs), and the labor relations authorities (LRAs). At the core of the personnel profession is a concern for the supply side of human resource management: the recruitment, selection, placement, and development of adequate numbers of personnel and skills to fill agency demands. Personnel offices typically want to know what kinds of existing skills and capabilities can be discovered from a simple set of descriptors about occupation, education, personal characteristics, skills, and so forth. The personnel problem is to forecast position requirements (demand) against which supplies of human resources can be matched through the management of personnel actions. The recent civil service reforms redraw the strict personnel charter. The new charter, in effect, authorizes OPMs to become more concerned with human resources budgeting and management and, thus, to become more involved with those occupational classification elements associated with resource constraints placed on the demand side of management (budget) and the means by which demand and supply are brought into balance (management).

Workforce Budgeting and Management Users. Both the offices of management and budget and the Congressional Budget Office (or legislative services) manage the demand for workers by establishing the ceilings that constrain the demand for personnel services. The heart of the budget discipline is making resource allocation decisions. Because budgeting in the United States involves decisions not just about money but about human resources—defined in terms of total ceilings—federal budget offices must be concerned with the mix of products and activities authorized and funded, the costs of human resources, and those factors—such as the skill mix or worker productivity—that affect program cost.

The direct consequence of a budgetary concern with program cost, especially aggregate program cost, is an emphasis on information that depicts from manning tables the mix of occupations associated with agency functions and programs. In this sense, the budget discipline is more concerned with the demand, or position, side of workforce information than the supply side. Budgeting is also concerned with grouping occupations to compare costs of alternative productive systems. Thus, the analytic use of occupational information from a budget and even a management point of view involves groupings of occupations rather than occupational transactions and raw data.

Program Planning and Management Users. Program planning and management involve conceptualizing and implementing programs whose purpose is the delivery of final governmental goods and services to citizens. Policy planners are officials and offices concerned with the analysis and advocacy of goals for public agencies. Program planners are concerned with the mobilization of resources required to deliver public policy results and to project program requirements under alternative scenarios. The costs of failing to account for both the employment effects of public policy will be reckoned in the delays that must be endured before a policy goal can be converted to reality. In instances where *timing* is strategic to policy success, failure to assess the workforce effects of policy choice can result not just in implementation delays but in complete policy failure.

Because program planners are, by definition (Dimock, 1978), essentially concerned with the delivery of final products to consumers within budgetary constraints, government program managers must be concerned both with the demand and the supply side of occupational information. Thus, program managers typically want to derive workforce demand by converting program needs into work load and staffing standards against which projected demand is compared to the availability of people and their occupational qualifications. The program planning and management need for workforce information goes beyond merely balancing occupational demand and supply within a *single* government agency. Its concern is with the competitive evaluation of alternative ways different workforces can be joined through the management of payrolls, contracts, grants, and cooperative agreements. Thus, program managers are charged with ultimate program accomplishment and, as a consequence, are increasingly led to consider the use of private and nonprofit enterprise as well as government workforces. As a result, program planners and managers require comparative information about workforces.

Oversight Agency Users. Oversight agencies are of two types. They may be charged to oversee all aspects of workforce management, in which case their charter for occupational data overlaps all five user categories. The General Accounting Office and many legislative committees fall in this category. Second, they may be charged with specialized oversight responsibility, in which case a special aspect of workforce management, such as affirmative action, pensions, or employee health and safety, define their regulatory responsibility.

An excellent example of specialized oversight responsibility is affirmative action, where Title VII of the Civil Rights Act of 1964 and the 1972 amendments of the Equal Employment Opportunity Act (EEOA) mandate the elimination of workplace discrimination based on race, color, creed, national origin, or sex. The use of the Equal Employment Opportunity Commission (EEOC) and the U.S. Department of Justice as regulatory bodies for the private and public sectors, respectively, requires a knowledge of occupational information depicting upward mobility opportunity for women and minorities, in particular. This means, in short, that EEOC/Justice needs information about occupational level, such as apprentice, full performance, and senior level, and occupational data depicting bona fide occupational requirements. Therefore, the EEOA agenda requires occupational data that depict position duties and responsibilities against which personal qualifications—defined as knowledges, skills, and abilities—can be certified as job

related. Furthermore, the Office of Federal Contract Compliance is empowered to encourage compliance in its supervision
of jobs created for minorities by patterns of government contracting.

Public Information Users. There are two categories of public
information users. The first includes the general public and
those mediating organizations, such as the press, that interpret
general public demands for occupational information to public
workforce managers and report the results of workforce studies to their respective publics.

One aspect of the general public's concern for public
service information, as articulated by the media and its representatives, is with the size and cost of government. Size is measured in two ways: (1) by static comparisons of the government
workforce with other governmental and nongovernmental
workforces; and (2) by longitudinal comparisons of trends in
the growth of government employment and cost. Another aspect of the public's concern with employment information is
with the distribution of employment across occupations, agencies, and regions of the country. For instance, government pay
policy is of obvious general public interest because of the impact salaries have on local economies. The general public view
is often developed through the activities of subgroups that demand specialized information about government workforces.
These groups are too numerous to name here, but the user list
would certainly involve the following illustrations:

- The general public's desire to know the size and cost of government as reflected in inquiries such as the Grace Commission (see Chapter One).
- Organized populations who wish to chart the progress their
  members have made over time in public service.
- Regional interests of the country that want to know the regional impacts of government employment and spending.
- Professional associations that demand information about
  certified practitioners in government service.

In addition to the general public, there are specific organized publics with special information needs. One major group consists of *students and trainees* and their advisers and counselors. This part of the population has yet to enter the labor force and must contemplate an investment in education and training to begin or change careers. They require information about public workforces that will accomplish the following:

- Inform them about kinds of work and pay levels, to help them make decisions about whether to pursue public employment.
- Advise them about ports of entry to the public service and educational investments that would entitle them to compete for employment.
- Indicate the career prospects that exist in the public service.
- Suggest the career prospects and outlook for those who elect one of the several ports of entry to public service.

In short, students and trainees (and their advisers) require information about public-sector career structures that identifies the routes to long-term employment.

A second group of organized interests is schools and education commissions. The concern of all schools, especially colleges and universities whose graduates generally find public employment attractive, is with their need to make curriculum investments. Such decisions often involve increasingly expensive equipment, a tenure-bound workforce, and conferring credentials on students. As state higher education commissions appear increasingly involved in decisions about investing in programs, especially the authorization of new programs, higher education actors acquire official standing in the pursuit of workforce information.

The interests of nongovernmental employers associations cannot be easily described. Both public- and private-sector employers need to recruit adequate labor supplies for their enterprises. Recruitment success depends, in large measure, on the pay structure and other incentives with which desired employees are attracted and held. Thus, all employers need information about the competitive adequacy of their compensation programs. Since the governmental workforce employs many people with professional and managerial skills also demanded by nongovernmental employers, there is great potential for increasingly stiff competition for scarce pools of trained talent. In addition, government data definitions and classification standards often serve as demonstration guidelines for private-sector occupational information.

Government employment is increasingly a collectively organized sector, and unions have an obvious interest in public employment information. Part of union interest is joined with the interests of employers who need compensation benchmarks. Unions also use labor market information to estimate the size and structure of the workforces they might organize. In addition, nongovernmental unions find government compensation data helpful as a bargaining benchmark, and unions are even tempted to compare different levels of government. For example, the American Federation of State, County and Municipal Employees (AFSCME) might well use federal data as a basis for bargaining about state and local government compensation.

Two conclusions can be drawn from even a cursory consideration of user information needs. The first is that oversight agencies and public information users are mainly concerned with structured information in which occupational classification elements are aggregated into occupational categories. Those users are not, for the most part, concerned with collecting and coding raw occupational data. Normally, they seek an aggregation of occupational classifications arrayed against occupationally related data such as pay, location, and population characteristics.

Only the first three categories are concerned in any significant way with collecting raw classification elements and raw occupationally related data. An occasional exception occurs when a union or professional group attempts to reclassify an occupation, but even then the concern is not data collection so much as data definition. Thus, operating personnel offices conduct job analyses and collect raw occupational data relating to position duties and responsibilities, qualifications of a workforce, and the pay, locations, and background of workers. Management and budget offices collect agency, program, and position data associated with agency workforce ceilings and payroll disbursements. Program managers establish the functional classifications to which are assigned the productive contributions of the workforce. Thus, two important categories of information consumer—oversight agencies and the general public—are dependent on the data collection services of the other three categories, whose internally oriented information requirements are not necessarily congruent with each other or with the requirements of oversight agencies and public representatives.

The second conclusion pertains to data requirement differences that separate personnel agency requirements (the first category) from the budgetary, managerial, and public policy information requirements of the second and third categories. The traditional preoccupation of operating personnel agencies with matching *individuals* with vacant positions, or, conversely, removing *individuals* occupying terminated positions, produces an occupational information system adequate for traditional internal personnel operations, but inadequate for public policy, management, and budget purposes. In other words, personnel information systems that usually serve as the source of workforce information are plagued with limitations imposed by the very definition of the personnel administration charter.

In particular, three data limitations typically impede a managerial use of most workforce information systems. First, organizational outcomes are not measured; in raw data terms, the function or product is often not attached to the other six classification data elements, resulting in an incomplete occupational classification data set. Second, of the occupationally related data elements, the type of enterprise and the basis for labor market comparison are not yet developed in most statistical systems to the point where program managers and planners can evaluate their program implementation options based on a knowledge of likely comparative workforce impacts. Finally, development of occupationally related comparisons by end users is also constrained by confusion about the operational definition of the term "occupation," a subject to which we turn in Chapter Seven, because what most stakeholders require is not raw occupational data but data organized in some intelligible and summary fashion about groups of occupations. Another way to state the obvious is to point out that the predominant stakeholder need is for information rather than raw data dumped on the management desk. But if confusion exists in the raw definition of "occupation," it is inevitable that confusion will also permeate any information system whose architecture is built on that confusion, and in this event workforce information systems will be unable to serve a real user need.

Information Supply and Use

Our conclusion is that multiple political and administrative demands for workforce data are a permanent feature of public accountability systems. Indeed, a permanent feature of the public management landscape vis-à-vis the private-sector environment is the extent to which an enormous number of public stakeholders compete to influence workforce decision making. Three broad categories of stakeholder exert controlling influence: (1) public policy agencies, (2) administrative agencies, and (3) certification and accreditation agencies, which are third-party stakeholders controlling large portions of public and private enterprise. Their pattern of information supply and use is depicted in Table 6.1. For purposes of simplicity, information in the third category is defined only in terms of health and human services enterprises.

Note that each actor is empowered to act on the public workforce in a politically significant way. Therefore they cannot be ignored, however much managers might wish to do so. Personnel system administrators can legitimately insist that merit or patronage rules of personnel access to jobs govern the employment of government employees. Budget offices can insist that budget ceilings and salary allotments not be exceeded. Legislatures and chief executives are empowered to control the overall size and cost of government employment and to ensure that employee expenditures of effort are designed to achieve

Table 6.1. Selected Public-Sector Workforce Information Suppliers and Users: Selected Examples from Health and Human Services.

Organization	Information Role	Nature of Data Supplied
Public Policy Agencies		
Governors, mayors, presidents, legislatures, councils	User	Uses comprehensive set of aggregate workforce data
Oversight and auditing agencies	User	
Administrative Agencies		
Budget agencies	Supplier	Staffing ceilings; Budget authorities and allotments
	User	Staffing costs
Personnel department	Supplier	Manning table; pay plan; position classification; merit/nonmerit administration
State and local auditors	Supplier	Data processing reports on staffing patterns
Certification and Accreditation Agencies		
State boards of health	User	Medicare certification
U.S. Dept. Health and Human Services	User	Medicaid certification
Joint Commission on Accreditation for Hospitals (JCAH)	User	Third-party reimbursement

public goals. Certifying bodies can insist that people who provide professional services by government are properly licensed and accredited for practice; this latter process often controls the release of third-party reimbursements for health and human services. Table 6.1 summarizes several actors now directly involved in the management of public workforces.

Multiple sources of data make information supply confusing and expensive, however. Public-sector reporting systems typically follow *functional organization lines*. Each operating division of a public agency has an institutional interest in owning a specific kind of workforce information. Each functional division physically possesses and controls its information through special data collection instruments and hard-copy batch reports. The personnel shop collects data on personnel transactions. The controller tracks salary obligations against budget authorities. The staff development director tracks in-service training, continuing education, and professional personnel licensure. The budget office attempts to cost out service delivery requirements. State boards of health seek information about patient-staff ratios for Medicare and Medicaid certification of public hospital units.

Functionally organized reporting systems are not management systems, however. Management information is created only when data are related to each other across functional divisions and support management decision making, as for example when managers attempt to relate on-board staffing with staffing requirements to assess the extent of staffing need, to discover whether there is room in the salary budget to hire more clinical professionals, or to assess the skill mix and training of the workforce. Integrative relationships among disparate operating divisions remain one of the great organization design questions (Galbraith, 1973; Lawrence and Lorsch, 1967). To date, it has been the painful task of public middle managers, for example, to convert raw data scattered among disparate reporting schemes into managerially significant information. The reports are hand crafted, slow in production, and occasionally inaccurate. That they are produced at such expense, however, is testimony to the importance of information and to the primacy of defining the user need for information. How to get that information and why the information is required are discussed in the following chapters.

Chapter Seven

Converting Data
into Useful Information

Satisfying the managerial appetite for workforce information requires a clear understanding of the fundamental strategies for classifying and collecting data about human resources. Clarity with respect to occupationally related data goes a long way toward establishing the design of managerial information systems. "Occupation" has never been clearly defined. Indeed, the term has many meanings that must be sorted out before useful workforce information can be made available to decision makers, for core stakeholder information needs can be met only when there is a clear notion of what an occupation means.

Structuring Raw Data

It is an operational definition of "occupation" that makes possible the conversion of raw occupational data into a form amenable to workforce analysis. Occupational information, correctly defined and collected, explains a great deal about who people are and what they are doing in an organization. Capturing the information in raw form is a complex, but not unfathomable, exercise. Thus, while dictionary definitions indicate that an "occupation" is that which "occupies" a person's time and attention and, hence, defines the work that person does, refinements are necessary before "occupation" becomes a concept useful in the handling of raw data. Not only does there exist no standard operational definition of what really constitutes an occupation, the literature suggests many different approaches to workforce classification exist (Scoville, 1969; Scoville, 1972; Miller, Treiman, Cain, and Roos, 1980).

The fourth edition (1977) of the *Dictionary of Occupational Titles* (DOT) provides some operational meaning to the term "occupation" as a "collective description of a number of individual jobs performed, with minor variations, in many establishments." Six elements constitute each DOT occupation: (1) a unique occupational code number; (2) an occupational title; (3) an industry designation; (4) alternate titles (if any); (5) a narrative definition, including a summary statement, a description of the task elements, and a list of the optional items that may be included in an occupation; (6) any undefined, related titles that may apply to the definition. "Occupation," in short, represents a grouping of many uniquely described "jobs" into more generic occupations based on an analysis of the similarities of structure and content of basically similar jobs.

The DOT definition is incomplete, however, where administered workforces are involved. In administered systems, such as public employment systems, the premise of all occupational classification is the existence of goal-driven effort in which *people* occupy organizational *positions* for the purpose of producing final *products*. Viewed from a managerial perspective, therefore, an occupation defines the productive contribution employees make to occupational goals. A corollary is that the heart of *occupational classification* is the classification of information rather than positions, persons, or products. In essence, what are classified are the salient facts about people working in occupations, rather than an indivisible essence of "occupation" that can be abstractly defined. "Occupation" can be defined many ways. The classification exercise is simply a way of sorting the many dimensions that collectively identify the boundaries of an occupation in terms relevant to management strategy and decision making.

Occupational classification should be viewed, therefore,

as a practical undertaking directed toward the production of useful data where utility is judged by the users enumerated in Chapter Six. To be sure, when administrative machinery is established on position-based premises and managed according to what in personnel circles has been known as a rank-in-the-job personnel system, occupational classification and position classification become almost synonymous. But to equate occupational classification with the unique administrative practices of time and place is to ignore the many ways that exist to classify and describe who people are and what they contribute to organizational productivity. Thus, if the point of occupational classification is to develop a pliable information instrument useful to decision makers, how can raw occupational data be converted to useful information? The beginning of the answer is to recognize the different foundations on which occupational classification can rest (Fine, 1968; Scoville, 1969).

At least three fundamentally different kinds of data need to be carefully distinguished. The first defines the "product," the outcome of work effort. Product can be either a good produced or a service performed. Product-oriented classification is often referred to as an "industry," where the private sector is concerned, or a "function," where government is involved. "Industries" have already been defined by the Standard Industrial Classification (SIC) and government "functions" have been defined by the Bureau of Census. But regardless of the term or the precise categories used for coding purposes, the basis for occupational classification remains the same: classification of occupations according to the final outcome of productive effort.

A second dimension refers to the "duties, requirements, and responsibilities" of the position that may exist apart from the characteristics of the person who occupies it. In this dimension, the major tasks performed, regardless of the personal characteristics of the performer or the products produced, become the basis of classification. In effect, one classifies the things a person does in a position or as a consequence of holding a position. The strength in a position-based approach is that resulting classification schemes are not dependent on the credentials of people, which can vary, or on the products they produce, which can also vary.

The third dimension consists of the qualifications and personal characteristics of workers. A person-based classification system focuses on the personal knowledges, skills, and abilities that inhere in persons rather than either positions or products. A typical approach would concentrate on personal qualifications, as represented by educational credentials, or the intellectual discipline of peers with which a person might be classified and compared. For example, most standard classification systems include such professional fields as nursing, accounting, engineering, economics, psychology, and social work, all of which are based on personal specifications that, in effect, define the position.

The result of this conceptualization is a three-dimensional approach to occupational data collection and codification from which precise occupational classification can be established. Figure 7.1 shows the basis of occupational classification where occupations are distinguished by each of the three single dimensions. An economist might be classified in terms of such qualifications as the possession of a professional degree (Ph.D. in economics). A more refined description might use combinations of the three dimensions: "defense [function/product] economist [personal qualification] serving as the administrator [position] of a policy planning office [subfunction]."

Keeping analytically distinct the three dimensions used to define occupation has numerous advantages, three of which are mentioned here. First, raw occupational information can be refined in a manner that permits the definition of the important respects in which occupations truly differ. For some occupations, a single label connotes both the content of position and the qualifications of the occupant. "Physician" seems a good illustration, where the domain of a person's qualifications and the domain of the position are congruent. The result is that the statistical report of occupational data for physicians is comparatively easy. On the other hand, many occupations,

Figure 7.1. Basis of Occupational Classification.

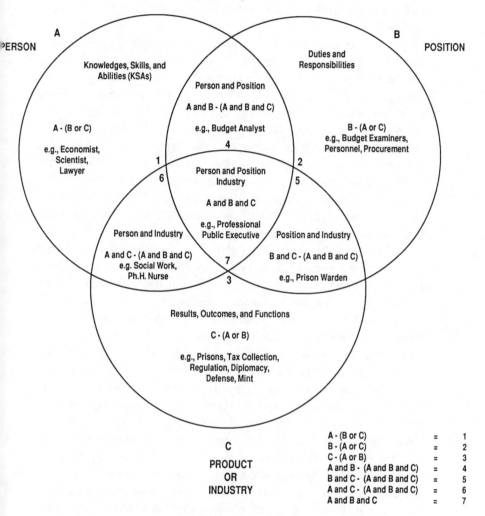

such as budget examiner, program analyst, and procurement official, are really position-based descriptions in which people with widely varying qualifications might well be suited for employment. Furthermore, position-centered descriptions are typically associated with widely varying industries, functions, and product lines. Clarity with respect to the possible divergence of position-based duties, personal qualifications, and final products and outcomes can be observed and catalogued accurately.

A second advantage of a multidimensioned classification system is the ease and efficiency with which occupational data can be processed in a manner consistent with user interest. Since the object of the classification exercise is to convert raw data into occupational codes and categories, the existence of a classification instrument that already reveals the critical differences among occupational types eases the coding burden. At the very least, multidimensional classification facilitates the coding of occupational distinctions based on empirical reality. What is avoided is forcing an occupational classification specialist to spend time debating fine distinctions among occupations with a unidimensional measuring device.

The third advantage is that a multidimensional scheme facilitates the timely delivery of occupational information to users. As noted in Chapter Six, different users require different kinds of information. Some users need position-based data; others need product-based data; other users need person-based data; still others need various classification combinations to answer their questions. Multidimensioned classification obviates the need to undertake a new collection or recodification of raw data each time a different reporting need is discovered. All that is required for report generation is a knowledge of basic data elements and a few simple rules of counting. Figure 7.1 shows how logical combinations of data elements representing the three occupational dimensions can be identified and counted. As we will see more clearly in the next section, such a scheme for classification is precisely what is needed to answer the difficult questions users are now asking, which often require precise comparisons among several workforces, such as between governmental and nongovernmental workers, who perform similar functions and in many cases are in competition for the same work. User questions are answered only when groups of occupations can be identified and compared using a common, or standardized, set of raw distinctions.

Finally, occupational information is only rarely useful

when cast in terms of raw data. To be useful, occupational data must be organized and transformed to acquire form and structure. It must, in other words, be converted to information. Simply put, most humans cannot make sense of the facts associated with the more than 20,000 occupational titles and descriptions found in the DOT. Analysts are only slightly more able to work with the 751 occupations listed in the Standard Occupational Classification (U.S. Bureau of the Census, 1977) or even the 437 occupational series of the federal white-collar classification system (Bureau of Policies and Standards, 1973), or similar numbers of occupations employed by state and local government.

Useful information is acquired only when elaborate classifications of endless detail can be reorganized and aggregated into an intelligible number of categories such that comparisons among categories can be made. Comparisons that interest users almost always involve measurement. Measurement is involved any time a user asks: "To what extent is one group larger than another? Growing? Shrinking?" Or, "To what extent are the characteristics of one group different from another group?" Or, "How many supervisors are there in a given workforce? How many managers? How many executives?" Thus, measurement becomes the only way generalizations about occupations can be drawn from raw occupational data, and classification is the only way to pull generalizations—deliberate simplifications—from the mass of a more detailed and accurate, but unintelligible, set of occupational data. The result is less detailed, perhaps slightly inaccurate, but understandable findings that have the final virtue of responding to specific user questions.

Occupational Grouping

One example of the kinds of comparisons that a multidimensional classification system facilitates derives from the principal classification dimensions themselves. To illustrate this point, Table 7.1 groups selected federal white-collar occupations from the federal *Handbook of Occupational Groups and Series of Classes*

(Bureau of Policies and Standards, 1973) in terms of which dimension predominates as a possible basis of grouping common occupations. The same analysis could have been conducted for any large public or private workforce, but the federal example is well described in publicly available documents. In other words, Table 7.1 shows how the federal occupations could be grouped, or structured, if an analyst were willing to simplify classification data by designating either position or person or product as the basis of aggregation.

Three groups emerge. Each group is an analytically created aggregation derived by emphasizing a single element of occupational classification as the distinguishing occupational feature. It bears emphasis that the raw data do not create the point of emphasis; only analysts striving to supply meaning to raw data determine the basis for aggregation. Thus, the first grouping in Table 7.1 is product dominated. Occupations are grouped according to the "thing" (good or service) they produce. For example, the description of a "Theater Specialist" (Bureau of Policies and Standards, 1973, p. 100) says that they: "(1) plan, supervise, administer, or carry out educational, recreational, cultural, or other programs in theater, such as children's theater or creative dramatics; (2) produce, stage, or di-

Table 7.1. Groups of Federal Occupational Classifications.

I. Production-Oriented Occupational Descriptions
   GS-436   Plant Protection and Quarantine Series*
   GS-1054 Theater Specialists
   GS-1176 Building Management Series*

II. Position-Oriented Occupational Descriptions
   GS-212   Personnel Staffing
   GS-221   Position Classification
   GS-501   General Accounting and Administration Series
            (but not Accounting Series GS-510)

III. Person-Oriented Occupational Descriptions
   GS-460   Forestry Series
   GS-510   Accounting Series
   GS-602   Medical Officer

Source: Bureau of Policies and Standards, 1973.
*Single Agency Standard

rect theatrical productions; (3) instruct or serve as a specialist in direction; technical production; dance production; performance techniques; playwriting; play or music theater production; or theater administration, management or promotion." Group II is distinguished by tasks, duties, and responsibilities that are positionally defined. Group III is distinguished by the personal credentials and qualifications specially trained persons bring to a position.

The importance of such potential groupings is not purely analytic and academic. The groupings seem tied to the organization of the public and, perhaps, the private workplace. Group I is descriptive of those occupations most closely associated with the production of final goods and services. Hence, position duties and responsibilities and personal qualifications are, in reality, determined by the substance of the productive process. Group II aggregates those occupations that are neither "product distinct" nor are the people employed therein best described as possessing a single kind of personal or professional qualification. Such occupations are most generally described as the cross-cutting occupations found in all organizations, public and private.

Group III can be viewed in a similar way. Those occupations for which personal qualifications are the distinguishing feature are the professions, the knowledge-based occupations. These occupations are distinguished by the fact that they are not bound to a single product line, or industry. Furthermore, they are not accurately portrayed by a recitation of position duties; it makes no sense to say that the distinguishing characteristic of the occupation called research scientist is that of "a person who occupies a position the holder of which submits monthly reports and oversees the efforts of a staff of ten." While all positional and personal dimensions of a group III occupation may be duly recorded by the occupational analyst, the *strategic* productive role of the occupations grounded in personal knowledge, skills, and abilities is determined only by a managerial evaluation of occupational data elements as they relate to productivity.

Three discrete conclusions are implied. The first is the

most simple and basic. Workforce information systems require continual refinement in terms of explicit treatment of each of the seven fundamental classification data elements that establish a raw data base capable of meeting the information needs of the many information users mentioned in Chapter Six. Confusion with regard to the core dimensions of occupational classification, for example confusing position with product data or merging personal qualifications with position duties and responsibilities, makes resulting information systems both expensive to collect and of limited use. Conversely, clarity about occupational data makes data collection more routine and less disruptive of operations.

A second conclusion is that clarity about basic occupational data elements means that data collections will be cost-effective because classifiers and job analysts will spend less time debating and confusing fine distinctions between occupations in terms of a single occupational dimension, for example position duties and responsibilities, and can more easily focus on critical differences among occupations based on a complete set of occupational data. Managers, rather than classifiers and data gatherers, can establish the significance and decision-making relevance of the data in terms of strategy and purpose.

Finally, one of the great strengths of an adequately defined data base is the flexibility of use that comes from capturing the several basic dimensions of occupations in one data base. An adequately defined data base will provide an information platform capable of supporting multiple reporting schemes. The technical basis for converting raw data into usable and useful information will be shown in later chapters. However, once the critical elements have been defined, collected, and encoded, a multidimensional data base is available that can serve diverse reporting needs including government needs for labor statistics, affirmative action reporting, planning requirements for multiyear forecasts, and other management needs defined in Chapters Eight and Nine. The costs of reporting, like the costs of data collection, are defined by the cost of designing report formats and generating the code required to convert rules of data base counting into information to fill the report shells.

Rules of Aggregation

We have already established that very few information users require highly refined, detailed, and raw occupational data. Most managerial users need information that is aggregated in some way and related to the other occupationally relevant data elements. Only operations managers have an end-user need for direct access to counts of raw data elements. The difficulty comes in determining how the aggregation is to occur. A good example of incipient confusion lurking in any data base exists in the case of the white-collar portion of the federal service, where 437 federal general schedule (GS) occupational "series" are collapsed into 22 groups, one of which is a "miscellaneous" category covering roughly 46,000 people. Table 7.2 shows the results of the federal attempt to create convenient groupings of series such that broad bands of federal employment have been created in seemingly related disciplines or areas including biological sciences, accounting and budgeting, engineering and architecture, and so forth.

However, grouping by broad discipline without regard to user need for information creates several problems. First, the *basis* of aggregation varies over the twenty-two categories, and no single classification element or standard of information use organizes the federal occupations. Some categories are dominated by positionally defined occupations, such as would be found in the personnel management and industrial relations group (GS-200). Other groups are better characterized as clusters in which the qualifications (such as education) of people working in similar disciplines serve as the organizing rubric; an example can be seen in the biological sciences group (GS-400). Still other groups appear to be organized according to the mission, or product, associated with the occupation, such as the copyright, patent and trademark group (GS-1200). Each of the groupings, therefore, supplies discrete chunks of infor-

Table 7.2. Federal General Schedule Information Structure:
Occupational Groups, Series of Classes, and Single Agency Standards.

Occupational Group	GS No.	Number of Series or Classes	Number of Single Agency Standards
Miscellaneous occupations (N. E. C.)	000	28	6
Social Science, psychology, and welfare	100	29	2
Personnel management and industrial relations	200	16	4
General admin., clerical and office services	300	40	0
Biological sciences	400	34	7
Accounting and budget	500	19	4
Medical, hospital, dental and public health	600	45	5
Veterinary medical science	700	3	0
Engineering and architecture	800	30	0
Legal and kindred	900	23	7
Information and arts	1000	21	0
Business and industry	1100	25	5
Copyright, patent and trademark	1200	11	5
Physical sciences	1300	26	0
Library and archives	1400	5	1
Mathematics and statistics	1500	11	0
Equipment, facilities and service	1600	9	0
Education	1700	7	0
Investigation	1800	26	12
Quality assurance, inspection and grading	1900	4	1
Supply	2000	8	0
Transportation	2100	17	0
TOTALS		437	59

Sources: Bureau of Policies and Standards, 1973, pp. 5–13; Chapman, Maharay, and McGregor, 1979.

mation useful to users who want to know, for instance, the size of the federal health establishment (GS-600 group). But when the user requirement is for a comparison of the federal white-collar workforce with *other workforces,* the federal aggregation structure does not provide comparability.

A second problem users encounter is the variety of occupational "series" found within each "group." As much or more occupational variety is found *within* groups as is found *between*

and among groups. The result is that the ability of any one particular group to satisfy a variety of user needs is curtailed to
the extent that a user requires a consistent, or at least a clear,
standard of aggregation on the basis of which meaningful counts
and comparisons can be made. A good illustration of the difficulties inherent in casual bundling of seemingly related occupational data without regard to user need is found in the
legal and kindred group (GS-900), which embraces twenty-three
different occupational series. The series are varied both in terms
of the personal qualifications and types of employees classified
in the 900 group and in terms of the basis of classification. For
instance, GS-905 is a "general attorney" series, covering attorneys admitted to the bar. This is a substantially different occupation from the "social insurance claims examiners" (GS-993)
or the "claims clerical" series (GS-998). Furthermore, the basis
of classification varies. The "general attorney" series, for instance, is distinguished principally by an employee's personal
qualifications, namely passage of the bar examination for which
possession of a law degree is a prerequisite. The "social insurance claims examiner" series is a single agency occupation, employed by the Social Security Administration, most significantly
defined by the product or function associated with processing
entitlement claims. The "claims clerical series" appear, in the
Handbook description, to be more positionally defined; employees so classified can be found in many federal agencies (Bureau
of Policies and Standards, 1973, pp. 89–97). Thus, the major
federal white-collar groupings shown in Table 7.2 are, in reality, diverse aggregations of occupations serving no discernable
user need for information.

What alternative information structure might be created
to facilitate workforce comparisons involving at least 1,500,000
federal employees now classified in more than 437 occupations? One possibility is to make the raw classification dimensions themselves the basis for occupational aggregation. In such
a scheme, occupations characterized by all seven of the classification elements could be grouped according to those elements that distinguish the unique and important (to the user)
features of an occupation.

Table 7.3 shows how comparisons among different workforces might be made using different standards of occupational aggregation, particularly the basic distinctions of person, position, and product. Indeed, precise comparison is possible *only* when an occupational standard is held constant across more than one workforce. Thus, category I occupations are distinguished by the products or functions associated with each occupation. Occupations most involved with line operations or the final products of an agency would be included. Examples of federal occupations that fit into category I are found in those occupations established under single agency standards, meaning they are nearly unique to a particular agency and its dominant product line. In all cases, the positional and personal dimensions of line occupations are determined by a final agency product.

Category II occupations are those in which position-based duties and responsibilities serve as a distinguishing characteristic. Such occupations are found in all large, formal organizations, public and private. The basis of aggregation cuts across both product and personal standards of classification since both product and personal qualifications can vary enormously at the same time that duties and responsibilities remain relatively fixed. Administrative staff occupations, such as budget, personnel, and procurement occupations, fit into category II.

Category III occupations are those in which the basis of aggregation is personal qualifications rather than a product or a set of duties and responsibilities. Professions typically fit into category III, especially since the occupation of professional economist, attorney, engineer, or research scientist is largely the same regardless of whether the employer is a government agency or a private corporation. Neither is the practice of a profession adequately defined in a list of position duties and responsibilities, since the definition of a profession inheres in the knowledge and personal skill of a qualified practitioner.

A final conclusion is that establishing an occupational instrument useful for workforce management presents a special challenge to analysts. In bald form, the comparisons increasingly demanded by users require instruments that distinguish the extent to which government workforces are similar to other workforces and the extent to which they are unique. The definition of "uniqueness" poses special problems. As Table 7.3 shows, federal uniqueness is defined largely in terms of the purposes (here equated with terms such as "product," "mission," or "program," or "function") of the federal government. Category I defines the kinds of comparisons necessary to establish the uniqueness of federal, state, and local workforces. Public-sector "uniqueness" is not predominant in categories II and III, whose distinguishing characteristic consists, respectively, of positional or personal dimensions. Occupations easily grouped into categories II and III are widely distributed throughout both the public and private workforce, notwithstanding stylistic and substantive differences defining operational methods, practices, and routines. Indeed, category III is the least publicly unique sector. Thus, to the extent that *both* public- and private-sector workforces are becoming more professionalized and knowledge-intensive, as argued in Chapter Two, public and private workforces are becoming more alike.

How can the "uniqueness" of a governmental workforce, or any workforce, be defined and operationalized? In Table 7.3, the deliberately simplistic use of the Bureau of Census's sixteen government functions reveals the basic nature of the classification problem. However, the sixteen categories do not properly distinguish the purpose and products of the many governmental workforces. To be sure, as Table 7.3 shows, the federal government provides "police protection," but the extent of similarity between the federal police "products" of the FBI, the IRS, or the Park Police and the products of state and local police is not yet established.

What is the strategy by which the government functions and products can be defined? Several possibilities exist. The first approach is that public managers might proceed to develop a new set of work output classifications that permit deliberate and competitive comparisons between alternative public suppliers of services and private suppliers of the same services. This might be done purely and simply by reviewing the functions of the major subunits of government and creating a clas-

Table 7.3. Occupational Classification Comparisons: Governmental and Nongovernmental Workforces.

I. Product or Function-Based * Classifications Common to All Workforces

Classification	Local Gov't	State Gov't	Federal Gov't	Non Gov't
Education	Teachers	Teachers	Teachers	Teachers
Hospitals				
Highways	Streets	Highways		Construction
Police protection	Police	State police	FBI, Park police	Security guards
Public welfare				
Financial administration				
Local fire protection				
Correction	Jails	Corrections	Prisons	
Local utilities, nonwater				
Health				
Natural resources				
Local parks and recreation	Park and rec.	State parks	Federal parks	
Sanitation, nonsewer	Solid waste			Solid waste
Water supply				
Employment security		Employ. sec.	Social sec.	Insurance
Sewage				

II. Position-Based Classifications Common to All Workforces

Administrative ---------------------------------------→
   —finance
   —budget
   —personnel
   —procurement and purchasing
   —public information/public relations
Clerical
Housekeeping
Facilities management

III. Knowledge and Skill-Based Classifications Common to All Workforces

Engineer ---------------------------------------→
Architect
Physician
Attorney
Accountant
Scientist

*Categories are functional definitions used by the U.S. Bureau of the Census.

sification scheme for the significant functions and product lines. For example, governments at several levels are involved in such services as policing, education, research and development, production of statistics and published information, transportation planning, and the like. A functional classification and grouping of the public workforce allows direct comparisons both within the many levels of the public sector and between public and private sectors. Table 7.3 illustrates further some of the comparisons that might be made. Thus, it becomes possible to engage in competitive evaluations of the productive contribution of each workforce relative to approximate peer groups. Managers then come into possession of a tool facilitating decisions about whether to invest in one workforce rather than another based on some ability to understand what such investments are likely to involve and produce.

A second strategy would be to use a set of standard program categories as surrogates for the major products of public agencies. Such a system of product classification could be adapted to the program categories used by budget agencies to assign program allocations and costs. Indeed, it appears both feasible and desirable for public personnel offices to consider using available budget program identification systems as a basis for product classification. Such an approach would involve the merger of selected personnel and budget data files. This strategy involves working with data files and classification systems that, for many levels of government, already exist. The result is that workforce decision makers could relate employment in like kinds of occupations—executives; supervisors and managers; professionals; administrative staff, clerical staff; labor, trades, and crafts; machine operatives; medical staff; and so forth—to the significant programs and product lines of public agencies.

A third strategy is even more ambitious: to develop workforce groupings and methods of analysis that are tied to "strategic outcomes of human resource management" (Evans, 1986, p. 150). Strategic outcomes represent the multidimensional nature of workforce management defined in terms of broad categories of organizational achievement where management failure creates strategic performance breakdowns. Among the possible strategic outcomes are the following (Evans, 1986):

- *Internal equity:* the development of formal systems for establishing equity, improving human relations, and enhancing the quality of working life; managers here are concerned with such internal workforce comparisons as would facilitate policies that promote, for example, "equal pay for work of equal value."
- *Competitive performance:* the development of feasible objectives and distinctive competitive competencies that permit the firm and agency to meet the challenges posed by external threat, opportunities, and competitors; here, managers focus on comparisons between internal and external workforces.
- *Innovation and flexibility:* the creation of elasticities and flexibilities that enable the organization to adapt organizational boundaries and internal systems to environmental turbulence; managers concerned about innovativeness concentrate on changes and trends over time, such as trends in personnel flows and the rate at which human capital is formed.
- *Integration:* the creation of effective interunit integration that is required within any complex, multidivisional firm or agency; in this area, managers might be concerned with internal consistency in the design of information systems so that internally valid and comparable user-oriented reports can be generated.

The essence of the strategic approach is that managers must be able to compare multiple workforce dimensions simultaneously. While work in this area is still theoretical, the great strength of this approach is that workforce managers are forced to specify the "ends or outcomes by which human resource policies should be evaluated" (Evans, 1986, p. 149). In effect, workforce managers who focus on strategic organizational outcomes cease to be mere administrators of an important functional activity—human resources *administration*—and become true strategists making direct contributions to the productive bottom line.

Finally, additional possibilities might be considered. An adaptation of the Bureau of Census's functional categories to reflect government functions more explicitly is still another option. Here, the focus is on changing the official instrumentation used to guide public statistical systems. Modifying the Standard Industrial Codes to reflect more accurately areas of public productivity is yet another strategy. In the end, however, the end-user need for aggregated workforce information will determine the best approach. Regardless of approach, we must conclude that without an explicit account of the true nature of productivity, the comparative classification and analysis of any workforce, especially the public workforce, will be incomplete and of service only to a limited list of administrative specialists; strategic managers and decision makers, however, will not be among the beneficiaries.

Chapter Eight

Managing
Workforce Information

It should be apparent by now that the key to workforce management is the successful, or strategic, management of massive amounts of information. Previous chapters have documented the many issues that must be tracked simultaneously. Public managers must comprehend the connection between productivity and human resource requirements. They must know current on-board availability of personnel. They must manage current and future resource requirements and constraints. In the end, workforce requirements and availability must somehow be equated consistent with organizational goals and resource availability. The fact that greater progress has not been made in this quest is due in no small measure to the monstrous information demands made of managers. The availability of an end-user information technology capable of handling the information mass would radically change the possibilities for workforce management, however. It would mean, for instance, that information could be stored, transformed, retrieved, aggregated, analyzed, and printed out at the decision maker's op-

This chapter represents a revision of an article co-authored with John Daly, who also compiled the tables in Appendix A, to whom thanks is owed for permission to revise the following: "The Strategic Implications of Automation in Public Sector Human Resource Management," *Review of Public Personnel Administration*, Fall 1989, *10*, (1) 29–47.

tion in the form of user-oriented reports designed by managers to influence decisions.

Information Management Technology

One encouraging sign is that the availability of information management technology (abbreviated IT) holds some promise of supporting the intellectual requirements of strategic management. At least five types of IT capabilities are required by all managers.

- *Word processing.* The electronic creation of text that can be edited and printed in desktop publishing configurations on management demand. Word processing packages can also be used as text editors to generate programming code in nondocument files to be executed with any number of program compilers.
- *Spreadsheets.* Electronic ledgers composed of columns and rows into which characters and numbers (row and column headings and cell entries) can be stored, edited, and manipulated. User-friendly report generators produce simple calculations, tables, and graphically displayed summary data.
- *Data base management.* Record-based information organized as a stack of electronic file cards on which are recorded alphanumeric characters grouped into fields of variables describing each record. In relational data bases, records and fields from multiple data bases can easily be combined and reorganized, sorted, transformed by calculations, and edited.
- *Graphics and statistical analysis.* The job of statistics involves one of three activities: descriptive statistics in which measures of central tendency, for instance an "average," and dispersion are presented; associational statistics in which relationships between variables are displayed; and inferential statistics in which hypotheses are tested for significance. The purpose of graphics is to give a visual representation of patterns and trends in the form of bar graphs, plots, pie charts,

line graphs, and other instantly recognizable ways to display major findings.

- *Communications.* The transfer of information from collection and coding locations to locations where analysis and decision making occur. Data communication refers to the exchange of information between computers in which data files can be uploaded to larger, more powerful computers, or downloaded from servers into smaller, end-user–oriented computing environments.

The design of any management information system involves the use of all five technologies integrated with hardware configurations including computers, printers, modems, mass storage devices, and connecting communication lines. The application of the five technologies varies with the level of decision making, as summarized in Table 8.1. Masses of data are collected and coded in data bases at operational levels and summarized and transmitted to tactical and strategic levels, where they are aggregated and cross-indexed with other relevant bodies of data—such as cost, program, and productivity data—and subjected to increasingly sophisticated statistical analyses. Strategic levels of organization are furthest removed from the activities that produce raw transactions data and make the greatest use of summary statistics, graphic displays, and special studies.

Can IT be configured to make strategic workforce management feasible? Among the most significant demands placed on public managers is that they must convert transactions data and information—hiring, firing, promoting, paying, disbursing—into decisional information (Camillus and Lederer, 1985) relevant to whether or not to expand or reduce the workforce, increase pay, contract for services, and so forth. The task is compounded by the fact that different combinations of IT are required. Raw personnel data are still handled by larger mainframe computers that process transactions. Yet, end-user needs for analytic decision-relevant information are most easily and cheaply met through the use of microcomputers producing an-

Table 8.1. Information Management Technologies and Decision Levels.

Decision Level	Organizational User	Information Management Technologies
STRATEGIC	Chief executives, Legislature, Significant interest groups, operating departments and agencies	Statistics, Graphics, Word Processing, Spreadsheet Analysis, Integrated Software Use, Microcomputers
		COMMUNICATIONS UPLOAD AND DOWNLOAD
TACTICAL	Operating Divisions, Centers, Institutions	Statistics, Word Processing, Spreadsheet Analysis Networked Micro, mini, and mainframe computers
		COMMUNICATIONS UPLOAD AND DOWNLOAD
OPERATIONAL	Operating branches, Wards, Treatment units, Individual worker	DataBase Management and Report Generation, Communication Systems, Word Processing MainFrame Computers

Sources: Castro, Hanson, and Rettig, 1985; Camillus and Lederer, 1985.

alytic products based on end-user decision needs (Camillus and Lederer, 1985) at middle and strategic management levels.

Fortunately, many of today's personnel functions can at least be partially automated. The cumulative advantages of automation include enhanced retrieval of employee information, simplified updating of personnel files and records, increased ability to address "what-if" scenarios, and the potential for saving valuable labor. The availability of microcomputer and related human resource information system (HRIS) software is an important development for personnel managers; use of automated HRIS may well provide an avenue for expending greater emphasis and energy on critical human resource management issues and less on the clerical routines of personnel operations. Appendix A describes the salient features of a sample of the more common, commercially available HRIS software packages on the market in the middle and late 1980s.

Personnel administrators now confront the question of whether to purchase or create human resource management software. The reality is that most available software has been designed for private-sector applications. Interested public managers may find it productive to purchase demonstrator programs from HRIS software vendors simply to understand the possibilities. Prices for evaluation disks are well within reach of even the most financially constrained personnel facility, generally from $25 to $100. Disks are configured to run on standard, microcomputer-based systems that can double as word processing and data management work stations.

Software consumers using personal computers (PCs) should note that most vendors have migrated toward packages that require minimum storage capacity of at least a 10 megabyte hard disk. With a 20 to 30 megabyte hard disk, however, current PC hardware and software can easily handle personnel data bases of 5,000 to 7,000 employees. In addition, continuing improvements in technology—chiefly enormous increases in storage capacity, machine speed, and multiuser accessibility—together with substantial declines in the price of computing power mean that inexpensive microcomputer-based applications for larger organizations are becoming increasingly feasible. Indeed, because of their speed and power, microcomputers have begun to replace mainframe computers in core, transactions-oriented corporate data-processing centers (Bulkeley, 1990). In many cases, microcomputer software vendors also have programs for larger hardware systems. Indeed, in many cases microsystems have been "downwritten" from larger systems.

The Automation of Personnel Operations

If end-user–oriented applications software is available, is it necessary? Does current personnel software serve a valuable purpose? Appendix A presents a sampling of the more popular available software packages and shows that there is no single personnel function for which automated systems are *not* available. While the study that produced Appendix A (McGregor and Daly, 1989) found no microcomputer system dedicated to preparing the certificates of eligibility required for merit systems, many of the recruitment, testing, and selection packages can be adapted to the requirements of public-sector employment.

The software survey of Appendix A does reveal both the enormous complexity of personnel operations and the diversity of software options available with which to automate the major personnel functions grouped into five broad areas: staffing and employment, compensation administration, career management, industrial/employee relations, and public policy regulation. The coverage of each area in Appendix A is indicated by symbols that show whether the module is included in the basic estimated price or is a supplemental package, or enhancement, available at some unreported cost.

Software Evaluation. It is clear from Appendix A that software vendors target software toward multiple human resource management markets. Human resource managers will need to consider carefully their needs and available resources when deciding whether to purchase off-the-shelf software. In general, most vendors provide core software programs that cover a full range of compensation administration and career management functions. In addition, a significant number of vendors produce staffing and employment software. Only a few vendors provide software dedicated to labor-management relations and public policy regulation, although nearly all vendors dispense modules that track equal employment standards for private corporations.

In all this, there is a tradeoff between ease of use and advanced reporting capabilities (Nardoni, 1985). The intuitive explanation of the tradeoff lies in recognizing that menu-driven software featuring easy-to-use data entry and report generation involves the use of preformatted screens and report forms based on a resident data base management system. A preformatted system works well so long as user need and system architecture are matched. Should unanticipated information requirements arise, then special programming is required to adapt the system to end-user information requirements, in which case the power and ease of programming use become issues. While much has been written already about the tradeoffs involving system costs, long-term maintenance, ease of use, capacity, power, and speed (Nardoni, 1985; Ceriello, 1984), what is clear is that no one system can do all things for all people. Workforce managers will need to define their central concerns and design systems that will meet specific office requirements. Also clear is that automation need not be accomplished in one great leap. It can be implemented incrementally, testing functional modules that serve a specific and limited purpose. A prototype for doing this is presented in Chapter Nine.

Organizational Impacts

Thus far, perhaps the feasibility and the cost effectiveness of automating part of the personnel management function have been demonstrated. What is curious is that so little is known about the organizational impacts of installing this new technology. Speculation and early analysis are far-reaching and often contradictory. One potential line of inquiry concerns general organization design. Some theorists posit the rise of the "dispersed organization" in which communications technology permits the loose coupling of numerous remote workforces to a central organizational unit or program (Louis and Sieber, 1979; Magee, 1985). A corollary finding is that forging direct data links between a strategic decision-making center and remote operations potentially undermines traditional industrial hierarchies staffed by large cadres of middle managers who manipulate instruments of authority and resource control through the routines of bureaucratic management. Postindustrial scenarios literally envision the death of hierarchy as an organizational principle, given the rise of complex information systems in which "power centers are wherever the brightest people are using the latest information in the most creative ways" (Cleveland, 1985a, p. 195). Some scholars have even begun to envision a world of "management without managers" (Martin, 1983; Zuboff, 1988).

Notwithstanding the futuristic excitement generated by the appearance of advanced technology, three puzzles remain for future research to ponder. The first is a discontinuity between the reported rush to adopt the latest microcomputer technology and the reports of only a modest revolution in organization design and management decision making in both the public and private sectors (King and Kraemer, 1984; Rockart and Scott-Morton, 1984; Rockart and Treacy, 1982; El Sawy, 1985). Progress is reported in the areas of paperwork reduction, office productivity, and automating the routine operations of business and government. Yet hard examples of information systems applications that drive planning and management decision making are difficult to find in the private sector (Rockart and Scott-Morton, 1984; Ward, 1987) and appear nonexistent in the public management literature (King and Kraemer, 1984). The absence of a detailed literature (Ulrich, Geller, and DeSouza, 1984; Meyer, 1983) on *successful* IT applications to both public and private strategic management augments a suspicion that there is more to the story than merely some button pushing in an automated personnel office driven by user-friendly applications software configured for microcomputers. Indeed, there is even some suspicion that the computer hype may undermine successful human resource management (Foegen, 1987).

A second puzzle concerns the organizational and office designs that result from the installation of a new technology (Zuboff, 1988; Markus and Robey, 1988). For example, the division of labor in the automated personnel office is not yet clear (Larson and Zimney, 1990). Thus, whether personnel jobs will become more or less interesting, whether the application of smart machines to human resource management will enrich and develop the working lives of the office workforce, and whether the rigidities of bureaucratic hierarchy can be loosened all remain undetermined.

Speculatively at least, the availability of end-user information software produces a number of results. First, the personnel function is freed from the batch-job, mainframe computer and all the intervening constraints on software production, report generation, and controls imposed by a centralized information systems staff. Central data processing of workforce transactions can still be used as a data backup in which to store archival data, as a server for other analytically oriented computers, and as a routine report generator. But current technology means that computing can be widely distributed throughout the corporation or agency with network hookups that link decentralized grass-roots parts of the organization to the strategic center. In addition, current applications software has removed the requirement that personnel office staff be computer programmers in order to enter, store, and retrieve data. This, in turn, places a powerful tool in the hands of managers and reorganizes the office. Clerical staff can be trained to work in the microcomputer work station environment and can increasingly assume administrative responsibilities for the maintenance and retrieval of human resource management information. The result is that personnel managers are freed to reallocate their time toward the design and installation of information systems and formal analysis (Ward, 1987) that supports decision making at middle and strategic levels. These are merely organizational speculations. Presently, there is little empirically grounded literature on the organizational effects of modern office automation (Bell and Steedman, 1967; *Scientific American*, 1982; Zuboff, 1988).

A third puzzle lies in the lurking suspicion that in public-sector organizations, things are different. Indeed, they may be so different that the prospects for successful, comprehensive, and large-scale IT applications may be regarded as congenitally limited by the political and public policy facts of life. This conclusion is one reading of the absence of published reports on public-sector successes. Indeed, the absence of sophisticated IT applications in government is a costly anomaly, given the size of government payrolls and the problems that arise when, as discussed in Chapter One, a strategic management of the public workforce does not occur. Progress in public-sector applications may depend on a better understanding of the many managerial needs for human resource information.

More on Management Information Needs

Managers have many information needs that automated personnel information systems are capable of fulfilling. Table 8.2 lists several managerial needs defined in terms of the different levels of decision making at which human resource managers operate. For example, personnel operations managers require on-line, real-time personnel data about individual employees and transactions. Operations data can be culled from data base management systems (DBMS) whose central function is counting, sorting, searching, and listing raw data pertaining to personnel transactions, such as hiring, firing, scheduling, pay-

Table 8.2. Public Management Decision Level and Associated Human Resource Information Requirements.

Decision Level	Decision Type	Time Horizon	Information Requirement
Strategic Decisions	Policy and unstructured decisions, planning	The future, long-term; for example 1–5 yrs.	Aggregate information, external and internal projections
Tactical Decisions	Management control evaluation resource allocation	Near-term recent past; for example, less than 12 mos.	Summary information functional areas reported weekly, monthly, annually
Operational Decisions	Structured decisions affecting routine activity	Current, on-line production processes	Precise and detailed data on individual employees and personnel transactions

Sources: Adapted from several writings that make the distinctions noted above: see, for example, Rosenthal, S. R., 1982; and Thierauf, R. J., 1982, pp. 72–73.

ment, and training. Compatibility of personnel applications software with the DBMS requirements of operations decision making is one criterion for evaluating the appropriateness of an automated system.

Middle-management decisions, by contrast, confront tactical questions of policy implementation. Middle-level human resource managers sit at the mid-point between the bottom-up realities and constraints of routine operations and the top-down demands of executives and strategic managers for innovation and change. The task of the middle manager is to convert strategic plans into operational realities. "Compressive management" is a current term referring to the creation and implementation of "concrete concepts to solve and transcend the contradictions arising from gaps between what exists at the moment and what management hopes to create" (Nonaka, 1988, p. 17).

The information needs of the middle-level human resource manager are very different from either the operations or the strategic manager. Middle managers make decisions grounded in two sets of problems—structured operating decisions represented by hard operational data and a strategic environment that generates unstructured problems affecting whole organizations. Thus, the immediate information need of a middle manager is for near-term information summarizing operational patterns rather than either raw operational data or aggregated strategic information. Tactically oriented managers need middle-range information that can be arrayed in digested format through the use of spreadsheets, statistics, and graphics packages.

The end-user needs of middle management suggest a second criterion by which the effectiveness of personnel software can be judged. In human resource management terms, compressive management requires report summaries about the alternative short-term effects of either maintaining or changing patterns of personnel management practices. In turbulent environments, middle managers are both users and creators of decision-relevant information (Nonaka, 1988). They *use* summary information about workforce cost, organization, deployment, and performance to make resource allocation decisions and for purposes of management control and evaluation. They *create* information, on the other hand, insofar as compressive management requires that the implications of alternative products, methods, and personnel usages be explored.

Finally, strategic management presents a third criterion for assessing personnel automation options. The strategic issue confronting all organizations is the achievement of a match between internal organizational capabilities, structures, and resource allocation patterns and the opportunities, threats, and challenges posed by the external environment. Strategic planning involves the identification of the most significant problems, opportunities, and constraints confronting an organization and the development of scenarios, or strategies, by which executive-level choices can be informed. Furthermore, strategic problems are, by definition, unstructured and involve choices of product, clientele, competition, and institutional investment affecting whole organizations.

Strategic decisions depend on the analysis of information that can be derived only from strategic data. Strategic data emanate from many sources tied in part to events and activities in the external environment in which a corporation or agency must operate. Even gossip can qualify as strategic data. However, insofar as strategic data can be systematically gathered and stored on a regular basis, the structure of a strategic data base (SDB) is fundamentally different from other information systems. For one thing, truly strategic information addresses at least four conceptual areas: organizational strengths and weaknesses; what it takes to be successful; the nature and strength of the competition; and relevant environmental opportunities and risks (King and Cleland, 1977). Moreover, SDBs seek to collect strategic *information* rather than raw operations data or even tactical information. Thus, large quantities of data and information must be organized, compressed, and arrayed in a strategically relevant way to create an SDB. Indeed, one of the benefits of SDB development is the training opportunity provided middle managers who are forced to develop strategic insights (King and Cleland, 1977).

Thus, the development of SDBs poses a challenge to personnel systems automation. Executives need strategic information support systems to understand the workforce effects of strategic decisions on large and complex workforces in turbulent environments. In private-sector applications, such a "strategy support system" would permit a multidimensional analysis of at least five issues (Fredericks and Venkatraman, 1988, pp. 48–49):

1. The extent to which investments can add value to the organization's product line.
2. What products to offer clients and the marketplace.
3. What customers want the product and why.
4. The nature and location of the competition.
5. The significant trends over time.

In more general terms, strategic support systems provide information that informs executives about significant trends that bear on the internal organizational adjustments required to meet externally generated threats and opportunities.

Strategic Workforce Data bases

Whether a strategic workforce data base (SWFDB) analogue of the SDB can be developed from the data reposing in automated personnel operations systems is a question for personnel information systems managers. In strictly managerial terms, the problem appears not to be intractable. The human resource analogues of the five strategic issues noted above might be illustrated as follows:

Strategic Issues	*SWFDB Questions*
1. Financial	Fixed-cost payroll effects on budgets and breakeven points of agencies and firms (Briscoe, O'Neil, and Cook, 1982).

2.	Products	Proportion of the workforce assigned to programs and final products as opposed to support functions.
3.	Customers	Types of clients served and mix of services provided by the workforce.
4.	Competitors	Comparative workforce cost and quality.
5.	Time periods	Workforce trends over time.

Developing public-sector adaptations of growing corporate practice will be a challenge to public management ingenuity. The kinds of strategic outcomes that might be the focus of SWFDB development are discussed in Chapter Nine. The most obvious conclusion is that regardless of the precise detail of an SWFDB, the basic structure involves the aggregation and juxtaposition of several different kinds of data elements, including the characteristics of people, workforce costs, products and services, and consumers. Furthermore, data must be arrayed over time. But here lies the challenge to public management. Private firms have functionally compartmentalized data elements associated with personnel, payroll, products, and customers housed, respectively, in human resources, accounting, program, and marketing offices. The technical and political problems associated with achieving an SDB integration within a private corporate structure are technically and politically difficult, but they are manageable. In the public sector, however, information integration involves data transmissions and interactions among legislated and sometimes constitutionally established offices including personnel departments, budget offices, government auditors, operating agencies, and program offices. Political realities constrain technical possibility in the public sector.

A further development is that some progress has been made in linking the multiple levels of managerial interest in human resources (King and Cleland, 1977; Szewczak, 1988). Technology is available such that SDB and SWFDB systems can be developed either from a centralized data-processing source or from decentralized SDB system levels. Telecommunication packages exist that allow the broadening of information linkages among and between groups of public decision makers; local area networks (LANs), for example, are becoming commonly used methods of information coordination and planning across diverse decision-making groups. Indeed, more than half of American corporations link their computers in networking arrangements and the number is rapidly growing (Bulkeley, 1990). Moreover, academic institutions and businesses now use group decision support systems (GDSS) technology to allow decision makers in decentralized settings to engage in decision-related meetings. For instance, C.A.C.I. Inc., Cleveland State University, EXECUCOM, and Georgia Institute of Technology, among others, have used GDSS technologies for group decision-making purposes (Huber, 1984). Thus, wide sharing of information and ideas among interested parties can be facilitated by today's LAN technology.

The result of IT development is that decision makers can, without leaving their organizational settings, communicate with other organizational elements even when offices are hundreds or even thousands of miles apart. In the state of Florida, for example, it is possible for a state human resource planner in Tallahassee to communicate with a field budget analyst in Miami about future human resource needs in the Miami/Dade County area. If desired, group brainstorming sessions can be arranged. Ideas can be generated from each participant with the added benefit of preserving the anonymity of each participant's identity, thereby negating rank as a factor in the selection of ideas for further consideration (Szewczak, 1988). In effect, distributed decision-making systems can be developed from a workforce information design (Rathwell and Burns, 1985) that supports multiple levels of decision making (Huber, 1984).

What is needed in public-sector applications is an analytic scheme that explains how data suppliers will be motivated to supply accurate and timely raw data to a managerial end user who has the ability to transform data quickly and easily into information serving a specific decision-making purpose. The problem is both technical and political. It is technical in the sense that human resource managers will want to move raw data maintained by the information systems into analytic environments where information can be aggregated, reorganized, and displayed. Purchasers of applications software with policymaking and managerial aspirations will want to ensure that data files can be exported from operations-level personnel management software modules by communications systems that serve data base management systems, spreadsheets, and statistical systems needed to support tactical and strategic levels of decision making. While the technical problems of hardware connectivity and strategic systems integration have largely been solved, great care must be exercised in software system selection for overall compatibility.

The more difficult problem in decision support system design is political. Public-sector human resource management, in particular, is a fragmented domain, with multiple information management requirements that depend on data elements captured by disparate, independently tenured jurisdictions. The personnel office, or civil service commission, collects information about people. The budget office allocates resources to authorized positions that may be filled and guards the data on budget authorities, obligations, and costs. The auditor's office encodes the information about disbursements (to be distinguished from budget estimates) required to meet a payroll. The program and project offices and line managers know what it is that people actually do for work, regardless of classification and levels of pay. Furthermore, in many levels of government, each management actor enjoys a statutory or even a constitutional basis, such as in the case of an elected auditor in a "long ballot" state, for participating in workforce management. To add to the confusion, not only do many political actors lay legitimate claim to some part of management decision making, but the human resource information supplied and required by each decision-making level (operational, tactical, and strategic) is different at each level. Thus, there are intellectual differences in the decisions made, questions asked, and information required. Even when information technology proves tractable, the public-sector workforce management task is to design schemes that make it both legal and rational for information suppliers and users to install and maintain multilevel workforce management information systems. This is an important and complex problem that cannot be solved without at least a partial automation of personnel operations.

Chapter Nine

Using Data Bases
to Support Decision Making

Those who would be strategic managers confront a massive information problem. Strategic management has an appetite for aggregated and analytic information rather than highly detailed, descriptive data. However, strategic information is designed to address specific macro questions whose answers establish a basis for choice. Unfortunately for strategic decision makers, most workforce data originate in a transactions environment in which minute details of day-to-day activity—hiring, firing, selling, training, investing, treating—are recorded. A discontinuity typically exists between the kind of information workforce managers need and the kind of information most easily supplied. Creating effective decision support systems for workforce management decision making out of transactions-based information environments is not a trivial task. Yet strategic workforce management depends on solving this difficult problem.

The decision environment and the transactions environment are two very different worlds (Camillus and Lederer, 1985). In transactions environments, information about people is kept functionally compartmentalized according to the particular transactions such as hiring, firing, payroll, benefits, or merit systems actions. Transactions-based information is highly detailed simply because the very nature of transactions is detailed, involving particular exchanges between specific parties, at specific times, and recorded in precise ways. By definition, then, transactions-based information is merely a voluminous recording of minute occurrences at working levels of organization and is not obviously related to management decisions.

Management decision environments, by contrast, contain actors who seek to link different sources of information to specific decisions either by pulling from the information welter the relevant transactions or by aggregating the details of transactions to detect relevant summary patterns. Facts, in other words, do not speak for themselves; decision makers manage facts in order to inform the act of choice. The goal of creating decision-relevant information is to answer precise questions— management questions—whose answers establish the foundations of management choice. Information systems that accomplish the task of connecting data to decisions are called, as mentioned in Chapter Eight, decision support systems (DSS).

How can the two information worlds—transactions processing and DSS—be linked in decision-relevant ways? The answer lies in resolving three initial problems. The first problem derives from the many public management *actors* affecting workforce management, each of whom is a specialized supplier and user of workforce information (see Chapter Six) who establish the multiple *dimensions* of workforce management. The second problem derives from the existence of multiple *levels of information* about the workforce. The third problem is technical and involves data base management where the multiple levels and dimensions of information required by workforce decision making are linked. The last two problems are discussed here, followed by a discussion of the significance of crosswalks that mediate the connection between data bases and decision environments. Crosswalks are information tools that link multiple workforce classification levels and dimensions.

Levels of Information

As noted earlier, the three levels of management decision making—strategic, tactical, and operational—have different workforce information needs. Strategic decision making is the policymaking level of an organization, involving issues such as organizational survival, basic goals and objectives, and environmental constraints (such as resource limitation, regulations, and sources of political support). To illustrate the practical issues that arise, consider these concrete examples, taken from mental health and social service administration.

- A governor makes a commitment to full institutional certification of state mental health institutions and loss of certification threatens an institution's survival.
- A court or external regulatory body establishes staffing standards for an institution necessary to be in compliance with state and federal law.
- Strategically placed external organizations—courts, major professional associations, legislatures, budget agencies, and interest groups—require workforce information necessary to their regulation and control of public agency business.
- A technological advance, such as psychotropic drugs and behavior modification techniques, creates new mental health treatments for which trained personnel are necessary.

Tactical decisions, by contrast, deal with questions of organization design and resource deployment that convert policies and strategic plans into programs of work effort. Tactical issues often appear in the guise of a need to evaluate program areas to discover opportunities for reorganization, targets of productivity improvement, and structural weaknesses in service delivery. Middle-level managers are most often concerned with the productive capacity, the cost performance, and the opportunities for financial and personnel shifts that would enhance the efficiency and effectiveness of a service delivery system. Some illustrative *tactical* questions asked by the budget analysts, personnel and procurement managers, and program evaluators include the following:

Are there sufficient numbers of personnel to service the work load?

Are salaries sufficient to attract the right numbers of
personnel?

What are the total workforce costs associated with different modes of service delivery?

What are the most productive ways to organize service
delivery?

Finally, operations managers are concerned with the day-
to-day operating routines and schedules that determine individual-level contributions of public personnel. The focus of *operations* management is on the real-time details of personnel
hiring, scheduling, training, compensation, and mobility that
directly affect production activity. The level of detail is the most
refined, in the sense that operations managers are the supervisors of production personnel concerned with such things as:

- Whether around-the-clock coverage of particular facilities is
available given the current staffing levels.
- To what extent a service provider must be overstaffed to
compensate for personnel attrition.
- Whether a particular kind of certified professional can be
found to cover the needs of a treatment facility.
- Whether adequate numbers of clerical staff are available to
support professional staff.
- Whether personnel with unused overtime can compensate
for staffing shortages at a given institution.

Thus, three levels of management make very different
types of decisions and ask different kinds of questions. Strategic decisions are policy decisions that determine the long-term
goals and directions; by definition, they are future-oriented
planning decisions that constrain all other decisions at the tactical and operational levels. Tactical decisions, by contrast, deal
with disaggregated portions of enterprises, such as can be found
at the directorate, institution, ward, module, or operating division level, where the focus is on near-term decisions and evaluations of service delivery patterns in the recent past. Finally,
operational decision making occurs at the level of the day-to-

day production process, where individual workers, treatment units, and patients must be linked; operations managers are therefore concerned with the efficiency, effectiveness, and quality of current production, since the aim of operations decisions is real-time intervention in the routine production process.

Clearly, different levels of management decision making require different kinds of information to be included in a decision support system (DSS). In general, however, the more that decisions involve operations-level problems, the more detailed, precise, and dense must be the DSS based on transactions-level data. By contrast, the more that decisions involve strategic planning and management levels, the more that workforce decisions require aggregated, rather than refined data; summary approximations, rather than highly detailed information; and episodic, rather than continuous, flows of data.

Based on these differences, it is even tempting to conclude that the design of a workforce DSS must involve the design and execution of a comprehensive and complete multilevel scheme, where operations information systems become the foundation for tactical systems on which, in turn, strategic systems are based. It is reasonable to conclude, therefore, that the entire information structure must be conceived and built as a coordinated whole. This, however, is the ambitious synoptic approach. Information system design that waits to achieve a complete, accurate, and comprehensive coverage before implementing a decision support system may wait a very long time to achieve results. The problem in decision support and information system design is that different management decision levels produce different managerial questions. Each type of question also presents a unique information management problem. Understanding the kinds of information required by each level is the basis for workforce DSS design.

Operations Decision Support Systems

Classic operational concerns revolve around the day-to-day routines and problems of scheduling and managing a workforce. Because the level of detail is so fine, the volume of data can be enormous. For purposes of concrete illustration, the following categories and questions are taken from the field of health systems administration.

STAFFING

Vacancy reports: What are the vacancies by occupational classification, hospital, ward, module, and building? How long has each vacancy existed? What is the extent of turnover in each position?

Work load reports: What is the work load of *each* staff member?

Licensure reports: What employees have an active license, current certification, or meet state requirements for certifications or professional standing? How many employees have failed to maintain current licensure or certification? What licenses are about to expire?

Staff activity and scheduling: What portion of staff time is spent in direct service delivery? Continuing education? Clerical tasks? Quality assurance? Staff development? In-service training?

JOB EVALUATION AND COMPENSATION ADMINISTRATION

Compensation level reports: What is the compensation average and range in each job classification? How many merit increases were approved or denied for each job class for each time period? What is the beginning compensation in each job class?

Benefits record: Has the employee sustained on-the-job injuries? How many work days have been lost due to illness or injury? How many days of accrued leave are left?

Overtime report: How much overtime and overtime pay has been accumulated in each time period by each employee? What are the overtime costs for each job classification working each shift?

Performance appraisal: What are the performance ratings for each person? What personnel have accumulated ratings of unsatisfactory?

Seniority: Does the employee have civil service status or standing? As of what date? How many years has the employee worked for government? Does the employee qualify for veterans preference protections in hiring, promotion, and reductions in force?

EMPLOYEE RELATIONS

Grievances: How many and what types of grievances have been filed by individual employees? What has been the disposition of each grievance?

Attrition: What is the average tenure in each position classification? How long has the incumbent been in the present position? If an employee leaves the position, what is the stated reason for leaving?

Unionization: What is the union affiliation of each employee? What is the bargaining unit?

Discipline: What disciplinary actions or adverse actions have been taken against each employee?

TRAINING AND DEVELOPMENT

Pre-service training: What academic training and degrees were obtained by each employee? On what dates?

Continuing education: How many paid hours were spent on continuing education? How much time has been spent on continuing education to date? What are the continuing education and training needs for each employee?

Skills inventory: What potentially job-relevant skills does each employee possess?

These questions are designed as illustrative. They simply suggest the kinds of issues that arise at operational levels. All the questions clearly relate to day-to-day personnel management decisions that require individual-level data reflecting current workforce characteristics. The data must be organized into reports based on an extensive sorting and manipulation of raw data about individual workers.

Tactical Decision Support System

Tactical decision support, by contrast, derives from the conversion of raw transactions facts into digested summary information. The information management task is one of data reduction; the chief concern at the tactical level of organization is the assessment and effectiveness of a workforce and its organization, cost, and productivity for purposes of budgeting, position management, and program evaluation. Examples of tactically oriented decisions involve the following kinds of questions:

STAFFING

Vacancy: What occupational classifications appear in chronic short supply?

Work load: In what divisions, institutions, centers, wards, and treatment modules are the work loads the heaviest?

Staffing patterns: What percent of staff in each area is full-time permanent? Temporary? Part-time? Contract staff?

COMPENSATION ADMINISTRATION

Compensation costs: What are the total personnel costs by job classification? What are the total costs of merit pay increases?

Benefits and overtime: What are the costs of lost time due to injuries? What are the total overtime costs for each division, institution, treatment module, and job classification?

Performance appraisal: What is the overall performance rating by job classification? What is the relationship between merit increases and performance ratings?

EMPLOYEE RELATIONS

Grievances: What are the average numbers and types of grievances in each division and institution? What types of personnel are involved?

Attrition: What is the average turnover rate for each major occupational classification? What divisions, centers, and institutions endure the worst attrition?

Discipline: What divisions, centers, and institutions experience the greatest number of disciplinary and adverse actions? What types of personnel are involved?

TRAINING AND DEVELOPMENT

Pre-service training: What is the average level of pre-service education and training? What is the average date of the training and the age of the recipient?

Continuing education: What is the average rate at which continuing education credit is accumulated in each occupational area? What is the total cost of continuing education in each area?

Skills inventory: What skills are in surplus? What skills are in shortest supply?

Once again, these questions are merely illustrative. They represent the types of questions that might be asked by a division chief, a budgetary analyst, or a program evaluator concerned about the allocation of resources. Some are diagnostic questions that reveal problems of personnel administration where unusual attrition, grievances, and disparities between salary and performance ratings suggest the need for organization design and development activity. Some of the questions simply help top management evaluate the overall performance of constituent units. All are questions asked in support of decisions made by middle managers.

Strategic Decision Support Systems

Different still is the information processing done in support of strategic planning and management. (In the interest of saving space, another full set of questions is not presented.) The interest of strategic managers rests with the overall direction of basic trends that if not managed, lead to outcomes that either threaten the survival of key components of an enterprise or alter fundamental directions. Thus, personnel data acquire strategic importance when aggregate trends reveal staffing inadequacy, unusual costs of operation, inadequacies of employee relations, and training and development that prevent effective service delivery and threaten either the survival of an institution or its ability to achieve its goals. In the health management example, a chronic shortage of licensed personnel that threatens the certification of whole institutions and hospitals is a strategic issue, for instance.

    Whatever the scheme, the aim of a strategic decision support system is to generate the informational indicators that alert top management about the direction and viability of constituent systems. Indeed, it would be possible to develop at least four categories of ways a strategic manager might view the workforce: internal equity, external competitiveness, innovation and flexibility, and internal integration as noted in Chapter 7. By comparison to operational and tactical decision support systems, strategic systems involve a frequent reporting of data that is more highly aggregated and analyzed. Whereas operational and tactical reporting involves either summaries of raw data or statistical summaries, strategic information invariably involves comparison with some standard, or yardstick, by which overall directions and outcomes can be assessed.

Data Base Management

What kind of DSS design satisfies the multiple uses of workforce management? In fact, while there are many design options and it is not possible to define a single data base, software package, or set of reports that will satisfy all management needs, in general, a multilevel, multiuser data base is the foundation of a workforce management decision support system. Furthermore, the DSS would be end-user–oriented such that on-line executives and managers can pose their queries directly to a data base to derive immediate answers. To illustrate this notion, what follows is a conceptual outline of a prototype data base system whose development can be tested and used as the basis for a full-scale, operational DSS. Once again, the best and most concrete way to show what is involved is to contrive a prototype workforce information system that can be applied to a real situation. This example is the basis for a mental health workforce information system (MHWFIS) that shows both the complexities and possibilities for data base development.

Prototype information systems are built in order to acquire a scaled-down model of an information system that can be installed, tried, revised, and evaluated regarding its cost, usefulness, technical performance, and feasibility of operation. The development of a prototype also serves a training purpose; it can train the people who will eventually run a real system. Normally, a prototype model permits a period of testing before large resource commitments are made to a system that may not meet an end-user information need. Because the foundation of a MHWFIS is data base management, what is presented are the conceptual model, the logical model, and the data elements and data dictionaries that define the basis for data base management in a mental health service system. In order to form a DSS from a MHWFIS, however, a means of pulling summary information from the data base is required for which a crosswalk, introduced at the end of this chapter, is an indispensable instrument.

Conceptual Model. The beginning of information system design lies with the applications to which the system will be put. Our previous discussion indicates that no *single* data base will simultaneously serve all requirements. Defining user information requirements is normally done by developing a conceptual model. In the MHWFIS case, user needs can only be satisfied with the development and aggregation of at least five different, but related, data bases. Each data base contains the collection of data elements organized by records (case observations) descriptive of workforce institutions, persons, payroll, positions, and a "crosswalk" that links multiple *levels* of workforce management. The five data bases are depicted in Figure 9.1, along with the basic kinds of management reporting that derive from each. The illustrative list of data bases and reports is not exhaustive. The conceptual model merely demonstrates in concrete terms that no one data base contains all the data relevant to workforce management and underscores the conclusion that the design of a management information system is, of necessity, multidimensional.

In effect, data about public workforces are found in four basic categories: institutional descriptors (*Institutions* in Figure 9.1) indicating the treatment unit, operating division, or ser-

Figure 9.1. MHWFIS Conceptual Model.

Institutions	*Persons*	*Payroll*
Production unit characteristics and services provided	Employee characteristics, backgrounds, continuing education, inservice training, work history	Financial authorities, obligations, costs, disbursements reporting

Positions	*Crosswalk*	
Manning tables, position authorities, classified (i.e., merit) positions	Occupational classification crosswalk	

vice module characteristics of the work area; personnel records *(Persons)* containing biodata, application information, and work history; financial allocations *(Payroll)* that control the funding of positions and people; and the manning or position control table *(Positions)*. The fifth data base *(Crosswalk)* provides the intellectual transportation between management levels and among data bases where occupational information is required on either a highly refined set of classifications as employed, for example, in an agency manning table, or a much cruder set of classifications as required in the state budget documents or by occupational groups such as unions recognized by a government-wide personnel system. The crosswalk will be discussed in the last section of this chapter.

The list of data bases that might be included in the conceptual model can be vastly expanded. We do not, for example, include data bases on the services and treatments being produced, the institutional subdivisions (wards, floors, branches, work groups, cottages, buildings) that might define the productive units, and the training and development programs that are so important to certain classes of professional service delivery, such as health, human services, and education. The point of the conceptual model is merely to show the structure of a multiple data base strategy and the different types of data required by different managerial users.

Logical Model. Converting a conceptual model into a set of schema that can be presented to a computerized data base management system (DBMS) requires a logical model. The logical model defines the data sets to be coded such that DBMS software can be mapped to the physical storage units (floppy disks, hard disks) for accessing, indexing, and report generation. The current availability of end user IT means that data bases, records, and fields of information can be coded in many flexible ways that permit end users to query, search, and update data in a data base without overweening reliance on technical personnel. End users can also manipulate data and generate reports and documents. Files can be moved along different data base environments and expanded and contracted as required.

Thus, logical schema represent a more precise specification of the contents of the five workforce management data bases than is developed in the conceptual model. Specification includes defining the fields, or variables, to be included in the five data bases, together with the list of indexes, or key elements, that permit data elements from different data bases to be mapped together. The mapping function can be accomplished because the indexes establish a common record number or character through which all data elements associated with the record index can be retrieved and manipulated for report generation purposes. We do not now require bubble diagrams and other graphic representations of the schema and subschemas, since modern, relational DBMS software makes it possible to relate all records and data to each other, provided the "keys" establish lines of connection between and among data bases.

The general structure of subschemas can be indicated, however; see Figure 9.2. For example, the association of *Persons* and *Crosswalk* permits the summary reporting of available personnel characteristics by occupational grouping. Relating *Institutions, Crosswalk,* and *Payroll* allows the generation of reports summarizing personnel costs and on-board staffing strength. Relating *Institutions, Crosswalk,* and *Position* allows the generation of reports on staffing standards that can be used to define institutional workforce requirements. Bear in mind, for the present, that *Crosswalk* merely represents a way to aggregate occupational information in ways that meet the reporting needs of different kinds of management users.

Data Elements and Data Dictionaries. The tool that enables managers to understand, control, and, indeed, to convert disparate data bases into an information system is the data dictionary. Data dictionaries provide the operational definitions of the data elements in each of the data bases as well as the basis for coding and storing data. The categories in Figure 9.2 are common elements included in a MHWFIS.

Figure 9.2. MHWFIS Logical Schema.

Institutions *(Treatment unit)*	*Persons*	*Payroll*
Average work load	Personal data	Salary base
Certifications	(age, sex, race)	Benefits
Facilities	Education	Status
	Certifications	Salary increment
	Transactions	Action
		Account
Key: Account no.	Key: Classification no.	Key: Position control
Organizational I.D.	Account no.	no. (PCN)
	Social Security no.	Classification no.
		Social Security

Positions	*Crosswalk*
Job title	Job title
Class code	Class code
Employment status	Group code
Key: PCN	Key: Classification no.
Classification no.	
Account no.	

CORE WORKFORCE DATA ELEMENTS

Employment status: Full-time, part-time, contract, tempo-
    rary, or permanent
Job title: Occupational classification
Degree date: Date of highest professional degree
Education level: Highest degree attained
School: Name of school from which degree was earned
Field: Discipline of professional/academic education
Birth date: Date expressed as some order of YY/MM/DD
Gender: Male or female
Race: Standard EEO classification
Previous employment: Organization of last employment
Service: Years of service calculated from appointment date
Salary: Annual pay
Licensure: State license to practice a profession
License date: Original date of license attainment
License exp. date: Date of license expiration
Work history: Promotions, dates, disciplinary actions

OPTIONAL DATA ELEMENTS

Private practice: Private practice/consulting
Staff activity: Hours spent in program elements
Performance rating: Summary rating of performance
Continuing education/training: Current educational investment by hours, discipline, degree programs
Address: Mailing address
Phone: Home telephone number
Injuries: Employee injuries for workman's compensation
Shift: Shift coverage
Special work assignments: Unusual detail
Special skills: Skills available but not used by the current job classification
Handicap: Legally recognized disabilities
Training need: Summary assessment of training needs
Privilege level: Admitting, treatment, teaching privileges at recognized institutions
Credentialing: Professional certifications/memberships

This list does not include all the indexes, or keys, such as Social Security, position control number, organizational I.D.s and report dates, that define the data base records. The aim is not to exhaust the possibilities, but to suggest core data elements in the development of an information prototype that can be augmented to suit specific management reporting needs.

Crosswalk Design

So far, so good. All the pieces appear to be falling into place easily. It would appear that all that we need is a fair understanding of the management questions to be asked, access to the latest information management technologies, a knowledge of elementary programming, and *voilà*, a DSS springs to life! What is missing?

Reality is missing. There is still not an effective way to capture what people do for work and how they fit into some organized effort. This requires a clear definition of the occupations that capture workforce effort. In effect, "occupation" is not defined. Is it tasks and duties? Personal qualities? Function? Does it derive from levels of mastery and expertise? Some combination of the several dimensions of occupations? And assuming that we know what an occupation is, are there ways to code it so that comparisons and analyses can be made?

The way to see the overall complexity of occupational classification is to compare four leading systems for occupational information collection: the federal white-collar (FWC) classification system, the massive *Dictionary of Occupational Titles* (DOT), the U.S. Bureau of the Census employment series, and the recently issued (1977) and once revised Standard Occupational Classification (SOC). The SOC was devised to sort out the incompatibilities extant among the many classification systems currently used in the United States. Table 9.1 shows the comparisons among the four systems (Chapman, Maharay, and McGregor, 1979) in terms of whether work descriptions are provided to accompany occupational titles, whether the meaning of "occupation" is actually defined, whether the basis for assigning alphanumeric codes to titles is explained, whether the occupational level is indicated, what the basis is for aggregating, or grouping, occupational titles, and what the end uses for the information appear to be.

An illustration of the complexities of comparison is found in federal personnel management.* The federal white-collar (FWC) service is perhaps the most sophisticated of public-sector personnel systems. Yet, even in that case "occupation" has never been precisely defined for the more than 2 million white-collar workers paid on the general schedule salary plan or its equivalent. The closest the federal system comes is to equate an occupation with a "position" (Bureau of Policies and Standards, 1973, p. 2) as follows: "'Position' means the work, consisting of the duties and responsibilities, assignable to an officer or employee." The equation of occupation with position-based duties and responsibilities is fully consistent with the position classification and position management basis of the federal civil

*I am indebted to George Maharay's insights on the structure of federal personnel information.

Table 9.1. Four Major Occupational Classification Systems.

Classification Dimensions	Federal White-Collar Work-force (GS)	Dictionary of Occupational Titles	U.S. Bureau of the Census	Standard Occupational Classification
Work descriptions in addition to title	Yes	Yes	No	No, except for master titles
Definition of occupation	No, but under development	Yes, partial	No	No, except by reference to the DOT
Existence of criteria for assigning codes to occupations	No	No	No	No
Hierarchic levels within an occupation	Yes, through grades	Yes, partial	Partial	Yes, crude
Basis for occupational grouping	Career patterns Qualifications Discipline Function	Discipline Function	Discipline Level	Qualifications Discipline Function
End uses	Internal management	External dictionary for employment purposes	External social, political, and economic comparisons	Undetermined

Sources: Adapted from Chapman, Maharay, and McGregor, 1979. See Chapter 6.

service. It is also compatible with the *Dictionary of Occupational Titles* (U.S. Department of Labor, 1977), which defines "occupation" as a "collective description of a number of individual jobs performed, with minor variations, in many establishments" (p. xv).

Confusions appear upon closer inspection of other federal personnel documents. For instance, Section 1501 of the U.S. Code enables the gathering of raw occupational information in a manner useful to personnel data users. The relevant portion of Title 5 asserts: "individual positions will, in accordance with their duties, responsibilities and *qualification requirements* [emphasis added], be so grouped and identified by classes and grades . . . that the resulting positions-classification system can be used in all phases of personnel administration." So, there are "qualifications of persons" dimensions to occupational definition that may be blended with positions requirements. A dimension has been added to the meaning of occupation.

The complexity does not stop with the U.S. Code. As noted in Chapter Seven, information about the federal white-collar workforce—2 million people—is aggregated on the basis of 21 occupational "groups." However, groups are merely the crudest of organizing rubrics for a classification invention called a "series." Each "group" contains as few as 3 and as many as 40 "series of classes." Thus, there are 437 "series" listed in the old *Handbook of Occupational Groups* promulgated by the now-defunct U.S. Civil Service Commission.

What, then, is a "series"? According to the *Handbook,* a "series" is "one or more classes of positions similar as to specialized line of work but differing in difficulty or responsibility of work, and therefore in grade and salary range. A series may be thought of as composed of steps in the *most natural line of promotion*" (Bureau of Policies and Standards, 1973, p. 1). Still more confusion. One source of difficulty is clearly that each "series" may embrace many different positions or occupations. Another is the introduction of yet another occupational dimension: a hierarchic organizational *level* through which a person may be promoted. But what is the "natural line of promotion?" Is it positional and defined by levels of organizational responsibility? Or is it defined in terms of qualifications and personal expertise?

One more level of confusion displays the complexity of the problem of defining what, after all, people really do for work. At the operating level, many operating bureaus and agencies keep two sets of books—one for reporting governmentwide information and the second for operations management. Great variety can exist in the operational systems used to classify a workforce at the most detailed level. A classic illustration of this variety can be found in the National Aeronautics and Space Administration (NASA), where an internal set of aerospace technology (AST) classifications have been developed within the structure of the FWC "series" classifications. For example, the *Handbook* includes the aerospace engineering series (GS-861) within the broader occupational group entitled "engineering and architecture." Yet *within* NASA, GS-861 really represents a very crude agglomeration of at least 46 AST knowledge-based specialties and disciplines, including magneto fluid dynamics, materials and structures, propulsion systems, flight systems, and research piloting. In short, clearly NASA GS-861s do very different things under the heading of "aerospace engineering," in part because they *know* different things and have different competencies.

There are further distinctions, however. Not only are there AST specialties based on knowledge, there are *subgroup* distinctions that specify the *function or product* of an occupation. For example, the following subgroups are recognized within the GS-861 construct:

Flight system
Measurement and instrumentation
Data systems
Facilities and operations
Management

In other words, classification systems can be used to specify an occupation's contribution to agency goals by virtue of an incumbent's productive *function.*

It is not uselessly pedantic to conclude that the definition of "occupation" is a very complex business. It is complex because there are many dimensions—pay, position, function, and personal qualifications—potentially involved in cataloguing human resources and the many elements associated with productive work. Moreover, precise definitions of each dimension and element will change from one administrative level to another. The task of strategic management is to determine which of the potentially operative definitions is most relevant to organizational outcomes on the basis of which executive and managerial stewardship will be evaluated.

A further conclusion is that the connection between the potentially unintelligible mass of transactions level data—the raw stuff generated at operating levels of organizations—and management decision making lies in the development of an information instrument connecting the two domains. However, this merely begs the next question: How can the connection be made, particularly in view of the many decision levels that affect the management of a complex workforce? The answer lies in developing some sort of crosswalk that provides the intellectual "transportation" among the several layers and competing definitions. Crosswalks have many characteristics, chief of which is that they record the impact of decisions taken at one level of an organization and reflected in decision-relevant terms at another level. Occupational, or workforce, crosswalks generate information that can aggregate highly refined workforce distinctions and activities so that overall patterns can be discerned.

The basis for crosswalk development remains an area of management connoisseurship, however. As we know, there are many ways to aggregate and organize multiple levels of information. Indeed, there are as many ways to structure crosswalks as there are dimensions to occupational classification. The complexity of potential crosswalk development is depicted in Table 9.2, where four decision-relevant variables are listed: pay plan, position characteristics, functional role, and personal qualifications. Computerization of such information is easy, for each dimension and element is codable with simple alphanu-

Table 9.2. Basis for Workforce Classification Crosswalks.

Classification Dimensions	*Classification Elements*
Pay plan	Salary
	Wage grade
Position-based definition of occupation	Employee classification number
	Occupational group code
	Occupational level code
	Occupational supervisor/not
Function	Program or support staff
	Product line
Personal qualifications	Knowledges
	Skills
	Abilities
	Certificates
	Degrees

meric codes that do not require elaborate discussion here. This, in turn, means that there are numerous methods by which codes can be attached to the multiple dimensions of occupation already discussed. Furthermore, current IT development makes it inexpensive and relatively easy to experiment with crosswalks as managerial need dictates.

To illustrate the point, an example of a crosswalk developed for mental health workforce management purposes is provided in Appendix B. It was developed with the assistance of many state mental health officials knowledgeable about the major occupational groupings in a state institutional system and the basic productive contributions made by a mental health workforce. A crosswalk program was written for use with a dBASE III+ compiler simply to show how an end-user data base management software package could be easily configured to generate a crosswalk report. While there are many ways to construct such instruments, the example illustrates the extent to which managerial leverage can be generated from seemingly endless and useless data about workforce transactions. Using a properly constructed crosswalk allows the manager to know the overall effects of personnel operations on the size, composition, cost, and productivity of the workforce broken out into as fine a level of detail as a manager could desire. Crosswalks and data bases provide the information platform on which DSS development can proceed, and they support both management analysis and workforce decision making.

PART FOUR

WORKFORCE DECISION MAKING

The payoff in a "double strategic" approach to workforce management is reckoned in terms of enhanced decision-making capacity. Workforce analysis is required to convert data into information that supports the knowledge requirements of the decision maker. Even with an adequately designed decision support system, actual decision making involves an extraordinary number of operational choices associated with converting forecasts and plans into programs of action. Indeed, once choices are theoretically made, a series of implementation barriers must be negotiated.

Chapter 10

Analyzing
Workforce Information

The connection between workforce information and management decision making is forged through workforce analysis. The great paradox of analysis is, however, visited on all workforce managers (Ludwin, 1988; Greer, Jackson, and Fiorito, 1989): the most sophisticated analytic techniques for analyzing workforce information apply to the easiest problems, particularly operations-level supply-side forecasting problems; yet the most difficult problems, particularly demand-side strategic choices, prove to be the most unyielding to elegant analysis. Thus, the paradox contains a double puzzle. One is that formal analysis typically makes unreasonable assumptions about the time, patience, and resources available to practicing decision makers who must act on large problems in short times frames. The second is that the available workforce analysis armament has been pointed toward the softest target—the details and algorithms of supply-side operations management. Furthermore, the paradox is unlikely to be fully resolved even with assistance from powerful computerized decision support systems that can save hours of prospective claims on executive time.

Notwithstanding barriers to real-world application, we can still explore the logic of workforce analysis and with that the possibilities for integrating formal analysis with line management decision making. The point of workforce analysis is to inform management choice. In simplest terms, the analytic objective is to help managers, employees, and other relevant parties visualize desirable balances between the supply and demand sides of the problem. Workforce analysis, therefore, is nothing more than systematic thinking about the choices confronting managers. Such thinking is logically organized into three categories: forecasting, planning, and programming. In reality, all three activities are linked and may even occur concurrently, although they are considered serially for purposes of discussion.

Forecasting is the prediction of likely patterns of workforce availability and requirements. It is the most technically sophisticated of the three activities. A wide array of technologies, data bases, and complex mathematical models useful in predicting labor requirements and availability has been developed over the years (selected citations are provided in Appendix C). Workforce planning is a consumer of forecasts and involves the formulation and evaluation of alternative strategies for balancing requirements and supply; by definition, then, planning changes forecasts. The core of the planning exercise is the anticipation of future realities and the development of scenarios by which short- and long-term demand and supply can be balanced. The third stage of analysis involves programming generally defined as the development of a schedule of actions required for the implementation of plans. Programming analysis requires that the line manager actually envision the practical implications of workforce decisions, for without programming, forecasting remains an unused intellectual exercise and planning produces unimplementable scenarios, perhaps theoretically interesting but unattainable in reality.

The main characteristics of forecasting, planning, and programming are summarized in Table 10.1 according to the nature of the time horizon, the key variables involved, and the link to requirements and availability-side management. Clearly, forecasting, planning, and programming activities are interdependent. Programming decisions depend on the quality of plans,

Table 10.1. Workforce Analysis: Factors Associated with Forecasting, Planning, and Programming.

Analysis Problem	Short-Term Factors	Long-Term Factors
Forecasting availability	Separation and accession rates	Individual development plans, labor force demographics, career mobility patterns
Forecasting requirements	Organizational goals, labor productivity, skill mix, budget constraints	Public policy goals, technological change
Planning	Adjusting external recruitment and internal availability to meet requirements; defining workforce needs	Realignment of internal and external markets
Programming	Implementation of plans through job design, hiring, firing, performance appraisal, compensation, transfers, promotions, downgrades	Implementation of plans through job redesign, employee training and development, organizational development

Sources: Adapted from Walker, 1969, p. 156; Burack, 1972, p. 72; McGregor, 1977, p. 226.

which, in turn, depend on careful forecasts. Analysis is the key to all these activities.

While scholars agree about the contents of formal workforce analysis and the need to do it, the precise way to proceed remains a point of sharp discussion (Greer, Jackson, and Fiorito, 1989; Ludwin, 1988). In practical terms, workforce forecasting and planning are necessary to facilitate human resource development, to avoid shortages of qualified personnel, to generate decision-relevant information, to support affirmative action decisions, and for purposes of budgeting and career planning (Greer, Jackson, and Fiorito, 1989). Furthermore, the turbulence caused by global competition for economic markets and the discipline of attempting to manage workforces under severe cost constraints and cutback conditions creates circumstances under which sophisticated workforce analysis is the *sine qua non* of effective choice. For example, both public- and private-sector agencies now feel the effects of a whole society confronting competitive challenge on a global scale. In theory, all strategies for enhanced competitiveness of public agencies and private corporations create conditions that require substantial increases in workforce analysis. The leading formulae for competitive success include the wholesale redesign of old industrial-style organizations in order to create flatter structures with fewer middle managers (it should be noted, however, that new designs do not eliminate middle-management problems); the development of innovation strategies for fast, new product development; and the enhancement of product quality.

All strategies represent long-term decision options whose implementation must be achieved in turbulent environments, changing markets and technologies, and under competitive conditions (Greer, Jackson, and Fiorito, 1989). Furthermore, the success of all strategies depends on enormous investments in human resources and in forecasting and planning systems to support management decision making. For example, workforce managers are being asked to develop employees and managers to work in information-based organizations, retrain displaced middle managers who must be moved into more productive roles or outplaced, and plan the development of future top managers who will have fewer middle positions through which to develop and serve an apprenticeship (Greer, Jackson, and Fiorito, 1989). In addition, innovation strategies require enhanced selection of highly skilled employees and significant investments in human skill in support of innovation. Strategies founded on continuous enhancement of product quality require a continuous focus on training and development (Schuler and Jackson, 1987). Virtually all strategies place enormous pressure on the accuracy and realiability of workforce analysis.

Paradoxically, however, the conditions that accompany strategies of competitiveness and innovation may also sow seeds that undermine the formal analysis that accompanies forecasting, planning, and programming. For one thing, the structure of problems stemming from environmental uncertainty involves short planning horizons and flexible forecasting and planning procedures, circumstances least hospitable to overly formal and complex analytic manipulations. In addition, linking strategic problem solving to human resource management ensures the direct involvement of top management in workforce management, yet top executives are least likely to invest in formal analysis. Instead they are likely to economize on scarce time by using simple charts, inventories, estimates, and crude rules of thumb to simplify complexity and move to conclusions within the time allowed by a changing array of problems that do not sit on a manager's desk waiting for analyses to be completed. The unsurprising finding that turbulent environments have led to attempts to simplify workforce analysis (Greer, Jackson, and Fiorito, 1989) remains an interesting empirical characterization of current forecasting and planning practice, albeit ironic when considering the arsenal of formal analytic capability built up over the past twenty years (see Appendix C). Our strategy is simply to examine the intellectual problems and possibilities for workforce analysis. It will, in the course of discussion, be obvious how simplifications of the formal analytic manipulations can be achieved. Once the logic of workforce forecasting and planning is understood, the development of charts, inventories, estimates, and nonstatistical rules of thumb that substitute very nicely in applications of the illustrated numerical exercises can be readily envisioned. In this way, busy line managers whose fields of intellectual specialization do not include workforce planning can follow the discussion of the problems addressed in formal analysis even though the tools themselves may not be adopted in literal real-world applications where severe constraints of time, cost, and complexity are placed on analysis.

Forecasting Workforce Availability

Forecasting the availability of personnel at a given time depends on a model of labor mobility that calculates the effects of mobility on labor stocks. This is done through a stock-and-flow model that depicts how a given on-board employment level (a stock) will be augmented by accessions to (a positive flow) and deletions from (a negative flow) the labor force. The resulting projection is a forecast of the new level of employment (a new stock) taking into account the many different ways workers can be added to and removed from the labor pool. The basic outline of the model is provided in Figure 10.1.

Since the initial aim of availability forecasting is to guess, or estimate, the number of people in selected workforce classifications *before* the impact of planning and programming actions, supply-side managers must do two things to be effective. First, they must have an accurate count of the populations of

Figure 10.1. Availability Forecasts: Estimates of On-Board Strength, Accessions, and Separations Over Time.

Fiscal Year 1 (Actual)	End-of-Year Strength Previous FY	=	Beginning On-Board Strength (Actual)	+	Accessions (Actual)	-	Separations (Actual)

Fiscal Year 2 (Estimate)	End-of-Year Strength Current FY (Estimate)	=	Beginning On-Board Strength (Actual)	+	Accessions (Estimate)	-	Separations (Estimate)

Fiscal Year 3 Next FY (Estimate)	End-of-Year Strength (Estimate)	=	Beginning On-Board Strength (Estimate)	+	Accessions (Estimate)	-	Separations (Estimate)
	Work Force Categories		Work Force Categories		Work Force Categories		Work Force Categories
	1		1		1		1
	2		2		2		2
	.		.		.		.
	.		.		.		.
	.		.		.		.
	N		N		N		N

each relevant classification—no mean feat, as demonstrated in earlier chapters. Second, they must understand the actions, or transactions, that can affect accessions to and separations from the workforce. More specifically, two types of transactions must be understood and managed: those that cannot be controlled, but nevertheless affect workforce populations, and those that can be controlled. Obviously, the *uncontrollable* accessions and separations command first attention. Neither automatic promotions and transfers in the accessions column, nor deaths, retirements, resignations, and voluntary transfers in the separations column are subject to manipulation by the manager. To the extent that uncontrollable accessions and separations can be forecast, then managers can begin to formulate planning and programming strategies for dealing with the mobility patterns that they do control. (Review Figure 5.4, which enumerates the many workforce transactions that affect human resource flows.) Workforce planning consists of developing scenarios for managing controllable accessions and separations in light of forecast workforce availability calculated in terms of the net effects of uncontrollable mobility and compared to the workforce requirements mandated either by corporate strategy or public policy.

The calculations accounting for the availability of onboard personnel are reasonably straightforward. Total stocks of personnel are mathematically described by the general form of a stock-and-flow difference equation in which:

$$P_i(t) = P_i(t-1) + A_i(t) - S_i(t),$$

where

$P_i(t) =$ a personnel stocks vector defining the number of on-board personnel in occupational category i at time t (t may be any time period such as a month, quarter, or year).

$P_i(t-1) =$ a personnel stocks vector defining the number of "on-board" personnel in occupation category i at time $t-1$.

$A_i(t) =$ a personnel flows vector defining the sum of personnel accessions to occupational category i during time period t.

$S_i(t) =$ a personnel flows vector defining the sum of personnel separations from occupational category i during time period t.

Furthermore, since accessions and separations result from two kinds of personnel actions—controllable and ·ncontrollable—operational forecasting systems will have to track personnel actions in precise categories of personnel activity. Thus, the types of accessions are illustrated below:

Controllable accessions	*Uncontrollable accessions*
Discretionary promotions (dp_i)	Automatic promotions (ap_i)
Hires (h_i)	Transfers based on retreat rights (t_i)
Reinstatements (r_i)	
Transfers (tr_i)	

In addition, examples of controllable and uncontrollable separations are also listed below:

Controllable separations	*Uncontrollable separations*
Firings (f_i)	Deaths (d_i)
Reductions-in-force (rif_i)	Retirements (ret_i)
Involuntary transfers (it_i)	Resignations (res_i)
Suspensions (sus_i)	Voluntary transfers (vt_i)

When all forms of accession and separation are accounted for, the result is a new net stock of personnel. This can be presented in a formal way simply to show the ease with which such data and tracking can be computerized. The general definition of the total on-board personnel strength for occupations i of a given agency or set of agencies at time t is given by:

$$P_i(t) = P_i(t-1) + [dp_i + h_i + r_i + tr_i + ap_i + t_i] - [f_i + rif_i + it_i + sus_i + d_i + ret_i + res_i + vt_i].$$

The result is simply netting out the effects of all sources of mobility on an original workforce stock:

$$P_i(t-1).$$

Requiring operating agencies and businesses to produce an annual account of the stocks and flows of personnel has many advantages. The most obvious is that a regular and periodic account of personnel can be obtained in a cost-effective manner simply by taking advantage of the information systems discussed earlier and automating the data-collection and report-generation system. A second advantage is that the available data are derived not from analyses and theoretical projections that may or may not be right, but from actual workforce decisions made by operating divisions about the on-board workforce size and skill mix and from the actual number of accessions and separations. A third advantage is that the supply-side forecasting and planning outlined here can be flexibly implemented; there are many accounting methods and technologies available to make the data collection and reporting easy.

Regardless of the data collection and forecasting methods used, the beginning of a serious workforce planning effort depends, to a large extent, on crude counts of personnel stocks and flows. Over time, however, better historical records and greater forecasting skill can result in increasingly refined record keeping and, ultimately, sophisticated forecasting ability. The process becomes increasingly easy as experience grows. What is important for managers to understand, however, is that the mathematical and arithmetical manipulations are elementary compared to the strategic decisions that are encoded in the classification and information system on which all analysis depends.

Once an appropriate data base is established, there are many different ways to organize raw personnel data to create analytically grounded forecasts about personnel availability. First, there is the batch of ordinary statistics available for compiling data on controllable and uncontrollable accessions and separations. "Average" rates of occupational separation based on historical data are certainly better than "guesstimates" promulgated without the benefit of data or careful analysis. Turnover rates have several classic difficulties, however, even when trends are seasonally adjusted and normalized by time series analysis.

Three are mentioned here. First, turnover statistics do not indicate the interconnected flows from one occupation to another; turnover simply records the fact of separation from an occupational category. Second, turnover rate analysis typically is not sensitive to "risk," that is, to the likelihood that an attrition rate will in fact occur. Third, crude turnover data are not sensitive to and cannot anticipate sudden shifts that produce "lumpy" mobility, such as would occur where cohorts of workers move en masse through an employment system because of a clustering of hiring or retirement actions caused by the bunching of workforce age structures, external labor market conditions, and other perturbations.

Several kinds of models are available to help forecasters recognize more complex patterns of workforce movement. One of the most common is Markov chain analysis, which provides an easy way to map flows of people among personnel classifications, or states. Markov models can assist with the problems of assessing the interconnections *among* occupations as well as the analysis of attrition risk. The intellectual foundation of a Markov chain rests on two things: first, the enumeration of the possible states, or classifications, into which personnel can be sorted and either enter or leave over time; and second, an estimation of the probability that personnel mobility (transitions, or flows) will occur between pairs of states. Once the mobility map is drawn, either in network or matrix form, the best guesses about the transition probabilities of moving from one state to another can be inserted and the effects calculated. Markov models have been used to forecast both stocks and flows of people for whole administrative systems (Burack, 1972; Vroom and MacCrimman, 1968; Bartholomew and Forbes, 1979).

The development of a clear and explicit personnel system design (recall Chapter Four) enhances the accuracy of workforce forecasting. For example, closed personnel systems staffed on a career basis are highly structured. Entry occurs only at the level of entering probationary positions from which movement into a protected position with tenure, or civil service standing, is allowed. Once civil service status is achieved, however, mobility is internally managed until the employee dies, retires, transfers, or is involuntarily separated from the workforce.

Open personnel systems staffed on a program basis, by contrast, work very differently. Regardless of whether the classification states are based on rank-in-job or rank-in-person structures, flows between internal and external labor markets are permitted and perhaps encouraged by strategic planning at every level of the organization. The result is that there are positive transition probabilities connecting external states to internal states; that is, there are no examples of zero probability that a person from outside the workforce can enter the internal labor market. Thus, one of the main benefits of formal Markov analysis is that it forces an explicit modeling of the employment system within which workforce management occurs.

Formal Markov chain analysis can yield counterintuitive surprises and insights that would be overlooked in analyses that depend on simple replacement charts, supervisor estimates of attrition, and crude rules of thumb that do not take complex mobility patterns into account. A simple example depicted in Figures 10.2 and 10.3 shows the basic management contribution of the Markov logic. The analytic premise of Markov chain analysis is that reasonably stable patterns of movement through a manpower system can be approximated by probabilities—the betting odds that people in one category at time 1 will be in the same or some other category at time 2. Note the implication of such a premise: if instability and uncertainty characterize *either* the states or the *pattern* of movement between or among available states, the value of Markov analysis is reduced. Figure 10.2 shows a simple hypothetical example involving transitions between only two personnel categories: line manager and professional staff. If we count "exit" as a third category, then Figure 10.2 shows that from year 1 to year 2, only 20 percent of line managers left their original category, while 50 percent of the professional staff left theirs.

If we assume that the workforce need in year 2 was 100 line managers and 100 professional staff, and this was the same need as in year 1, then the matrix shows the size and kind of

**Figure 10.2. Mobility Probabilities for Line Managers
and Professional Staff: Year 1 to Year 2.**

| | | Year 2 | | | Row Sum |
		1	2	3	
	Line manager 1	.80	.10	.10	1.0
Year 1	Professional staff 2	.20	.50	.30	1.0
	Exit 3	0	0	1	1.0

the "new" personnel need; no new line managers are needed, but 40 new professional staff are required. This is because 80 line managers—.8 times 100 managers—remained as line managers while 20 professionals—.2 times 100 professionals—became line managers. At the same time only 50 professionals remained and only 10 line managers moved into professional staff positions. The result is a deficit of 40 professional staff persons.

If the analyst is willing to make the sometimes heroic assumption that this general pattern either *will* or *should* hold for several years and that shifts of occupational category from year 2 to year 3 are independent of shifts from year 1 to year 2, then Markov chains can be used to show the distribution of personnel for as many years in the future as workforce planners dare or need to extrapolate. Thus, if one wishes to project the probable mix of human resources in year 3 from the earlier matrix, one can take the "second power" of the matrix, which is shown in Figure 10.3.

The probabilities are calculated by summing, as in a tree diagram, the probabilities that after two moves (year 1 to year 2 and year 2 to year 3) managers and professional staff will end up in year 3 in cell $p_1 1$ (i.e., (first row and first column), cell $p_1 2$ (first row and second column), and so on. Thus, if we wish to know the probability that those who began year 1 as line managers will end up as line managers in year 3, we would *multiply* .80 (the probability of remaining in the same category

**Figure 10.3. Mobility Probabilities for Line Managers
and Professional Staff: Year 1 to Year 3.**

		Year 3			Row Sum
		1	2	3	
Line manager	1	.66	.13	.21	1.0
Year 1 Professional staff	2	.26	.27	.47	1.0
Exit	3	0	0	1	1.0

from year 1 to year 2) *times* .80 (the same "independent trial" probability applies for year 3) and *add* that product to the very slight probability (.02) that line managers in year 1 would move to professional staff positions in year 2 and back to a line management position in year 3 (.10 times .20), for a total of .66. We assume in this example that those who exit do not reenter. This says that of the original 100 line managers in year 1, 66 will end up in that position in year 3. To that 66 will be added, however, 26 line managers who began in year 1 as professional staff. If the *need* for line managers in year 3 is still thought to remain at 100, then it is apparent that only 8 managers will have to be acquired either by a program of career development or by recruitment from outside the organization. Similarly, if the *need* for professional staff is also thought to be 100 in year 3, then 60 professionals will have to be acquired.

As noted earlier (Greer, Jackson, and Fiorito, 1989), the actual use of formal analysis to solve workforce management problems is sharply debated. One benefit from such analysis is that even if the probabilities are wrong, regular and quick approximations can be made about the likely staffing mix under several sets of probable assumptions. A second benefit is that even crude approximations often reveal helpful and nonobvious conclusions. In the above example, an examination of annual turnover rates in the two occupational categories might plausibly suggest (see Figure 10.2) that since 20 percent of line managers and 50 percent of professionals leave their original categories each year, one ought to recruit two line managers for every five professionals per year. In fact, if the predicted mobility pattern prevails over just two years, such a recruitment policy could have disastrous consequences for an organization—in the absence of expanded line manager needs—caused either by glutting the organization with line managers or failing to provide career development prospects for professionals. Markov chain analysis reveals that no new line managers will be needed after one year, and the recruitment ratio over the two-year period should be something like one line manager to every seven and one-half professionals. Emphasis needs to be given the pliability of these tools, which do not produce solutions to problems, but only suggest likely outcomes if management accepts such approximations as either the actual picture of mobility or the "desirable" picture (Mc-Gregor, 1972).

While Markov chains provide handy summary pictures of mobility, studies suggest (White, 1970) that the dynamics of mobility are even more complicated. Markov chain models simplify what in reality are "bumper chains" of movement, in which a person moves from one job to another only when the person ahead in the queue moves. Thus, mobility may be best described in terms of chains of opportunity, created either by a person at the front of a queue vacating his or her position, or a new position being added. Eventually, however, everyone in the opportunity queue is affected by even one move.

The implication of this is that occupational queues either become escalators or deescalators of opportunity, depending partly on the skill with which the workforce is managed. In the absence of organizational expansion, what looked like a rapidly moving escalator can quickly become clogged as expansion slows or ceases. The problem is compounded when workforce planners fail to make even crude short- and long-range forecasts of human resource needs.

A more esoteric, but intriguing, use of Markov models is in forecasting risk (McGregor, 1977). Models of risk assess the likelihood that a particular end state, such as a workforce ceiling, will be reached. Probability density functions depicting the likelihood that a workforce will be a certain size or larger for a particular organization or occupation cohort can be generated simply by treating attrition rates as a series of trials ("Bernoulli trials" in finite mathematics language) that may be applied to the on-board workforce. Probabilities for several time periods in the future can also be calculated. Thus, a 100-person organization with a 10 percent annual attrition rate will have a particular probability of ending up with 90 people at the end of the year; but there are also calculable probabilities of having 89 people, 91 people, 88 people, 92 people, and so forth. Such a model might well be useful in allowing a central planning agency to evaluate staffing plans.

Markov models are particularly useful in highly fluid situations in large organizations where people move among different occupational and organizational roles frequently enough to say that there are, in fact, transitions. Alternatively, Markov forecasting can be useful in planning situations where the manager wishes to understand what the effects of a complicated series of personnel changes might be before deciding. Markov models are less useful in the following situations: where little or no mobility occurs; when an adequate personnel classification system does not exist; where personnel movement depends upon a previous mobility sequence and thus the "trials" in each time period are not truly independent; and where the mobility that does occur is so simple that developing a Markov model becomes uninformative activity (for example, where organizations are either very small or large and relatively undifferentiated). In very small organizations, a Markov model is not a useful forecasting tool simply because there are other informal ways to assess workforce availability: succession planning or replacement charts, taking a personnel inventory, or relying on supervisor estimates based on their knowledge of the workers (Greer, Jackson, and Fiorito, 1989).

Immobile, career-based employment systems are another example of a workforce management situation for which Markov models are not helpful. In static situations, where hiring is done only at entry levels under career-selection assumptions, the mobility that does occur is simply that of attrition, which either occurs early in a person's career or not until retirement. In such static career systems, the person who remains in an agency beyond the high-risk early years will spend a career in a single occupation at a single institution. The problem of forecasting in such systems is one of predicting the likelihood of attrition in both the early years of service as well as during a career in which disability, mortality rates, and rules of retirement—all uncontrollable separation factors—govern the rate of separation. One model for forecasting attrition under such circumstances is the log-probability model (Clark and Thurston, 1977). The model is built on the assumption that attrition is a career phenomenon which peaks at the beginning of a career in an organization, rapidly diminishes over the first few years of service, and slowly decreases thereafter until retirement age. The log-probability function describes the pattern of decelerating attrition among cohorts of personnel hired at the same time and predicts personnel availability over time after attrition has taken its toll. Such a model can also be used to predict the actuarial process of "aging out" by which personnel will leave a system because of death, retirement, disability, and so forth.

The availability of a large number of models and techniques for forecasting mobility means that staffing plans should, in time, be supported by some sort of analyses, although there are in fact many options. Large public agencies, particularly, should profit from such analysis since their "no growth" budgetary position means that attrition is one of the nonradical tools for adjusting workforce skill mixes over time. Thus, only careful forecasting and planning will permit the resource husbanding required in turbulent policy environments. In particular, while there is debate about the applicability of some of the fancier tools of analysis, the Markov logic still yields useful insights with respect to the *net effects* of complex mobility patterns, where large numbers of people are placed in motion by strategic plans to upgrade the workforce over time. The circumstances under which this conclusion is reached are discussed in Chapter Eleven.

Forecasting Workforce Requirements

The old question beckons: How many people does it take to run the public railroad? Ironically, the greatest analytic investment has been made in building the analytic muscle of the more tractable of the two basic problems; forecasting workforce availability is easier than forecasting workforce requirements. This conclusion applies particularly in cases where public policy goals are "squishy," or where commercial yardsticks (commercial providers whose staffing patterns can be compared with public agency staffing) are absent, or where there are not industrially engineered staffing requirements that can reasonably be said to be correct. The first case obtains for large agencies associated with collective goods such as national security, defense, diplomacy, and environmental protection, where the goals themselves are difficult to define and measure. In the second case, one can find unique public services, such as are provided by the FBI, the Park Service, and the Forest Service, for which commercial competition is only partly available. In the third case, analysis would place research and development agencies, such as NASA, and a range of social and health services (depending on how their purposes are defined) whose staffing levels are driven by program requirements and patient and client need where there is not a clearly "correct" staffing standard that can be established through engineering principles.

How can analysts ever hope to forecast workforce requirements? In the public sector, forecasting workforce requirements is done frequently by working through the mechanics of a "manning table," which lists the resource requirements of an organization for fixed periods of time. Manning tables vary in form depending on the variables important in producing the figures and the time periods for which needs are to be established. Major variables linked with short-run needs include work load or productivity measures, estimates of budgetary expansion (or contraction), and employment mix. In the long term, environmental and technological change must be taken into account. Private enterprises, by contrast, typically tie personnel requirements forecasts to production and sales of goods and services. Whether or not public-sector enterprises, which do not engage in market transactions and whose outputs are subject to constant redefinition, can apply the same kinds of forecasting technologies is not clear.

The state of the art of requirements determination now seems crude. Several obstacles may prevent the use of sophisticated forecasting methodologies. One is an organizational dilemma afflicting both private industry and government agencies: "plans for acquisitions, mergers, conglomerates, and other organizational developments frequently fall into the category of privileged information" (Heneman and Seltzer, 1970, p. 5). Thus, even if the forecasting tools were available, those responsible for human resource planning may lack the minimal information—because it is denied to them—to apply available forecasting technologies. Such secrecy may be especially prevalent when major technological or organizational change is being installed. Premature revelation of technological shifts can make basic change difficult. While instances are recorded where manpower forecasting and planning have been conducted in a reasonably open manner (Mosher, 1967), the extent to which sufficient openness can be maintained to use requirements forecasting tools is not established.

A second problem that is endemic in public organizations is that human resource requirements are determined by public policy. Yet public policy environments can be highly turbulent and goals can change in response to electoral outcomes as well as evaluations of program successes and failures. Thus, the definition of some agencies and programs as requiring more or fewer employees can derive as much from political values and conflicts that allow some functions to grow and others to decline (Thompson, 1975) as from any alternative, objective analysis. Policy analysts have yet to develop a political derivation of staffing requirements.

Notwithstanding forecasting constraints, several variables seem immediately relevant to forecasting short-term human resource needs. The most important public-sector variable is the budget, in which the ancient public practice of making incremental adjustments in the input base is a dominant practice (Wildavsky, 1964). The standard practice finds policymakers using manning tables to make an across-the-board percentage increase or decrease in both dollars and the manpower ceiling authorized to the agency. The public agency finds it expedient to regard the new ceiling as an outlay target, to make the case for an expanded budget in the next fiscal year.

A hypothetical example of the budgets-as-requirements strategy is to define requirements as the maximum number of people that the budget will allow. The objective here is to hire a mix of employees who will be paid salaries that the budget can sustain consistent with pay plans and negotiated wage and benefit packages. To illustrate, if the on-board number of employees is depicted by employment row vector and if the average salary that is paid each category in e is shown in column salary vector (s), then the following human resource budget totals $9.8 million, the product of e and s.

$$\begin{array}{cccccc} & \text{APT} & \text{SAM} & \text{COMOT} & \text{PF} & \text{LTC} \\ e = & (200 & 100 & 400 & 100 & 100), \end{array}$$

where

APT	= Administrative, professional, and technical employees
SAM	= Supervisory and managerial
COMOT	= Clerical, office machine operation, and technician
PF	= Police and fire
LTC	= Labor, trades, and crafts

and

$$\begin{array}{cccccc} & \text{APT} & \text{SAM} & \text{COMOT} & \text{PF} & \text{LTC} \\ s = & (\$15{,}000 & \$16{,}000 & \$8{,}000 & \$13{,}000 & \$7{,}000). \end{array}$$

If the agency budget for the next year is set at a 5 percent increase, a total of $10.29 million can be allocated in a variety of ways. For example, if there were no increase in the number of employees, then an across-the-board raise of 5 percent for all classes would produce a new salary vector $\acute{s}$ of

$$
\begin{array}{cccccc}
& \text{APT} & \text{SAM} & \text{COMOT} & \text{PF} & \text{LTC} \\
\acute{s} = (\$15,750 & \$16,800 & \$8,400 & \$13,650 & \$7,350).
\end{array}
$$

An example of the extreme alternative is to grant no raises but use the increased appropriation to hire proportional increases in personnel. Such a policy results in a new employment vector e' of

$$e' = (210, 105, 420, 105, 105).$$

Clearly, there are many ways managers can both assign salary raises and hire additional people to spend the budget authorization of $10.29 million.

The question in requirements forecasting is whether statements of human resource requirements can have a basis other than mere determination to use up authorized budgets. There have been several attempts to break the traditional budget logic of making incremental adjustments in the resource base. Performance budgeting, program-planning-budgeting systems (Schick, 1966), management-by-objectives systems (Newland, 1974; Brady, 1973), and zero-based budgeting (Pyhrr, 1977) are all strategies for tying budget allocations to statements of agency goals and measured outputs. All make different assumptions about the role of the budget agency in program and workforce management and depend upon different levels of analytic sophistication. In the end, however, all systems represent different strategies for "managing" marginal allocations of resources, for not even zero-based budgeting envisions a "zeroing out" of the government.

More sophisticated organizations link the determination of needs to the contributions that the various types of labor make to organizational productivity. For instance, one survey of private-sector practice reports that the most sophisticated organizations divide manpower forecasting into projections for "direct" manpower (those directly involved in production) and "indirect" manpower (support personnel). The forecasts of direct needs were derived from such variables as production schedules, workloads, and estimates of lost time. Indirect labor needs were forecast by dividing the group into variable manpower, whose work load varies with the size of the workforce and the productivity of the plant, and fixed manpower, whose work load is affected by neither variations in workforce size nor the productivity of the plant (see Heneman and Seltzer, 1970).

While forecasting direct labor needs seems a straightforward process of linking personnel requirements to measured output and schedules, forecasting variable and indirect private-sector labor needs seems relevant to governmental situations when the product of a police department, public works department, or planning office is not analogous to factory production and when the contribution that employees make to the product is not easy to measure. In such situations one approach is to develop conversion factors (Heneman and Seltzer, 1970), which represent the estimated amount of time required either for completion of certain actions or for "production" of certain units of output. The conversion factor ($_nC_i$) is the time (t_i) which n people require to produce N numbers of units of output (i) or complete N actions (i), and it is expressed as:

$$_nC_i = \frac{_nt_i \text{ (person days, weeks, or months)}}{_nN_i \text{ (output, actions)}}$$

Thus, $_nC_i$ can be calculated either for one person (in which case $_1C_i$ will cover several actions or output units (i) such that 100 percent of a person's time is accounted for) or for a group of persons.

When the total projected work load (L_i) for each action

or unit of output (i) can be estimated (by means not to be discussed here) and multiplied times $_nC_i$, the staffing standard conversion coefficient, then the human resource requirements, ($_nR_i$) for a single person or group of persons (n) can be expressed as follows for each activity (i):

$$_nR_i \text{ (person days, weeks, or months)} =$$
$$_nC_i \text{ (time/output or actions)} \times L_i \text{ (outputs or actions).}$$

For example, a group of ten welfare case workers may have their time apportioned among three activities: client office interviews and counseling, clerical work (processing forms), and client home visitation. In Table 10.2, if an average single case worker spent 50 percent of his time on interviews and counseling, 30 percent on visitations, and 20 percent on processing forms, then the conversion factors could be calculated if the numbers of actions could be reliably estimated. In this example, we assume that ten case workers handled 2,000 interviews, of which 1,600 resulted in processing forms and 500 involved visitations to the client's home.

If forecast work-load estimates for the following year are 3,000 interviews with proportional increases in visitations and forms processing, then the projected load (L_i) allows us to estimate future resource requirements for each activity (i). Adjusting $_nR_i$ to a base of ten person years, the projected need is

Table 10.2. Estimating Case Worker Needs in Person Years: Assume Initial Workforce of Ten Persons.

Activity Type	Percent of Time	Number of Actions/Years	Conversion Factor	Number of Projected Actions/Years	Projected Required Person Years ($C_i \times L_i$)
i	$10^t i$	$10^N i$	$10^C i$	L_i	$_nR_i$
Interviews	50	2,000	.0025	3,000	7.5
Processing forms	20	1,600	.00125	2,400	3.0
Visitations	30	500	.006	750	4.5
Totals	100				15.0

calculated at fifteen person years, or an increase in five person years of effort.

Whether five new case workers should be added depends not so much on the simple arithmetic shown above but on the conclusions that analysts draw. For instance, managers might restructure work so that computers would be used to process forms and reduce the clerical load. Or, work might be done on contract. Decisions can also be made to reduce the number of interviews subject to visitation from 750 to, say, 500, which would save 1.5 person years of effort. Such possibilities represent only a few strategies for eliminating the discrepancy between manpower needs and supplies.

In some public-management situations, it is difficult to decompose people's time into discrete actions and to calculate conversion factors. An alternative strategy is to use surrogate measures of output that can be plotted against the numbers of on-board personnel for specific times. Should analysis reveal that the plots can be reasonably described by some simplifying statement such as a regression line or a ratio, conversion factors can be generated easily. A practical example of this was once demonstrated by a student researching the relationship between manpower ceilings and output measures of a procurement division of a federal agency. The example is transferable to an urban management setting in cases such as administrative staff offices in which the real functions can be only partially or indirectly measured. In this case, the output of a procurement division was defined as the number of procurement actions (purchases) made per year. Such a definition of output is a radical simplification of the mission of a government procurement division that must balance the need to maintain an open marketplace with the need of operating divisions for timely deliveries of required and desired goods and services. Furthermore, a procurement action is often a highly variable output, embracing large, complicated, competitive procurements and relatively small, routine sole-source purchases.

While the data gathered were limited to seven years, a simple analysis of the basic trends provided useful information to resource planners willing to accept the data limitations. Table 10.3 shows for a series of fiscal years both the numbers of professional personnel on board and the number of procurement actions done in each year (Rosenthal, 1973). The simplest way to associate workforce size with output is with a ratio of actions to workforce size. The mean number of actions is shown to be 21 per person per year. Clearly, additional analysis (such as regression analysis) can be done to determine whether 21 actions per person is an appropriate work load figure from which a conversion figure of .048 (that is, 1/21) can be derived. (As this procurement division managed large, complex procurements, a figure of 21 actions per person seems reasonable.) In regression analysis the slope of a "least squares" line, where the X axis denotes actions and the Y axis denotes personnel, becomes the conversion factor.

The measurement of outputs for other government functions may be a more tractable problem than commonly believed, especially when there is a production process at least partially described by such measures as checks written, cases handled, tons of garbage collected, and acreage mowed. Productivity measurement is an elusive process, however. For example, the federal finding that 67 percent of the civilian workforce has been covered by some kind of productivity measure (Joint Financial Management Improvement Program, 1974) is important not because managers have completely described 67

Table 10.3. Numbers of Procurement Division Actions and Personnel:
1967 to 1973.

(1) Year	(2) Person Years	(3) Number of Procurement Actions	(4) Ratio:(3)/(2)
1967	40	790	19.8
1968	29	780	26.9
1969	31	716	23.1
1970	28	659	23.5
1971	32	493	15.4
1972	28	502	17.9
1973	24	475	19.8

mean = 21 action/person

percent of agency "productivity." The significance is that a tool for forecasting personnel needs is available that does not depend on strictly input-oriented budget strategies, such as what was allocated and presumably spent last year.

Notwithstanding productivity measurement advances, great problems remain in indexing public service outputs (Wise and McGregor, 1976). Not only are there organizational pathologies that develop as a result of measurement programs (Blau, 1955; Ridgway, 1956), there are also far-reaching policy consequences attached to any set of measures. Police services provide a good example. Elaborate output statistics can be developed to measure the productivity of police departments, such as the number of tickets issued and crimes "cleared" (Hatry, 1972). Yet, in communities where the function of the police is to provide such services as smoothing community relations, offering lectures, organizing community projects, and counseling, an entirely different set of productivity measures becomes appropriate (Wilson, 1968). Thus, the key to successful needs forecasting depends on measures of output consistent with the strategic objectives of the organization and not on mere quantitative manipulation. An illustration of the quantitative mechanics is found in Appendix D.

The end of the conversation about forecasting and planning is not, however, the generation of endless tables of numbers, transition matrixes, and forecasts, although it is likely that such analyses can and will occupy many computer runs easily programmed in a high-power language or designed to use the power of end-user–oriented spreadsheet software. The ultimate management challenge is to decide what to do about the forecasts, projections, and plans. In the workforce management model developed above, what can be done if workforce requirements and availability diverge? We know under the terms of an identity that the requirements-side and the availability-side of the workforce management problem will tend to equate one way or another. We also know that there are numerous strategies by which requirements and availability may be balanced. The question is whether the balance will be achieved on a basis compatible with organizational goals. What can the manager do to engineer a balance between the two sides of the equation? This requires a discussion of workforce programming, the third step in the process of workforce analysis.

Chapter Eleven

The Strategic Perspective in Making Choices

Managers are paid to act. Certainly they are also paid to think, study, analyze, assess, forecast, plan, and array the choices before them. Ultimately, however, they are hired (and fired) based on their ability to make choices and to act on those choices. How can public managers (as well as private managers) act strategically with respect to a workforce? The key is to see the choices that do, in fact, exist. A simple logic developed over several chapters focuses on the reconciliation of the requirements and availability of human resources in order to implement strategies and public policies. The key to success in that regard is to understand that there are many ways to reconcile policy-driven workforce requirements and the effective availability of personnel. Available to the workforce manager are all the tools of the human resource management trade through which the people side of enterprise may be managed.

Programming

Perceiving the full range of choices available is the first step in workforce programming. Part of the perception problem is to understand the alternative ways that exist to interpret forecasts and plans; a second part is knowing what to do about the problems developed in the planning process. Markov transition matrices are a good illustration of the first perception problem, for availability forecasting can be regarded in two ways: (1) *behavioral predictions* of likely patterns; or (2) *design statements* describing mobility levels and staffing patterns that must occur for an organization to be healthy and productive. Management programming decisions vary with each interpretation. In the behavioral view, transition probabilities may be regarded as the most precise approximations of workforce mobility patterns available to management. Clearly, the greatest predictive precision obtains in organizations operating in stable environments, using stable technologies, and either expanding or contracting at slow to moderate rates. Regardless of the numeric precision, however, the behavioral approach attempts to make the best guess about what will happen so that managers can decide how to react to the availability of personnel if *nothing is done*. The objective of behaviorally based workforce programming, therefore, is to react to empirical forecasts on the assumption that, absent managerial intervention, Markovian assumptions and numeric projections will, in fact, occur.

In the design view, however, the issue is not so much to discover "natural" patterns of mobility as to determine what mobility patterns are desirable and use the forecasts as determining the quotas placed on mobility. In this case, programming decisions are proactive and fused to forecasting and planning. The mobility transitions depicted in Markov analysis simply depict (forecast) ideal mobility patterns. In effect, forecasting becomes a policy statement defining the patterns that will be enforced in terms of the workforce proportions that *will* be moved through a personnel system.

An example taken from Chapter Ten may clarify the distinction between the two approaches and therefore the different linkages between forecasting, planning, and programming. The transition probabilities displayed in Figure 11.1 show the hypothetical mobility pattern in Chapter Ten that projected a mismatch between agency operating requirements and forecast availability of administrative, professional, and technical employees (APT) and supervisory and managerial employees (SAM) in a small agency of 200 persons. The discrepancy was caused by the mobility of the two types of personnel.

When the forecasts of Figure 11.1 are taken as behavioral statements, management confronts an enormous problem. The agency is losing large numbers of APT personnel who do the actual work of the agency. Furthermore, if the APT stock is not replenished annually, then the workforce loss begins in the second year to drain the managerial pool of SAMs. Ultimately, the forecast is for an agency with mostly SAMs and few APT workers around to do the work of the organization. The agency will soon close down. The workforce planning and programming challenge is to find a way to balance the projected requirement and availability of people *given* that the mobility patterns are what they are. Clearly, the recruiters will be busy.

In the design approach, mobility patterns can also be regarded as enforced movement, mobility that *will* occur. When viewed as policy, transition rates become decision attributes. In the illustrated example, the movement of people is designed and codified in the numbers as a matter of policy rather than prediction. Thus, Figure 11.1 shows that in a single year, the loss of departing SAM managers *will be* exactly replaced by upwardly mobile (if movement into managerial ranks can be termed an "upward" move) APT personnel. This is engineered mobility designed to achieve a proper flow of personnel through an organization. Such a strategy is common in closed, career-based, rank-in-person personnel systems such as are found in military officer corps, the foreign service, and even some re-

Figure 11.1.

| | | Year 2 | | |
		SAM	APT	Exit
	SAM	.8	.1	.1
Year 1	APT	.2	.5	.3
	Exit	0	0	1.0

search institutes and universities that rely on a continued circulation of personnel for organizational rejuvenation. The result is a kind of "up or out" system in which fixed proportions of personnel are retired, thereby making room for other professionals to test the managerial waters. Meanwhile, some number of SAMs are returned to regular professional practice each year.

Transition rates can be changed, however. The paradoxical result is that taking action with regard to the full range of human resource management options destroys the original forecasts and plans. Thus, real-world human resource *programming* constantly generates a need for new forecasts, new plans to balance availability and requirements, new programming options, and so the process goes. The dynamic nature of the programming process can be illustrated in the simple, hypothetical case of the two-class organization with the mobility transition rates noted in Figure 11.1. If one were to apply the transition rates to an organization that has, for purposes of illustration, an annual requirement for 100 SAM and 100 APT personnel, numerous programming possibilities are presented. In general, there are at least four strategic dimensions of human resource programming: the external labor market within which a workforce must be managed; the internal staffing and employment system by which personnel systems employ personnel; the internal appraisal and compensation system through which people are paid; and the internal appraisal and development system through which personnel are trained, developed, and changed.

External Market. The first scan of the problem requires a recognition of the points at which workforce programming impinges on the external environment. The "environment" could consist of a number of factors (Tichy, Fombrun, and Devanna, 1982), including external political, economic, and cultural forces, the extent of competition, the marketability of products, and the long-term trends (such as technology and demographics) that affect strategic decision making within the firm or agency. Leaving aside the long list of questions about the nature of market competition and equally long lists of complex questions about the political, economic, and cultural attributes of the strategic environment, an obvious external problem with which *all* human resource managers must cope is that personnel intake decisions are likely to be severely constrained by projections about external labor markets. In the hypothetical case of Figure 11.1, for example, current American labor force projections suggest an obvious strategic question: "Is it reasonable to conclude that an organization of 200 employees can add 40 new professionals to replace the forecast APT attrition?" The initial answer may well be: "Perhaps, depending on the precise types of personnel required and whether or not salary policy can be loosened up to allow competitive bidding for what may well be scarce talent."

A sensible external scan would, however, continue with its own response: "Mr., Miss, or Mrs. Management Decision Maker, recall that in the original problem, the operating requirement was for an on-board workforce of 100 APTs and 100 SAMs, while the net annual attrition was 40 APTs and no SAMs *if* the APT workforce was replenished with 40 new APTs every year." The cross examination might continue: "Casual scanning of long-term labor market trends suggests that other possibilities ought to be considered. After all, current projections find the U.S. labor force growing more slowly than at any time since the 1930s and a marked rise in the average age of the workforce indicating a declining pool of young workers" (Hudson Institute, 1987). The implication of this contrived discussion is clear: thoughtful managers might, at this point, start to think strategically about other programming options. In particular, the question would be whether internal programming options exist involving employment, appraisal, compensation, and development where action could be taken with respect to balancing workforce requirements and availability in ways that still meet organizational productivity and effectiveness targets.

Internal Employment System. One set of internal programming options consists of managing patterns of hiring and firing personnel, including recruitment, selection, and placement of workers. In the example above, the message is very clear: hire the required 40 APT employees per year or change the staffing requirements. But how might staffing requirements be modified? The answer to this pivotal question lies in digging into the heart of the work system (Hall, 1985). Work systems define in operational terms how people fit into a system of production. At least four dimensions (Leavitt, 1965, p. 1145) characterize work system design: systems, tasks, technology, and people.* They form the "staffing diamond" that is graphically presented in Figure 11.2.

The first work system option is to change the production *system*. This is accomplished through the definition of structures and processes used to produce a final product. Work systems can be modified by converting a job-shop or project management system into smoother, continuous, and even automated line operations processes. Another kind of production improvement might be to experiment with using groups and teams of people, rather than individual work units, as the basis of productivity. The point of this discussion is not to define all the decision options, but rather to suggest that numerous opportunities for equating projected workforce requirements and availability arise through the redesign of work systems.

Figure 11.2. The Staffing Diamond.

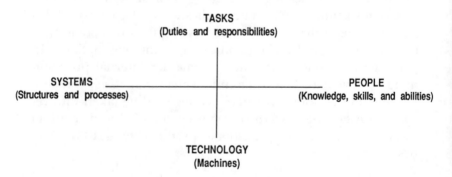

TASKS
(Duties and responsibilities)

SYSTEMS
(Structures and processes)

PEOPLE
(Knowledge, skills, and abilities)

TECHNOLOGY
(Machines)

*I am indebted to Jerry Mechling at the John F. Kennedy School of Government, Harvard University, for his insights on the four-dimensional scheme for assessing management change.

A second strategy is to change *tasks,* that is, the configuration of repetitive tasks, duties, and responsibilities that are programmed into individual jobs. For example, job enlargement and enrichment strategies are classic task-altering options. In terms of the hypothetical issue at hand, the one-to-one de facto SAM to APT staffing ratio implies a limited task repertoire assigned to highly paid personnel. For example, a top-heavy organization can well become overly administered with armies of SAM personnel coordinating, supervising, and otherwise producing intermediate products with rapidly declining marginal utilities to the organization (Downs, 1967). We can envision cadres of excessively zealous supervisors tripping over each other in attempts to police the work of APT personnel. An obvious target is to consider a reduction in the requirement that 100 SAM personnel supervise 100 APT personnel.

A third strategy is to change the work requirements by changing *technology.* The most obvious example would involve a partial or complete automation of the production process so that computers enhance the productivity of people. Recent applications of artificial intelligence and expert systems suggest enormous possibilities for technology applications as well as organization problems in absorbing new technology (Zuboff, 1988). Even administrative functions formerly requiring the labor-intensive services of middle managers are potentially subject to automation (McGregor and Daly, 1989). Thus, the potential for implementing this strategy must be rated as enormous. Indeed, the interaction between technology and organizations is its own massively varied and complex field, presenting myriad possibilities for organizational innovation and design (Tushman and Nelson, 1990).

A fourth strategy is to change the *people* in some significant way. This involves altering the workforce skill mix through hiring or realigning the on-board workforce using mechanisms, such as merger and acquisition of functions. The aims might be to produce workers who exhibit greater competitiveness and work intensity and master a growing array of knowledges and skills (Oka and Tanimitsu, 1985). "People changes" can accompany many strategic redirections of public and private enterprise, including the creation of new products, the

development of product improvements, and the enhancement
of the production process itself. Once again, as in the case of
the other three corners of the staffing diamond, whole books
remain to be written on the opportunities for work system design that depend on applications of human development. In
the hypothetical minicase, a question might be posed about
whether supportive training and development systems could
be put into place that would allow the APT employees to absorb a forty percent annual attrition rate in the short term and
still maintain case loads and effective client service. Quite obviously, other parts of the staffing diamond are affected by the
answer.

The result of this discussion is that the staffing diamond
represents a way to catalogue the four dimensions of work systems around which workforce programming decisions are made.
Clearly, it is difficult to separate the four dimensions, for changes
in one immediately affect the other three. Finally, the diamond
also suggests a fifth strategy, which is to consider all four dimensions simultaneously; indeed, truly *strategic* management
moves are aimed at solving complex and multidimensional
workforce problems in one stroke by simultaneously adjusting
systems, tasks, technologies, and people.

Internal Appraisal and Compensation System. Another way to
achieve a fit between externally imposed challenges and constraints and the internal details of workforce management is to
realign the compensation system. In the case of Figure 11.1,
both the original problem and any implied modification of organizationally ruinous career mobility patterns have enormous
potential compensation issues attached. In the case as originally posed, the staffing problem obviously arises because of
attrition in which a net of 40 people of a 200-person workforce
are forecast to leave in each year, assuming annual replenishment. The implication is clear: APT personnel are "bailing out"
of our hypothetical social service agency because the compensation package is inadequate. Thus, the compensation of APT
workers should be raised.

Once again, compensation is not a stand-alone variable.

Appraisal and compensation are also significantly affected in any scenario by which tasks, systems, people, and technologies are changed. In the radical change scenario, noted earlier, in which all four factors might be redesigned, enormous realignments can occur. Full-scale automation of administrative, professional, and technical functions might well be the only way to reach agency productivity goals, given the lack of significant growth in the external labor pool from which new recruits would be drawn and given the budgetary constraints placed on resources. The only reasonable option may be to squeeze productivity from the on-board workforce by radical restructuring of systems, tasks, technology, and people. People will be asked both to produce more and to be paid more as well.

Organizational restructuring can be substantial. Strategic managers might do well to borrow from the findings of recent case studies (Applegate and Cash, 1989; Brock, 1980) and studies of organizational competitiveness and innovation (Walton, 1987; Keen, 1986). One glimpse of the possibilities includes team-based production, automated operations with massive inputs of technology, and the elimination of layers of middle management. In effect, production teams could be made self-managing and involve substantial role flexibility such that workers are capable of filling many different production roles within an organization (Walton, 1987). In this case, compensation systems built on position-based, individually assigned rewards with hierarchic pay differentials between APT and SAM workers may well come under extreme pressure. Indeed, the compensation system may simply be an administrative dinosaur that has lost its relevance to current attempts to overhaul outdated and unproductive workforce management systems.

Internal Appraisal and Development System. The above discussion implies yet a third programming strategy: human learning and development must support a continuous process of organizational innovation. Thus, people learn, grow, and innovate by experimenting with new ways of doing things, adopting the experimental successes, and learning from the failures. In programming terms, this means that the strategic manager looks for ways to train and develop the workforce. In terms of the hypothetical social service agency, much depends on whether APT workers can learn to operate without constant managerial supervision, whether they can develop and apply automation technologies to work processes, and whether intellectual skills can be developed in order to work faster and more reliably. Strategic change depends on the development of such capabilities in the workforce. Indeed, the most daring developmental strategy would be to introduce large-scale work innovations that have the effect of obliterating hard workforce distinctions between narrow specialties and between "management" and "labor." Thus, for example, experiments in developing role flexibility, continuity in employment and assignment, increased worker participation, and more social integration have been attempted in such diverse areas as shipping (Walton, 1987), insurance claims processing (Brock, 1984), and financial services (Applegate and Cash, 1989). Virtually all such innovations depend on substantial investments in technical training and basic education required to support the innovation. Indeed, in some cases, innovation experiments themselves are investments in training and development.

Viewed in the most general terms, the aim of training and development is to affect significantly the workforce learning curve. The curve occurs when people perform repetitive tasks and become increasingly more skilled and efficient the longer the production process runs. The basis for learning-curve applications has a technical background that is summarized in Appendix E. Nevertheless, the essential insight of learning-curve analysis is simple and rests on the discovery that there are many productive endeavors that can be made increasingly efficient through either learning by workers or managerial innovations and other factors (plant layout, work group organization, procedures and lines of communication) that reduce the time required to produce final products. In very simplistic terms, if one were to plot the relationship between the *cumulative average* total units of final product produced and the direct labor hours required, the resulting function would be a downward sloping curve expressing a declining cumulative average number of hours required to produce the final product.

The extent of learning-curve application to workforce management still begs further research. For example, the geometry of learning-curve analysis is subject to widely varying assumptions and mathematical interpretations (Belkaoui, 1986). Theoretically at least, learning-curve analysis appears to have broad application, especially in labor-intensive, discontinuous forms of manufacture such as aircraft and ship assembly (Argote, Beckman, and Epple, 1990). However, learning improvements have been observed in continuous and capital-intensive industries such as petroleum refining and basic chemicals and in process-oriented manufacturing and job-shop production. It also appears in mature industries as well as start-up phases (Belkaoui, 1986). By inference from industrial experience, there is an enormous potential for learning in labor-intensive public services. Leading potential public-sector applications include permit issuance, technology transfer programs, and a wide range of urban services such as police, fire, sanitation, and public works construction.

What rate of workforce learning can management expect? There is no definitive research. In general, however, industrial experience suggests the following rule of thumb (Belkaoui, 1986): learning will be greatest in labor-intensive situations and least in capital-intensive situations. Empirical research suggests that 80 percent learning rates can be found in the former cases (Andress, 1954) and 90 percent rates in the latter case. Regardless of slope, basic learning-curve geometry involves a downward sloping curve in which the learning rate is the rate of direct hourly labor reduction required for every doubling of cumulative output. The result is the cumulative average learning curve shown in Figure 11.3.

The classic learning curve is, therefore, an exponential curve. That is, as cumulative production increases, the *total* hours required drops swiftly and then levels out at a declining marginal rate. Thus, as production doubles from two to four to eight to sixteen units, and so forth, each cumulative doubling takes an *average* of 80 percent less labor than the previous av-

Figure 11.3. Cumulative Average Learning Curve.

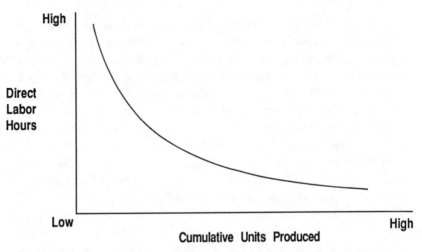

erage. Thus, the exponential effect that accrues from the com-
pounding of 80 percent productivity improvements produces
an enormous cumulative decline in human resource requirements over a long production run, although the total hourly
decline occurs at a declining marginal rate.

The cumulative effects of human learning have profound implications for both public and private enterprises; the
effects are felt most directly in program costs, budgets, space
utilization, speed of delivery, employee training, and wage and
salary structures. The brief excerpt in Appendix E contains a
perceptive analysis of the development of Japanese industry by
David Halberstam (1986). The vignette illustrates two strategic
implications of learning-curve analysis. The first is that enormous predictable reductions in workforce requirements occur
through the production life cycle as learning occurs. To illustrate the point from the original Frank Andress (1954) example, summarized in Appendix E, let us assume an 80 percent learning rate applied to a manufacturing situation where
12 total work hours were required to produce the first unit of
a manufactured good, 19.2 hours were required to produce
two units, 30.72 hours to produce four units, and so forth.
Thus, the early returns show a declining cumulative average

hourly requirement of 12 hours, 9.6 hours, and 7.68 hours, respectively. At a production level of 150 units, the total hourly requirement is 358.7 hours and the cumulative *average* has declined to 2.39 hours. Based on this cumulative experience, what should be the budgeted workforce requirement for a production run of 1,500 units? Certainly *not* the product of the production target—1,500 units—and the last known average, which is 2.39 hours. That would yield a common-sense conclusion that is wrong, namely that 3,585 hours, or more than 1.7 person years of effort, would be required to produce the desired 1,500 units. The truth is, however, that if anything like an 80 percent learning curve is realized, then only 1,710 hours will be required—slightly more than .82 person years of effort—or substantially less than fifty percent of the common-sense estimate.

Needless to say, there are major management mistakes attached to the failure to take learning-curve analysis seriously. In the public sector, particularly, productivity is defined in terms of cases handled, permits issued, households serviced, claims adjusted, public works constructed, and so forth. Large numbers of production units are involved because the size of public consumption is large when dealing with numbers of citizens, clients, cases, and claims. In instances where many thousands and millions of products—services, cases, actions—must be produced for a very large public customer, the costs of misjudgment are large. Even at a "mere" 90 percent learning rate, the failure to account for organizational learning results in huge misallocations of resources.

The second conclusion about the power of learning is the speed with which new products and industries can be developed once basic product research and development have been done and initial production processes have been put in place. For example, in expanding markets where service capacity might double every year, there is an *annual* application of the learning rate. In effect, this means rapidly declining costs and cheaper service on an annual basis. Clearly, both government budgets and private industry can benefit from applying the learning curve insight.

Recent research suggests that real-world learning curve

applications are vastly more complex (Ghemawat, 1985) than a mechanical imposition of a table such as is found in Appendix E to a production situation. Little is known about *why* learning occurs. As a result, little can be said about what factors favor an acceleration of learning (Yelle, 1979), whether learning persists within organizations (Joskow and Rose, 1985), and whether learning transfers across organizations (Argote, Beckman, and Epple, 1990). These are important issues because they lie at the center of current attempts to structure and manage knowledge-intensive systems in which the management of learning systems is the essence of postindustrial workforce management.

Learning persistence and transferability are particularly significant issues, because the productivity advantages of the cumulative learning curve must be depreciated by the extent to which events such as "forgetting," work interruptions, and organizational transfers lead to the degeneration of learning. In effect, there are many ways to imagine that the classic learning curve, based on some mathematically derived cumulative output function, significantly overstates the persistence of learning. Partial evidence for the significance of the cumulative learning loss phenomenon lies in a recent analysis of old production data taken from World War II Liberty Ship manufacture and a summary analysis of data from the more recent Lockheed L-1011 TriStar program (Argote, Beckman, and Epple, 1990). As in all good studies, the number of questions raised exceeded the answers given, but the strong empirical finding that learning acquired through experience does not persist, and indeed that learning depreciates rapidly, undermines simpleminded applications of the cumulative experience learning curve.

One obvious conclusion drawn from empirical analysis is that learning is a complex process affected by many possible factors including the rate of production and the recency of experience. Thus, the *rate* of production has a strong impact on learning persistence. In more practical terms, such a finding suggests that a firm or agency that is new to a competitive marketplace and, by definition, lacks the cumulative experience of a long production run can compete with more established (higher cumulative output) rivals if its "recent output levels are comparable to those of its rivals" (Argote, Beckman, and Epple, 1990, p. 152). In other words, early start dates are no guarantee of long-term success. Furthermore, while there was no evidence that personnel turnover contributed to learning depreciation in the Liberty Ship environment, which produced a uniform product from a standardized design controlled by a central management agency, it is likely that turnover affects less standardized environments employing highly skilled employees. Thus, the manner in which knowledge is embedded in such diverse work areas as manufacturing technology, standard operating procedures, methods of communication, and "shared understandings about how work is to be done" (Argote, Beckman, and Epple, 1990, p. 152) suggests some of the strategic complexities of work system design.

Toward a Strategic Perspective

This book has explored the implications of adopting a strategic approach to human resource management. The basis for the argument is that people have ceased to be mere operational inputs to traditional industrial production processes, either public or private, that are mass production systems designed for an era when environments were stable, production runs were long, competition among providers of services was slight, technologies were stable, and properly trained personnel were readily available in the external labor market.

The basic facts of life for both public- and private-sector managers are that the assumptions of the old industrial order have changed. Environments are not stable and controlled. Production runs are being configured to meet expanding and contracting market niches that open and close as populations and tastes change and competitive opportunities permit. Even public-sector providers must endure comparison with private-sector service providers who compete for public work. Furthermore, the technologies available to assist productivity ap-

pear to be constantly changing, forever opening up new opportunities for new products and productivity improvement.

There are many lessons to be absorbed by public and
private managers. One is to recognize the strategic significance
of human resources. In the emerging postindustrial order, human knowledges, skills, and abilities—an invisible resource
imbedded in people—rather than the availability of marginally
trained physical bodies define the prospects for productivity
improvement and national and industrial competitiveness.

A second lesson is that there is an extraordinary diversity of ways with which to manage this strategically valuable
resource. In this regard, the routines of personnel operations
are highly varied and subject to change. There is no single,
obviously correct design under which even public-sector merit
systems are best administered. For example, while the United
States has generally structured its public services around principles of open-career, rank-in-the-job, programmed-based staffing, many examples of closed-career, rank-in-the-person, career-based staffing can also be found. Both models have their
strengths (see Chapter Four). Both models also have their
weaknesses. For example, while the first model is a more per-
meable system that is better connected to external labor markets than the second system, it is also increasingly undermined
as the basis for postindustrial productivity shifts from position-
based strategies, structures, and systems toward the management of people, skills, and corporate or agency culture (Pascale
and Athos, 1981; Miller, 1989). Meanwhile, although the latter
model appears to be the more flexible system by virtue of vesting rank and pay in persons, a closed-career structure places
enormous pressure on recruitment and training and development systems—learning systems—to keep the workforce up to
date. Thus, the seeds of obsolescence are sown in the operational assumptions embedded in both systems, but the struggle
with ever-threatening obsolescence takes different forms.

How can the public workforce, in particular, remain
competitive and up-to-date? A strategic approach suggests experimentation with competitive alternatives. For example, there
is no reason why public-sector human resource managers can-

not experiment with blends of the two classic models for different types of employees. For example, position-based systems may be useful for administrative support personnel, while person-based systems might suit certain kinds of professional employees and production personnel whose personal knowledges and licensed skills are critical. Indeed, multiple systems can and are frequently used within the same bureau or agency. Each human resource management system can be designed with particular public goals and workforce mixes in mind.

Another lesson is that managers must learn to take strategic advantage of naturally occurring phenomena. Perhaps the most dramatic process is that people do learn and grow. Thus, new approaches to service delivery can be useful purely and simply because they enhance the capacity of a workforce to take on and solve tough problems. Much experimentation with computer applications (even the human resource information systems discussed in Chapters Six and Seven) can be partly justified as training activity; if the productivity goals are met, so much the better, but the development of a computer-literate workforce has a training value above and beyond nominal productivity improvement.

Another strategic implication of human growth and development has to do with the redesign of whole organizations. Unlike the learning curve that occurs naturally and presents alert managers with strategic opportunities for productivity improvements, the motivating force behind organization redesign in the private sector is externally induced by one of the most pressing of strategic issues—survival in competitive environments. Two examples illustrate the role of development, one from a study of international shipping and a second from strategic applications of telecommunications. Although both cases appear as private-sector issues, their implications affect workforce programming decisions confronting public workforce managers as well.

A recent study of shipping illustrates the trend—perhaps even a stampede—toward workforce role flexibility in response to strategic pressures of technology application, cost reduction, and general competitiveness in the shipping industry

(Walton, 1987). The detailed background to the conditions of competition and excess capacity that predominate among the companies that operate the world's oceangoing fleet need not occupy this discussion. What is relevant is that powerful strategic forces associated with competitive company survival and ambitious attempts to apply technology, such as remote sensing, microprocessor-equipped position finding and collision-avoidance devices, hatch automation, automatic alarms and communication equipment (Walton, 1987), have resulted in experiments designed to shrink crew sizes and costs. What happens to an organization when strategic management decision making moves in the direction of seeking a cost-competitive position by cutting costs and applying cost-saving technology? The result is a profound pressure to change workforce requirements radically by cutting payrolls and reducing crew costs and by restructuring the work environment. These changes typically occur *all at the same time* (Walton, 1987).

What then happens to the workforce? In the shipping case, a profound shift has been occurring in the structure of the job content. Whereas traditional staffing plans were built around narrowly defined jobs bound to collectively bargained rules that emphasized the repetitive performance of position-based tasks, duties, and responsibilities, the "new" staffing structures are built around broadly defined jobs based on the skills possessed by each crew member. The net effect has been that the most innovative shipping companies have changed the rigid, hierarchic shipboard structures consisting of separate deck, engine, and catering departments, each subdivided in turn into officers and several classes of seamen. Now they have cross-trained teams of general-purpose crew who are trained to operate both navigational and cargo systems as well as mechanical and electrical functions. Overly hierarchic and specialized occupational classifications reinforced by specialized labor unions preserving separate and distinct partitions among deck officers, engineering officers, masters, radio officers, and "ratings" (nonofficer or "unlicensed" members of the crew) have been relaxed. Instead, innovative work systems are being developed

that emphasize flexible work assignments, participative decision making, and on-board social integration (Walton, 1987).

Of equal significance, however, is that the basis for
workforce management has shifted from position management
to the management of personal knowledge and skill. Work roles
are based not on position classification and union membership
but rather on *knowing how to perform* the many functions associated with running a technologically sophisticated ship. This
is the only adaptation that satisfies the strategic requirement
for smaller and less costly crews to manage increasingly automated and sophisticated ships. In essence, a strategic change
in the external environment combined with choices of ship
management strategy has changed the workforce requirements. The same trends can be found in many other industries, both public and private (Brock, 1984; Miller, 1989; Applegate and Cash, 1989).

The development of "polyvalence" in the workforce becomes a management goal. Polyvalence is the means by which
workers perform or retain the ability to perform many different ranges of tasks. Polyvalence cuts across narrow bands of
job and skill classifications (Child, 1987) and poses an enormous and exciting challenge for workforce managers, who will
find that traditional occupational classification schemes are increasingly useless as tools of workforce management.

Yet a different study of competitiveness reveals a second
trend. Strategic applications of new technology are creating new,
knowledge-based jobs that did not exist before. A classic example is found in Peter Keen's analysis of the strategic application of integrated information technology (IIT) in private
enterprise. The definition of IIT includes the merger of data
processing, information systems, and telecommunications. A full
discussion of IIT is too extensive for this volume, but the principle of strategic applications of IIT bears brief consideration
in a discussion of workforce management. Organizations competing on a global basis have found it necessary to establish
electronic "highways"—satellites, fiberoptics, switching systems—that involve strategic applications of telecommunica-

tions technology to move data and information fast enough to provide a competitive edge.

One effect of the strategic application of computing and telecommunications technology, however, has been to change radically the staffing patterns of corporations. The automation of the office function with networked, point-to-point communications systems, teleconferencing, voice message systems, and other computer-aided devices permits major reductions in clerical costs and the elimination of entire layers of middle management that traditionally managed the interactions between the strategic center and the operational periphery (Keen, 1986). Even more profound is the whole new set of knowledge-based skills that had to be created and grown. Thus, Keen (p. 187) projects an array of new skills required for the new technology environment of the 1990s, including

> Document management specialists
> Videodisk specialists
> Product development planners
> Expert systems development staff
> Integrated services digital network (ISDN) specialists
> Videoconferencing planners
> Videoconferencing operations staff

Where do these new skills come from? They are not widely available in the external market. Indeed, they will have to be grown rather than brought or bought from the external marketplace.

This question raises yet another. How does the strategic workforce manager convert an aging workforce organized along hierarchic, position-based principles working with outdated technology into a competitive and innovative workforce that quickly and easily accesses and applies new technology? In more specific terms of the IIT example, how does the manager convert personnel tied to now aging technologies involving 1970s data-processing and telecommunications systems or 1980s information systems personnel into the integrated technologies of the 1990s? The literature responding to this question is sparse, but clearly workforce managers will be challenged (Zuboff, 1988; "Blue Shield. . .", 1983). Furthermore, the *public*-sector literature that documents successful organizational adaptation to changing technology is even more sparse (Bell and Steedman, 1967) and requires updating by experienced managers who also find time to conduct research and write.

The telecommunications and shipping examples illustrate one of the strategic puzzles for public and private managers alike. Advancing technology promises both to destroy and create work, jobs, and positions at perhaps an increasing rate. The evidence suggests that the one constant in this process is a growth in the formal knowledge and skill requirements necessary to learn the new technologies and jobs. Thus, the basis for work content becomes increasingly skill based. This means, in turn, that the invisible characteristics of people—their knowledges, skills, and abilities—become increasingly significant in the workplace. Strategic workforce management will become synonymous with the strategic management of this invisible resource.

Improved Public Programming

Where does all this lead public-sector managers? The evidence is overwhelming that the foundations of bureaucracy have already shifted and that government is not and cannot be immune to the forces of change. The same pressures for cost reduction and strategic uses of technology exist for government as for private business. Indeed, there is every evidence that, far from being immune to competition, public agencies not only compete among themselves for missions, resources, and political support (Bragaw, 1980), they also compete with the private sector to provide public service (Savas, 1987). The implications of such strategic realities are clear. Public managers have a mandate to experiment with new and better ways of doing things. The results of that experimentation have already been indicated. Gone are the structurally rigid organization charts. Position-based personnel systems are not the only way to structure personnel systems. Public policy and public missions appear to be constantly inventing new organizational instruments, new occupational skills, new product lines, and new ways to deliver old product lines. The results of the experimentation are likely to be new occupations, increased role flexibility, more participative decision making, and increasing reliance on knowledge and personal skill as the basis of productivity. If strategic programming is the essence of both public and private management improvement, what can be done in the short term to improve the prospects for effective workforce management? There are many things that might be tried, including the following:

Human Resource Accounting. The human capital insight produces a fundamental conclusion: While personnel represent large outlays in current operating costs, human resources are more significant as assets and not simply as a charge against the operating budget. Moreover, second-generation human resource accounting systems are being developed in the private sector that begin to account for the human asset and therefore for its management (Flamholtz, 1985). The reality of most public- and private-sector accounting systems, however, is that even the operating costs of human resource management are not well tracked. Experimental private-sector accounting systems, for example, operationalize human resource "value" in terms of personnel operations, that is, the replacement cost plus the investment made by the firm in terms of a person's recruitment, training, and development (Likert, 1967).

Despite creative early attempts at measurement, the future of human resource accounting remains in doubt. While all agree (Norkett, 1982; Beer and others, 1984) that the subject has great potential for development, no one yet foresees extensive practical use of human resource accounting systems developed to date. Some possible applications include (Norkett, 1982):

- Measuring return on human capital employed.
- Integrating human asset values in financial accounts for external reporting purposes.

- Valuing businesses (the private-sector case) where the human asset is a relevant factor in mergers and takeover decisions.
- Examining the disposition of human assets throughout an organization.
- Evaluation of personnel operations expenditures in relation to human resource value.
- Using human resource values as a basis for designing remuneration systems.

With the exception of some exploratory research for the Department of the Navy (Flamholtz, 1985), virtually no public-sector investment has been made in the development of even a prototype human resource accounting system. The stakes of the exercise are large because the value of the resource is so significant. For example, where final products derive from human resource knowledges, skills, and abilities—research and development enterprises and health care providers are the most obvious examples—the value of the strategic human asset—scientists, engineers, and doctors—dwarfs the value of all other assets combined. Human assets are profit centers that earn many times their salary in revenues generated from fees, contracts, and grants. Indeed, in the case of research centers, the absence of critical human assets converts a potentially productive organization into an organization whose balance sheet becomes the salvage value of the physical plant and equipment. There is room to experiment with public-sector human resource accounting systems.

Information Systems Development. Regardless of the directions taken in the accounting profession, there are now many simple opportunities to improve the information base on which public-sector workforce management might be conducted. Some thought could be given, for example, to restructuring governmental personnel information systems to include cost and productivity criteria. Revised information systems could also clearly distinguish position-, person-, and product-based personnel classifications and data. The federal government, for instance, could benefit from reorganizing its current structure of series and groups that now serves only operational personnel interests and beginning the process of connecting personnel operations with the budgetary and productivity-based issues of line management. Such a move would make personnelists almost instantly useful to top managers and the connection between strategic decision making and personnel operations would be greatly strengthened. Among the information systems development options that would support a truly managerial approach to workforce management are the following:

- Crosswalk development: connects end users with raw workforce information.
- Automating the personnel function: decision support systems and applications of artificial intelligence hold some promise for reducing the information barriers that stand in the way of effective workforce management.
- Begin to develop staffing standards: government should initiate a substantial staffing standards research program that would support productivity analyses of alternative staffing patterns and, ultimately, support workforce planning.
- Staffing plans: public managers can be encouraged to manage the workforce more effectively by using staffing plans as the basis for budgeting and personnel decision making; the plans need not, at first, be overly sophisticated and analytic; over time, however, the analytic component could be grown to suit management needs.

Civil Service Simplification. The foundations of public service have shifted just as surely as they have for all organizations in postindustrial societies. Merit systems administration was established at a time of industrial development when humans were a visible resource that could be managed through the positions that people held. Times have changed. It has been the argument here that much of modern government has less to do with position management and more to do with the semiautonomous performance of work by people based on personal knowledge and skill. Even the vast clerical bureaucracies of government have been reorganizing work processes and auto-

mating clerical functions (Brock, 1984). How are human resources to be managed when product portfolios of public
agencies shift in response to the demand for increasingly
sophisticated products? When production systems are automated? When products are experimental? When the instruments of production involve managing complex intergovernmental networks?

One potentially interesting idea moves in the direction
of simplifying civil service rules, regulations, and procedures.
A recent federal example of the issue is seen in the recently
proposed Civil Service Simplification Act (S. 1545, introduced
on July 24, 1987). In the proposed act, a complex federal classification system of large qualifications manuals, eighteen pay
grades, and ten pay steps would be reduced to a flexible system
of simple position descriptions and flexible pay bands. Managers would be free "to match labor requirements to mission
accomplishment and market conditions" (Colvard, 1987a,
p. 21). Line managers would enjoy reduced staff-control and
more freedom to manage the workforce.

Maybe. The great strength of the simplification idea is
that it provides an authorizing vehicle by which a single civil
service system can be adapted to fit the variety of people, products, and positions found in general-purpose units of government. The aim of the act, after all, is: "to promote better management of the Federal work force by establishing a Simplified
Management System that will vest in Federal agencies the authority and responsibility to use *flexibilities* [emphasis added] in
assigning rates of basic pay in order to recruit, motivate, and
retain a well-qualified work force." Yet passage of such legis-
lation is problematic. Congress did not immediately rise to defend the idea. Furthermore, the policy process generally ignores the subject of civil service reform. What do workforce
managers do if legislative authorization is not forthcoming? This
book suggests some possible lines of inquiry, none of which
requires legislative authorization or involves acts of high public
policy.

Aggressive Use of Demonstration Projects. Public managers can
also innovate and experiment. For example, Title VI of the

Civil Service Reform Act of 1978 explicitly authorizes and encourages experimentation with new federal personnel administration designs and practices. Only modest use has been made of the authorization to date, but the reported results of the two senior demonstration projects are particularly interesting. Both experiments involved a deliberate simplification of personnel policies and procedures governing the civilian workforces at two Department of Navy centers: the Naval Weapons Center in China Lake and the Naval Ocean Systems Center (NOSC) in San Diego. Both experiments began in July 1980 and were, based on promising results, extended to September 1990. The two experiments targeted four main areas: first, simplified position classification standards and shorter position descriptions; second, streamlining and targeting performance appraisals to establish performance expectations, assess achievements, and allocate variable financial rewards; third, establish flexible pay policies through the design of broad pay bands; fourth, recognize performance as a major criterion in the conduct of reductions in force (*Federal Register*, 1980, 1981, 1982).

The results of the experiments as found in reports (Wilson, 1985) and testimonials (Gore, 1987) have been encouraging. Indeed, several effects have been found: the classification system has been simplified, the ability of the navy to compete for talent appears to have been strengthened, the turnover rate has declined, morale has been sustained, support staff work has been reduced, and the line management system for final product production has been strengthened. The case for extending the experiment to the rest of the federal government seems strong (Colvard, 1987a). Indeed, state and local government could benefit by considering the results to be reported in the evaluations.

What is striking about the two demonstration projects is that the two naval civilian workforces involved in the experiment are precisely representative of the knowledge-intensive workforces (*Federal Register*, 1980) discussed throughout this book. In effect, it may be that the composition of the navy workforce and the nature of the "products" produced at the two centers have much to do with the effectiveness of the demonstration experiment. This theory could be tested by extending Title VI experimentation to other sites in which the final products and required workforce skill mixes are more varied; that is, production and clerical workers as well as research and development workers could be studied to discover whether morale, turnover, and productivity were significantly affected when different kinds of workforces were handled in different ways. The point is that there is much to be learned from careful experimentation with new ways to manage the public workforce.

Chapter Twelve

Implementing
Workforce Management
Improvements

Can improved workforce management decision making be made to work? It may have occurred to more than a few alert readers that I have made it appear too logical and perhaps too easy. Can it really be that the recipe for workforce management success merely involves following a few rules of employment system design, developing a classification scheme, creating a data base, flipping the switch of a microcomputer, and watching workforce management decisions either scroll across the screen or print to hard-copy output? The answer to this rhetorical question is, of course, that the simple-minded view of management has *not* been the thesis advanced here. The principal aim, rather, has been to make workforce management complexity more explicit so that management decision making can be supported by clear thinking and potentially useful information.

To this point, however, we have merely discussed an explicit set of managerial, organizational, logical, and technical issues associated with all workforce management. We have also explored the problems of linking strategic, tactical, and operational problem solving and the distinct information requirements of each decision-making level. Finally, we have tried to show some of the very subtle, but strategic, distinctions that come into play when operating work systems shift from traditional bureaucratic structures and processes to postindustrial designs. Nevertheless, even if all the foregoing chapters consisted of powerful logics, unalloyed precision, and penetrating clarity, there would still remain several practical barriers that introduce enormous complexities into real-world decision making.

Implementation Barriers

Implementation barriers are created because of the way people in large organizations deal with the intellectual, technical, and political requirements of management decision making. Failure to understand and deal effectively with these barriers can be the downfall of overly precious management improvement schemes. Fortunately, however, much descriptive research has been done on the problems of rationality in organizations (March, 1988) and, as a result, something is known about practical impediments plaguing deliberate attempts at rationality. Some of the most notable implementation barriers include problems of bounded rationality, information ambiguity, threats of automation, and the partisan manipulation of information. A few comments on each problem are offered, with the caveat that each one is a prospective topic for a separate book. The summary discussion here merely serves as a deliberately superficial warning about the potentially fatal challenges to the improvement of workforce management.

Bounded Rationality. One of the most commonly cited problems is lodged in the limited human intellect. The operating reality of the human brain is that man's capacity to perform feats of memory and calculation associated with most rational models of decision making is severely constrained. This means that if reasonably bright people confronting real-time decision problems cannot be expected to perform the formal manipulations associated with rational choice, then it makes no sense to claim that choices are somehow rationally or analytically "best" or "optimal." It makes sense only to speak of "limited or bounded rationality" (Simon, 1957), which is nothing more than acknowledging that when confronting problem situations, decision options that cross the threshold of being "good enough" for a given problem situation will be chosen as soon as they are presented. In such satisficing conditions, no one really knows or can ever objectively know whether a particular decision was rationally correct. Thus, the "correctness" of decisions becomes an interesting academic debate over whether a best, utility-maximizing, cost-minimizing, or optimal course of action was selected. The debate can be the occasion for wonderful displays of formal and informal analytics and argumentation, but not the final basis for real choices.

What leads to this satisficing behavior? Several factors have been discovered that militate against analytic rationality. One set of limits is neurologic. The ability of the human brain to perceive, absorb, retain, and process information with respect to practical problem solving is severely limited by comparison to the makeup of a complex, problem-producing environment (Simon, 1969). The practical result is that the human animal can be objectively rational only when the presentation of stimuli can be greatly slowed down or external memory aids supplied. People's brains, it seems, have limited short-term memories and confront bottlenecks in moving information from the very limited short-term storage to the nearly unlimited, large-scale and long-term storehouse (Simon, 1969). In short, the human brain was not made to be analytically rational when confronting dynamic problem-solving situations in real time, although static problems in stable environments are obviously more tractable and amenable to rational solution.

A second limitation is that gathering, storing, retrieving, and processing information (Simon, 1957; March and Simon, 1958) in support of rational decision making is expensive business. Just because formal analysis can be done does not mean that it will be or should be. In general, the analytic rule of thumb is that unless expected benefits of information processing and analysis clearly exceed the costs, it is not reasonable to expect real decision makers to invest greatly in expensive research simply for the satisfaction of being objectively "rational." It is more likely that they will engage in "satisficing" behavior and develop coping routines as an inexpensive way of simplifying complex problems.

A third limit inheres in the structure of real decision situations, where facts and values cannot be easily disconnected for purposes of estimating the empirical outcomes separate from an implicit or explicit normative evaluation of those outcomes. Thus, even if the human brain were not limited, or could be mechanically assisted (the solution to the first problem), *and* the benefit-cost ratio favored research (the answer to the second problem), the practical structure of decision making often conspires against a clean separation of facts and values, which represent the normative labels attached to outcomes. In other words, it becomes theoretically desirable but practically impossible to explore separately the factual consequences of all possible decision options. In situations where a complex management problem elicits more action options than the human intellect can process, the cost of analysis is prohibitive because the numerous outcomes are more than mere "states of nature." They are also normative conditions to which multiple stakeholders attach different interests and values.

What can the decision maker do? The practical answer is that extensive formal calculation is avoided in favor of a more realistic strategy where managers attempt to forge a consensus about acceptable ways to muddle through incremental changes that do not require analysis of a large number of decision options and heroic feats of information management and calculation (Lindblom, 1959). The incremental strategy is particularly appropriate in multiperson, multiperiod, and multiutility situations where problem complexity and scarce time conspire to prevent sophisticated formal analysis.

Do these theoretical objections to rational decision making apply to workforce management? Clearly they do. In earlier chapters, we demonstrated that there are many administrative and policy actors who are stakeholders in workforce management decision making, each of whom captures pieces of information and decision-making authority. Second, powerful disagreements rage over the basis for employment system design; budget people, personnel people, employee associations and general managers, for example, simply do not agree about the design rules that, in turn, have enormous implications for program costs (a budget concern), career structures (a personnel concern), job opportunities (an employee concern), and future decisions affecting the whole workforce (a concern of general management). Third, there are hundreds of potentially relevant decision variables describing in fine detail the many attributes of the workforce. Fourth, there is even the risk that misapplication of information management technology can compound the information management problem through an indiscriminate "dumping" of disorganized data files on the desk of any would-be manager who is not thoughtful about the decision relevance of data and information. Fifth, we have demonstrated that there are multiple levels of workforce management data, so that even if decision-relevant variables could be defined, the multiple levels of aggregation can frustrate the decision maker who does not possess validated crosswalks required to climb from operations to strategic levels and back down again. Given these realities, how can decision making be anything but severely limited?

There are two types of responses to the bounded rationality critique. The first, of course, is that the critics of rationality are correct, particularly in the workforce management case. The human brain assisted by a stubby pencil *cannot* perform the manipulations suggested here. The costs of time and human effort are simply too great to expect anything better than seat-of-the-pants decision making when the decision maker is not assisted by modern information management technology. Furthermore, practical decision making involves workforce outcomes that *simultaneously* affect people, tasks, technologies, skills, and work systems, each of which represents a cluster of empirical and normative variables that are very difficult to separate.

The conclusion, therefore, is not to deny the realities and the complexities of real-world decision making. The point is to take advantage of new systems that can support the decision maker. Remember that sophisticated, end-user technology is available, so it is reasonable to expect that managers do not have to forget facts about the workforce. Furthermore, managers can harness this technology and organize workforce facts in many helpful ways that do not take inordinate amounts of time and effort, once a modest investment in information management skill has been made. The further point is a founding hope of this volume: if the workforce management problem can be demystified and decomposed into its many puzzles, each of which can at least be partly understood, then sources of risk and confusion can be written down so we can understand the kinds of calculations that might help managers. In this way, some progress toward rationality can be achieved. One need not claim absolute rationality in order to press the case for advancement.

Information Ambiguity. The second possible implementation barrier implied in the literature is based on the ambiguous character of workforce information. Mere availability of information spewed forth in profusion from sophisticated information systems is, taken by itself, ambiguous (March, 1987). Data and information do not order themselves, suggest salience, tell decision-relevant stories, or pull strategic facts from the morass. For example, workforce characteristics, turnover rates, employment levels, and productivity rates are not inherently meaningful. Knowing such information does not automatically suggest conclusions or recommend actions. Thus, having information and information systems technology is not inherently meaningful. "Information entropy" committed on the desks of aspiring executives is an occupational hazard in an information-intense environment where there is an enormous technical capability to capture, store, retrieve, and manipulate multilevel and multidimensional information about the workforce.

Managers must recognize and acknowledge the danger. The way out of the inherent confusion and ambiguity, however, is the same as the route into the confusion: a managerial mind must make the connection between information systems and decision making. The connection is not automatic or inherent in the information itself (Ciborra, 1987), a point dem-

onstrated in earlier chapters. Clear management thinking about
the strategies and goals of organizations is required to convert
useless data to structured information that, when used to inform questions asked by decision makers, produce the knowledge they require. Only when data and information are converted to knowledge statements does information start to lose
its inherent ambiguity and become useful. That this task of
creating useful knowledge and information involves some soft
technologies—history, culture, literature, educated guesses,
gossip, hunches, and plain old common sense—needs no elaborate defense here. All these tools will be potentially useful in
teasing the workforce management story from a pile of in-
choate workforce facts. The lesson is that what matters is the
story, the workforce picture, that generalizes from the facts,
not just facts taken by themselves.

The attempt to make the connection between information and decision making and thereby overcome the ambiguity
problem, however, leads the decision maker to the next difficulty, which is that workforce information then becomes a threat.
This is one of the classic management paradoxes, since if information is inherently ambiguous, then the threat of information systems abuse is reduced. Indeed, such systems are
harmless and, if harmless, may be close to useless. If, however,
information systems do establish a connection with the knowledge needs of management decision making, then information
ceases to be completely ambiguous for it must in some way
respond to the knowledge needs of managers and executives.
Indeed, under conditions of connectivity, information management potentially becomes a very powerful tool.

Threats of Automation. At the point where connections are
forged between information systems and decision making, at
least two implementation barriers come into play. They arise
because of the multiple organizational threats posed by the introduction of powerful information management technologies
into work systems. In effect, massive organizational change is
threatened both in terms of operating work systems and in organizational effects of creating an "electronic text" of organi-

zational activity. The threat is felt most keenly by people in bureaucracies whose jobs have traditionally depended on a functional capture of decision-making responsibility and the data and information that support management decision making—that is, routine workers and middle management.

The source of the threat is worth a short digression, because it frames a challenge with which nearly all modern organizations will have to deal. The source of the difficulty lies in the nature of end-user–oriented technology being installed in all public and private organizations. In effect, the application of modern computer hardware and software to any work system simultaneously does two things: it *automates,* in the sense that smart machines are applied to production processes for the purpose of speeding up work and displacing the human worker; it also *informates,* in the sense that the automation process generates an information byproduct that is instantly "visible, knowable, and shareable" from any organizational point to any organizational point (Zuboff, 1988, p. 9). The combined effect of automating and informating poses strategic choices for organizations that are revolutionary and, by definition, threatening to settled patterns of doing business. The details of applying smart machines to work systems and organizations cannot be dealt with here at length, for detailed discussion would fill volumes (Zuboff, 1988; Briefs, Kjar, and Rigal, 1985; Bailey, 1983).

Perhaps most salient are two aspects of "computer-mediated work." The first is the enormous impact of automation on work systems. In effect, massive displacements of people by smart machines are now possible, with large-scale but as yet poorly understood consequences for workers. A reasonable summary seems to be that emerging technology is so flexible and powerful that an enormous range of work design choices is now possible (Zuboff, 1988). One scenario, for example, is that work can be enriched and made more interesting through the automation of dull and dangerous work and the empowerment of workers who can be allowed to manage complex systems of flexible manufacture. Productivity and pay can increase for workers remaining on the automated workforce payroll, and, in general, the workplace can be enormously enriched, making everyone in the workforce better off even though the aggregate workforce size will be smaller. The same technology also makes possible a contrasting scenario, however, which involves using smart machines to make jobs more routine and less enriched, all the while reducing worker control over operations through highly centralized information structures. In short, the application of smart and flexible information management technology to the task of automation does not predetermine organization and job design. Design remains to be fixed by management decision making.

The second impact is that a fully informated organization strips away sources of power, layers of bureaucracy, and restructures the interactions (Ciborra, 1987) associated with old industrial hierarchies that traditionally have incurred large transaction costs imbedded in the rigidities of organization structure. In traditional systems, a large number of middle managers are required to handle the coordination, interoffice memos, meetings, approvals, supervision, and other essential information transactions required to run complex organizations. In the postindustrial office, by contrast, information systems automate many information transactions and thereby informate as well (Zuboff, 1988, p. 10):

> The combination of on-line transaction systems, information systems, and communication systems creates a vast information presence that now includes data formerly stored in people's heads, in face-to-face conversations, in metal file drawers, and on widely dispersed pieces of paper. The same technology that processes documents more rapidly and with less intervention, than a mechanical typewriter or pen and ink can be used to display those documents in a communications network. As more of the underlying transactional and communicative processes of an organization become automated, they too become available as items in a growing organizational data base.

Organizational intelligence is no longer capable of being phys-ically captured as the personal property of middle managers whose power depends upon capture.

The stage is set for a wholesale redesign of organiza-tions. The informating power of computers is capable of strip-ping away layers of middle-management functions, eliminating hierarchies, and creating problem-solving networks. The or-ganizational impacts are not neat and surgical, for the tasks of the remaining workforce become redefined in ways that have not been definitively studied. Clearly, however, the substance and the distribution of work of an entire workforce, including the management of organizations, is up for renegotiation in the postindustrial organization. Hierarchies become replaced by teams and problem-solving networks. Power flows to people with relevant knowledge rather than to people holding posi-tions. Organization designs containing elements of both cen-tralization *and* decentralization become possible.

Will postindustrial designs strengthen or weaken indus-trial democracy? Will work systems become more or less dull? Will workers capture the wage benefits of automated organi-zations? The threat lies in the uncertainty inherent in auto-mated and informated designs that have an equal potential of becoming contrasting and contradictory things: they can either be democratic or totalitarian, sustain dull or interesting work systems, be generous or not with ordinary workers.

In organizational terms, the new technology presents a clear and direct threat to entrenched interests and traditional ways of doing business. The threat, however, is *not* simply the existence of intelligent hardware and software systems that au-tomate work. It bears repeating that a second threat lies in the informating potential for linking information systems to deci-sion making. Where information systems and decision making are separated, middle-management work multiplies in order to create a connection. On the other hand, where sophisticated configurations of end-user–oriented information management technologies are linked with decision-making applications, stra-tegic managers with access to the electronic text of a fully in-formated organization can, from any organizational position, climb into the operations of any other organizational operation merely by invoking information management protocols and bypassing all intervening layers of hierarchy and functional division. We have discussed the theory of such linkages in earlier chapters. Thus, implementing sophisticated workforce management systems is not a neutral organizational act, and aspiring workforce analysts and managers will need to deal with the natural human fear of uncontrolled change and the understandable instinct to self-protection that seeks to reduce uncertainty rather than undertake a rational assessment of the organizational costs and benefits of strategic change.

Partisan Manipulation. In cases where information systems and decision making are connected, there is the problem that "information is not innocent" (March, 1988, p. 387). Thus, even if managerial magic could remove the first three implementation problems, there remains the old-fashioned problem of man's political nature, which is potentially tempted to manipulate for partisan gain both the structure and the contents of any technically sophisticated system of organizational intelligence. Favorite strategies available to organized man, even "rational" man, include withholding information, confusing the coding and organization of information, and on special occasions reserved for espionage, actively engaging in the promulgation of disinformation.

Ironically, the incentives for partisan manipulation of information become greatest at precisely the moment when the connection between potentially ambiguous information and decision making is made and workforce information is about to become managerially useful. That is, at the point where knowing something has decision relevance, the incentives are greatest to manipulate and even to "game" the information system for private advantage and competition for scarce resources and rewards that accrue to successful gamesmanship. Indeed, the organization theory literature is full of accounts of the dysfunctional and organizationally perverse consequences of data-collection and measurement schemes. Social welfare workers engage in "creaming" the labor pool in order to lift productivity rates (Blau, 1955). Academic departments redesign curriculums in order to create more appealing course structures with which to attract students and manipulate credithour production (March, 1988). Police departments have the capability, if they wish, to manufacture increases in crime rates in response to productivity studies. On and on goes the gamesmanship designed to massage poorly designed and managed information systems. Paradoxically, at precisely the point where information systems give the appearance of driving decision making, both theory and practice lead analysts to expect partisan manipulation of workforce information.

Once again, it is not the aim of this volume to deny reality. Of course, a large and complex organization is not one big unified, happy family. Of course, firms and government bureaus are political coalitions that aggregate competing interests among operating divisions and disciplines (March, 1962). Under circumstances where a workforce is managed in a multimember, interorganizational environment, the temptation to engage in partisan manipulation of workforce information is even greater than original studies (Cyert and March, 1963) have suggested. If anything, as environments of public and private organizations become increasingly volatile and competitive, partisan pressures on information systems will probably increase in the future (Kaufman, 1985). The metaphorical depiction of the modern organizational condition as a purposeless garbage can begins to acquire substance (Cohen, March, and Olsen, 1972).

The response, once again, is that managers must acknowledge organizational reality. Political partisanship does pose a real challenge to any would-be manager of advanced postindustrial systems. The constant threat of organizational anarchy can probably be disciplined only by managers with a sense of strategic purpose and design who inspire trust in their motives, leadership, and managerial judgment. The threat of partisan manipulation of information also suggests the fate that awaits simple-minded models of information systems design. Absent a strategic sense of direction that determines the information that is required and the data-base distinctions that must be preserved, organizational confusion seems inevitable.

Proactive Strategies

While the difficulties associated with implementing a strategic management approach to a strategic resource are clear, the evidence seems equally clear that the costs and risks of avoiding the issue are vastly greater than risking failure in the pursuit of a strategically motivated, proactive approach to workforce management. Evidence and testimonial suggest that managers who either wittingly or unwittingly cling to an endless refinement of traditional and specialized personnel operations and practices without regard to the fit between human resource management and overall strategy and organizational outcomes are vulnerable to two sorts of fates, both associated with organizational decline (Cook and Ferris, 1986; Evans, 1986; Meshoulam and Baird, 1987): First, the evidence suggests that in a task environment populated by competitors, proactive firms that do systematically engage in strategic human resource planning outperform the reactive ones. In competitive environments, in effect, enterprises clinging to traditional routines and reactive, crisis-oriented decision making are candidates for decline, reorganization, and perhaps extinction (Kaufman, 1985).

A second fate is a scenario that follows directly from the discussion in this volume. Inability or unwillingness to balance availability and requirements on terms consistent with overall policies and objectives, by definition, will place the firm or agency in an increasingly vulnerable position, where the ability to meet goals of any sort (except possibly the goal of providing short-term, paid employment) will be compromised. In the long term, however, multiple sources of environmental turbulence—new problems, shifting policy goals, new constraints on operations, manmade and natural disasters, population shifts, the development of innovative technologies, to name a few—can destabilize both the availability and the requirement for human resources often very quickly. Thus, even without competitors, the mere pressure of events poses risk.

One typical scenario that currently threatens any easy balance between workforce requirements and availability involves both the supply and the demand side of the workforce management identity. On the availability side, population figures for an aging U.S. workforce suggest that labor shortages will be the norm in many areas, particularly in many high-skill, shortage occupations. This, in turn, means that the option of simply going to external labor markets to satisfy hiring needs may be severely constrained (Hudson Institute, 1987). Furthermore, strategies to increase labor availability by creating more employment opportunities for formerly underemployed persons—women, minorities, and foreign-born workers—must work through a series of snags at some cost both to the firm and to the employee. For example, there are natural limitations implied in rising workplace competitiveness caused by the "burden of out-of-work responsibilities" borne largely by women; no amount of equal employment opportunity rhetoric can erase the conflict (Kanter, 1986, p. 535). In addition, in the case of minorities and foreign workers, there are barriers of inadequate education and training as well as prejudicial attitudes and behaviors that threaten equal opportunity. All these availability barriers can be removed, but removal is not costless or automatic. Only proactive planning and management can create flextime jobs, day-care centers, flexible pay and leave policies, remedial and advanced education classes, language training, and affirmative action plans. In addition, work systems, corporate and agency cultures, and teamwork traditions will be required to deal with the very difficult availability issues found in the economies of the United States and Western Europe.

On the requirements side, equally substantial challenges can be found. A typical scenario for turning around a firm in decline (Cook and Ferris, 1986) consists of attempts to realize more work at higher quality from fewer people by simultaneously automating work, upgrading jobs that can be more productive and better paid, recruiting fewer and more capable employees, weeding out poor performers, shrinking aggregate payroll costs as a percentage of the productivity effort, and reducing administrative overhead. These are nearly universal requirements of all firms and public agencies attempting to implement some combination of the following strategies: develop new products and services quickly, compete on product quality, produce more complex products and services, meet productivity goals with an inelastic resource base (that is, one that does not expand with output demands), achieve a flexibility to respond to shifting market demands for products and services. In sum, typical workforce requirements attached to many corporate and public agency strategies for survival and prosperity appear to dictate an impossible and seemingly contradictory set of objectives: managers must simultaneously shrink and upgrade the workforce (good news in the face of a prospective availability shortage, but bad news in the face of mediocre public education systems), allocating fewer and fewer workers to middle-management and administrative overhead positions. It bears repeating that a reactive style of workforce management wedded to fixed personnel routines and practices cannot readily rise to meet the challenge confronting old-line operations. Reactive managers arrive at the workforce management table with too little, too late.

This conclusion leads to the final puzzle. If we accept the need for proactive, strategic management under current environmental conditions, what does the manager do? What steps can be taken to overcome the incipient anarchy implied in the sheer complexities associated with workforce management in the postindustrial era? Definitive answers are not sitting around in the available literature, but some guidelines are beginning to emerge from recent research and from the discussion of the previous eleven chapters. At least four kinds of responses are indicated for general managers who wish to be strategic and proactive players in the workforce management drama.

Recognize What Is Going On. The first answer is seemingly trite, but potent in its implications. The shift from position-based, industrial-style production systems with pay based on organizational status to knowledge-based, postindustrial production systems with compensation based on "contribution" is a major discontinuity in much of our organized activity. The shift destroys traditional hierarchies. It establishes human resources as a strategic resource, perhaps *the* strategic resource. It is found in both labor-intensive and in capital-intensive enterprises. It affects both public and private sectors. It promises to reward some and penalize others. While the shift can be accelerated or decelerated according to choices that managers wittingly or unwittingly make, early recognition of the postindustrial discontinuity is the key to prospective success.

Integrate Strategic Planning and Workforce Management Functions. The second response seems equally obvious, yet the merger of workforce management with line management decision making involves two kinds of integration: vertical and horizontal (Cook and Ferris, 1986; Meshoulam and Baird, 1987). The vertical dimension ties the management of people to strategic planning from which emanate the key requirements, constraints, outcomes definitions, and timetables that define workforce management success. The horizontal dimension involves an integration among the disparate disciplines *within* the workforce management domain. Since being proactive implies anticipating alternative scenarios that indicate what to do *in the event* likely scenarios develop, workforce planning and management are partners. Many organizational designs are available by which a structural and functional merger of these two seemingly disparate functions can occur, not the least of which involves sharing decision-relevant information.

It should be clear by now that workforce management can be designed in a near infinity of ways. Some of the options were discussed earlier. The significant point, however, is that it makes no sense to describe in precise detail each of the combinations of employment, compensation, evaluation, and career management practices that might exist, although we have tried to define some of the strategic decision variables. What is relevant is that the logic of strategic management implies that workforce managers *simultaneously* fulfill multiple roles and demands for responses to strategic issues. This can at least be partly illustrated by citing what can happen when strategic components do not support each other (Meshoulam and Baird, 1987, p. 499): "Money, time, and energy are wasted. Information is collected but not analyzed. Surveys and environmental scans are conducted but not used. Programs are purchased but not implemented. Many firms have purchased career planning, performance appraisal, succession planning, and other programs which figuratively or literally sit on the shelf because managers do not have the skills to use them. Managers become frustrated and angry because they don't have the support needed to work with employees effectively. Human resource professionals become frustrated because they can't accomplish what they feel needs to be done."

The anxious manager quite properly feels a growing sense of panic. Simultaneous integration of all aspects of workforce management with strategic planning? That is a tall order! It is too tall. No one develops simultaneously on all fronts. Paradoxically, a winning integrative strategy emerges in the form of staged development associated with strategic organizational outcomes. While there are different developmental sequences (Meshoulam and Baird, 1987; Evans, 1986), the key point is that workforce managers do not have to work on all fronts simultaneously. Indeed, in the words of one analyst (Evans, 1986, p. 163): "the unsuccessful pattern is to try to succeed at everything at one and the same time."

What, then, is the proper sequence? Different advice can be given but, in general, strategic planning will help sort out the developmental stages. One approach, for instance, is "outcomes oriented" (Evans, 1986), in the sense that the strategic outcomes of internal equity, competitive performance, innovation flexibility, and corporate integration all define management effectiveness. One study of leading-edge European corporations found that successful engagement of problems of equity and human relations occurred before management turned its attention to the challenge of competitive performance, followed by tackling the challenges of innovation and flexibility (Evans, 1986). Another study postulates the need to fit human resource management practice to the appropriate stage of organization development; thus, as an organization proceeds through the stages of organizational initiation, functional growth, controlled growth, functional integration, and strategic integration, human resource management practice must produce adaptive responses (Meshoulam and Baird, 1987). In addition, some writing suggests a logic for identifying targets of integration. One approach focuses on two prongs of action (Meshoulam and Baird, 1987, p. 499): First, invest in the workforce management areas that are lagging and threaten the whole enterprise; strong areas will pull their own weight. Second, invest in areas where critical constraints on organizational success are found. Thus, if a critical need exists for fast, cheap, and reliable information of use to strategic planning, for instance, then it is self-evident that time must be invested in developing strategic information systems.

Establish External and Internal Fits. The concept of strategic "fit" is perplexing. Proactive managers are exhorted to achieve simultaneously two different kinds of fit. One is between the external environment and the workforce management outcomes that must be achieved in order to achieve goals. This is the challenge of "doing the right things." The other fit occurs in the internal realignments of human resource management practice that drive workforce management operations. This is the challenge of "doing things right" (Meshoulam and Baird, 1987).

Whether both kinds of fit can be achieved together remains one of the fascinating management questions. Clearly, only a proactive and strategic examination of the double fit problem will stand a chance of success. For example, an emerging "external fit" scenario involves the challenge of creating a continuous workforce transformation where increasing productivity is generated from a declining number of workers who are recruited, organized, trained, and compensated in ways designed to achieve an overall productivity position that meets the challenges of the external environment. In some cases, the external fit also involves keeping up with changes in technology, learning about new strategy that guides a business or agency, and working in self-directed teams that do not require great administrative overhead and supervision to achieve productive results (Cook and Ferris, 1986; Ost, 1990). And, as if things were not complicated enough, the idea of "transformational management" (Kozmetsky, 1985) embraces the notion that constant innovation may be a further strategic external requirement. If one accepts the above capsule description as reasonably definitive of the notion of "doing the right things," then the question for internal fit is to realign human resource management practices so that "things are done right."

The external-fit conclusion implies a massive redesign of all internal aspects of human resource management practice. Often mentioned are such internal adjustments as upgrading recruitment and selection practices (Cook and Ferris, 1986), changing compensation plans and systems to pay skills and contributions rather than organizational status (Kanter, 1986; Ost, 1990), redesigning training and development programs to incorporate the subject of strategic management (Cook and Ferris, 1986), and the development of computer information systems (Ost, 1990), to name only a few options. The result is a strategic transformation of operational practice that is both unsettling and ambiguous.

Nowhere is the ambiguity of achieving a double fit more in evidence than in the attempt to design compensation systems that recognize new workforce realities. Gone are the tactical uses of compensation that attempt to use rewards only to manipulate individual behavior. Even traditional gain-sharing approaches that typically reward efficiency improvements are inadequate, although team-based compensation supplants narrowly competitive and destructive versions of merit pay plans. Truly strategic approaches to compensation design incorporate rewards based on achieving goals promulgated by external strategy, including but not limited to achieving bottom-line external outcomes, rather than merely performing a specific production process; acquiring new knowledges, skills, and abilities as the basis for organizational transformation; and assuming risk in absorbing the collective gains and losses of the enterprise (Hufnagel, 1987; Ost, 1990). Thus, according to one recent study (Ost, 1990), the use of strategically designed compensation systems—team-based compensation in this case—to support business strategy "requires adopting performance objectives that have less definition and clarity" than would be found in more narrowly focused, but precise, plans. Great trust between managers and workers is required to achieve strategic fit when important matters such as pay are involved.

There Is Innovation. Finally, there is the grand paradox. Leading thinkers (Evans, 1986; Kanter, 1986) have noted that strategic workforce management goes beyond the comfortable notion of "fit." For reasons that previous chapters have tried to suggest, the modern realm of workforce management implies that organizations and workforces will be in continuous motion. Changes in workforce composition will raise new problems that will frustrate, for example, the employment of women and minorities. Strategic changes in compensation systems will threaten the management prerogatives of comfortable hierarchies established to administer traditional systems of compensation. Indeed, the idea of strategic fit connotes a process of matching, or achieving a state of congruence between that which is required and that which is made available through management action. Yet, the notion of "fit" is itself subject to strategic examination, depending on the strategic aims of organization. One particularly perceptive account puts the paradox of fit in the following way (Evans, 1986, p. 158): "Fit is indeed the appropriate metaphor if the desired outcome is performance. Yet the closer is the degree of fit, the tighter is the interlock between different elements, so the more rigid or inflexible is the system. Fit is an inappropriate metaphor if the desired outcomes are innovation and flexibility. Order, and especially the machine-like order symbolized by the concept of fit, is the enemy of innovation, flexibility, and adaptation." While scholars can debate the implicit empirical assertion that "tight interlock" and "inflexibility" are necessarily linked, especially in modern, information-intense organizations, the point is well taken. Indeed, the pressures of postindustrial change suggest that overly comfortable notions of a fit are fatuous. The gale forces that sweep through modern organizations threatening hierarchies, traditional practices, and bureaucratic routines appear to have only begun. The aim of this discussion has been to examine the critical dimensions of workforce management that will need to be kept firmly in view as events and pressures place organizations and workforces in motion. The way to deal with motion is to acquire a compass, a roadmap, and a set of directions. This book represents a search for such navigational aids.

Appendix A

Human Resource
Information System
Availability

End-user software technology for desktop microcomputer systems demonstrates the widespread availability of support for computerized workforce information systems. A survey of commercially available software was described and classified in a recent article: Eugene B. McGregor, Jr. and John Daly, "The Strategic Implications of Automation in Public Sector Human Resource Management," *Review of Public Personnel Administration* (Fall 1989), *10* (1), pp. 29–47. I am indebted to John Daly for permission to reprint the two sets of revised tables showing characteristics of commercially available software packages. The first set (Table A.1) includes machine requirements, cost, operating system, programming language, compatibility with other computer environments, and report-generation capability. The second set (Table A.2) reports the functional areas of human resource management covered by each software vendor.

The names of vendors have been eliminated because the point of this information is to show the technical advances that have been made rather than to advertise programs that at the time of this printing are already out of date. The costs of these packages are generally dependent on a number of factors, including the number of personnel program modules resident within the software, the size of the workforce data base (and therefore the number of records), and the amount of memory required to load the software.

Table A.1. Human Resource Information System Availability: Selected End-User Packages for Microcomputers.

Vendor	RAM Memory Required (Kb)	Demo. Avail. (Y/N)	Demo. Cost ($)	Software Cost	Language Used	Operating System	Compiler Included (Y/N)
A	384	Y	$10	$6,500	COBOL	PC-DOS,Xenix,Unix	–
B	256	Y	Free Trial	$995	C. BASIC	PC-DOS	N
C	256	Y	Free Trial	$795	C. BASIC	PC-DOS	N
D	N/A	Y	$30	$98	BASIC	PC-DOS/CPM	N
E	640	Y	Free Trial	$3,000	Knowledgeman	PC-DOS	N
F	512	N	N/A	$7,200	Pascal	PC-DOS	Y
G	256	Y	$50	$499	C	PC-DOS/XENIX	N
H	–	Y	–	$12,000	–	PC-DOS	|
I	512	Y	$10	$3,993	C. BASIC	MS-DOS	Y
J	384	Y	$50	$2,500	dBASE III+	MS/PC-DOS	Y
K	256	Y	$25	$11,000	C. BASIC	PC-DOS	Y
L	320	Y	$25	$1,500	BASIC	PC-DOS	Y
M	640	Y	$100/Ref	$10,000	RBase	PC-DOS	Y
N	512	N	N/A	$1,200	BASIC	PC-DOS,Xenix,Unix	N
O	512	Y	$150/Ref	$9,970	DataEase	PC-DOS	Y
P	256	Y	$25	$3,250	dBASE	PC-DOS	Y
Q	–	Y	Free Trial	$6,000	COBOL	PC-DOS	Y
R	512	Y	Free Trial	$9,299	BASIC/FORTRAN	PC-DOS	N
S	640	Y	$50	$9,750	C	PC-DOS	N
T	512	Y	Free Trial	$12,500	dBASE III	PC-DOS,Xenix	N
U	128	Y	$30	$200	BASIC	PC-DOS	N
V	512	Y	$30	$6,700	Informix	PC-DOS,Unix,VMS	Y
W	640	Y	Free Trial	$6,925	Rev/Rbase	PC-DOS	Y
X	320	Y	$25	$995	C. dBASE III	PC-DOS	N

Table A.1., continued

Vendor	Upload to Mini System (Y/N)	Preformatted Report Gen. Included (Y/N)	Ability to Create Your Own Reports (Y/N)	Statistical Pkg. Avail. (Y/N)	Graphics Pkg. Avail. (Y/N)	Standard Reports (Number)
A	Y	Y	Y	Y	Y	35
B	N	Y	Y	N	N	10
C	N	Y	Y	N	N	10
D	Y	N	N	Y	Y	—
E	Y	Y	Y	Y	Y	75
F	N	Y	Y	N	N	60
G	Y	Y	Y	N	N	30
H	Y	Y	Y	N	N	45
I	Y	Y	N	N	N	—
J	Y	Y	Y	Y	N	60
K	N	Y	Y	Y	N	50
L	Y	Y	Y	Y	Y	30
M	Y	Y	Y	Y	N	80
N	Y	Y	N	N	N	—
O	Y	Y	Y	N	Y	50
P	Y	Y	Y	Y	Y	30
Q	Y	Y	Y	N	N	25
R	N	Y	Y	N	N	70
S	Y	Y	Y	N	Y	50
T	Y	Y	Y	N	Y	30
U	Y	Y	N	N	N	6
V	Y	Y	Y	N	N	40
W	N	Y	Y	N	Y	60
X	Y	Y	N	N	N	30

Table A.2. Microcomputer-Based Automation of Personnel Operations by Function.

	Vendor																							
	A	B	C	D	E	F	G	H	I	J	K	L	M	N	O	P	Q	R	S	T	U	V	W	X
I. Staffing and Employment																								
Applicant tracking	s	a	a	x	—	s	x	x	—	x	s	s	s	—	x	s	x	—	s	s	s	s	—	—
Job analysis and position classification	x	x	x	x	—	x	x	x	a	x	s	x	x	—	x	x	x	x	x	s	s	x	x	x
Job description and specification	s	a	a	x	—	x	x	x	x	x	s	x	s	—	x	s	x	x	x	s	s	x	x	—
Recruitment	s	a	a	x	—	s	x	x	—	x	s	s	s	—	x	s	x	—	s	s	x	s	—	—
Testing and selection	—	a	a	x	—	—	x	x	—	x	—	s	s	—	x	s	x	—	s	s	s	s	—	—
Placement	x	x	x	x	—	x	x	x	—	x	s	x	x	—	x	x	x	x	x	s	x	x	x	x
Vacancy	x	x	x	—	—	x	x	x	—	x	s	s	x	x	x	x	x	x	x	s	x	x	x	—
II. Compensation Administration																								
Accident tracking	—	—	—	—	—	—	—	—	—	—	—	s	x	x	x	—	—	—	—	—	x	x	—	—
Attendance	x	—	—	x	x	x	—	x	x	x	s	x	x	x	x	s	x	—	x	—	—	s	x	x
Basic pay and benefits	x	x	—	x	x	x	x	x	x	x	x	x	x	x	x	x	x	x	x	x	x	x	x	x
COBRA module	a	—	x	x	—	—	—	x	—	x	s	s	x	x	x	s	x	—	—	—	x	x	—	x
Hazardous pay	s	—	—	—	x	—	—	—	—	x	—	s	—	—	x	—	—	—	—	—	—	x	—	—
Incentive systems (bonuses)	s	—	—	—	x	x	x	—	—	x	—	s	—	—	x	x	—	—	—	s	x	s	x	—
Job evaluation	x	x	—	x	x	s	x	x	x	x	s	s	x	x	x	x	x	x	x	x	x	x	x	x
Medical and health	x	x	—	x	x	x	x	x	—	x	s	s	x	x	x	s	x	x	x	s	x	x	x	x
Overtime pay tracking	x	—	x	x	x	x	—	x	—	x	s	s	—	x	x	—	—	—	x	—	—	s	—	—
Pension adm., cafeteria-style module	x	a	a	x	—	x	—	s	—	x	s	s	—	x	x	s	x	—	x	s	x	s	x	—
Vacation time tracking	x	—	x	x	—	x	x	x	—	x	—	x	x	—	x	s	x	x	x	—	—	s	x	s

	1	2	3	4	5	6	7	8	9	10	11	12	13	14	15	16	17	18	19	20	21	22	23	24
III. Career Management																								
Career planning	—	—	—	—	—	—	x	x	—	x	—	s	—	—	x	—	x	—	x	s	s	s	—	—
Discipline and review	x	x	x	x	—	x	x	x	x	x	x	x	x	x	x	x	x	x	x	x	x	x	x	x
Personnel actions, demotion	x	x	x	x	—	x	x	x	x	x	x	s	x	—	x	x	x	x	x	s	x	x	x	x
Personnel actions, promotions	x	x	x	x	—	x	x	x	x	x	x	s	x	—	x	x	x	x	x	s	x	x	x	x
Personnel actions, reinstatements	x	x	x	x	—	x	x	x	x	x	x	s	x	—	x	x	x	x	x	s	x	x	x	x
Personnel actions, separations	x	x	x	x	—	x	x	x	x	x	x	s	x	—	x	x	x	x	x	s	x	x	x	x
Personnel actions, transfers	x	x	x	x	—	x	x	x	x	x	x	s	x	—	x	x	x	x	x	s	x	x	x	x
Personnel history	x	x	x	x	x	x	x	x	x	x	x	s	x	—	x	x	x	x	x	x	x	x	x	x
Scheduling (e.g. flextime)	a	—	—	—	—	—	—	—	a	—	—	—	—	—	—	—	—	—	—	—	—	—	—	—
Skills and educational attainment	s	x	x	x	x	x	x	x	x	x	s	s	x	x	x	s	x	x	x	—	x	x	x	x
Training and development	s	x	x	x	—	x	x	x	x	x	s	s	x	x	x	—	x	x	x	s	s	x	x	—
IV. Industrial/Employee Relations																								
Grievances	—	—	—	—	—	—	x	—	—	—	—	—	—	—	x	—	x	—	—	—	—	x	—	—
Bargaining unit	—	—	—	x	—	—	—	—	—	—	s	—	—	—	x	—	—	—	—	s	x	x	x	—
Communication tracking (feedback)	—	—	—	—	—	—	—	—	—	—	—	—	—	—	—	—	—	—	—	s	s	—	—	—
Employee relations	—	—	—	—	—	—	x	—	—	—	—	—	—	—	x	—	—	—	—	s	s	—	x	—
Job design	—	—	—	x	—	—	x	—	—	—	—	—	—	—	—	—	—	x	—	—	—	—	—	—
Organizational level	—	—	—	x	—	—	x	x	—	—	—	—	—	—	—	—	x	—	x	—	—	—	x	—

Table A.2., continued

V. Public Policy/Regulations

Appointment authority	—	—	—	—	—	—	—	—	—	—	—	—	—	—	—	—	—	—
EEO-1 module	x	x	—	x	x	x	x	x	x	x	x	x	x	x	x	x	x
EEO-4 module	x	x	—	x	x	x	x	x	x	x	x	—	x	x	x	x	x
ERISA module	x	—	x	s	—	x	—	x	x	s	—	x	—	—	x	—	—
Health and safety tracking (OSHA)	—	—	—	—	x	s	s	x	x	—	—	—	—	x	—	x	—
Security module	—	—	—	—	—	—	—	—	—	—	—	—	x	—	—	—	x

x = included in basic price
s = supplemental package available
a = enhancement available at an additional cost

Appendix B

Mental Health
Workforce Crosswalk

Crosswalks are databases that provide explicit linkages between different sets of observations about the same objects or cases. Thus, two different systems for classifying people, industries, communities, or any other item of interest often require some set of definitions that explains how membership in one classification of the first system accounts for a given classification in the second system. Crosswalks are perhaps most useful when multiple levels of data gathering about people, organizations, markets, regions, and so forth, exist and require linkages in the interest of aggregating data from highly refined and minute levels of analysis to broader classifications and groups for reporting purposes. Crosswalks provide, in essence, the intellectual transportation among levels of analysis, as seen for instance in attempts to tie operations-level activity to strategic levels of analysis.

Nowhere is the crosswalk of greater potential use than in occupational analysis where definitions of occupation differ greatly. A simple illustration of the principle is shown in a study of institutionally employed mental health workers in the Indiana state personnel system. In its most refined form, the state personnel department recognizes at least 338 different classes of personnel employed in the state system. This represents an operational level of analysis, where highly refined definitions of mental health occupations are used to manage the personnel actions—hiring, firing, paying, promoting—affecting approximately 7,000 individual employees. Other levels of management, however, may be less interested in reporting actions and resources attached to 338 different occupations and more interested in the summary patterns. For example, the most refined classification does not reveal which personnel are involved in direct patient care and which ones are serving in a support capacity. Nor does the operational system display the skill mix in terms of whether medical staff (doctors and nurses) predominate over behavioral case workers (psychologists, social workers, and several kinds of counselors). Thus, a crosswalk serves as a codebook that can convert operational workforce detail into summary data by displaying the rules of aggregation that can be added to any database.

In the example of mental health workers, the following codes were used to distinguish "program" personnel from "support" personnel and, within each broad category, the types of pay systems involved. In the summary below, letters indicate program code and numbers indicate pay plan categories.

Program Code	Program Description	Pay Plan	Pay Description
A	Direct-care staff	1	Direct-care staff consisting of medical, professional, and technical personnel
A	Direct-care staff	2	Dietetics and nutrition
B	Support staff	1	Labor, trades, and crafts (LTC); protective and law enforcement (POLE) personnel
B	Support staff	2	Executive; professional and administrative; clerical personnel

Occupational groups can be further broken out, as shown in the following intermediate classification of occupations.

A. Program Personnel
    1. Psychiatrists, physicians, and dentists
        a. Psychiatrists
        b. Physicians
        c. Dentists
        d. Intern/resident
    2. Psychologists
        a. Ph.D. level
        b. Master's level
        c. Intern
    3. Social workers
        a. M.S.W. level
        b. B.S.W. level
    4. Nurses
        a. Master's level (for example, M.P.N.)
        b. R.N. level
        c. L.P.N. level
    5. Pharmacy personnel, chemists, and laboratory technologists
        a. Pharmacists
        b. Other pharmacy personnel
        c. Chemists and technologists (for example, chemists, radiographers)
    6. Therapists
        a. Physical therapists
        b. Occupational therapists
        c. Audiologists/speech pathologists (incl. speech and hearing clinicians)
        d. Other therapists (for example, recreational therapists)
    7. Counselors, teachers, case managers, and associates
        a. Special education teachers
        b. Substance abuse counselors
        c. Pastoral counselors
        d. Guidance counselors
        e. Community workers

       f.   Case managers, module directors, health care planners

       g.   Medical records administrators

       h.   Other personnel (for example, clinical associates, behavioral clinicians, physicians assistants, developmental disability staff)

    8.   Dietary personnel

    9.   Attendants, aides, technicians, and assistants

B.   Support Personnel

    10.   Housekeeping, building and grounds, maintenance, and security personnel (such as LTC/POLE personnel)

    11.   Administration, clerical, and other personnel

These groupings merely establish the codebook through which a crosswalk can be developed. The crosswalk itself is the data base whose observations record the actual classifications for each job title and class code, and ultimately each person and position, in a given operating system. Crosswalks can consist of manual and automated systems. The ease with which computerized crosswalks can be created and augmented and modified is illustrated in Table B.1, a data slice taken from the state of Indiana and programmed in dBASE III+.

Table B.1. Crosswalk: Indiana Department of Mental Health Program Codes, Job Titles, and Occupational Group Codes.

D.M.H. Program Category	Job Title	Class Code	Occupational Group Codes
Program	Assistant Supt Modular Services E V	E14275	7f
Personnel	Audiologist III	14363	6c
1. Patient Care	Audiologist/SP Path III	14313	6c
(program	Behavior Clinician III	13043	2b
code = A1)	Behavior Clinician IV	13044	2b
	Behavioral Clinician III/WL	W13043	7h
	Biochemist E VI	E12106	5c
	Biochemist II	12102	5c
	Chaplain Educator II	23012	7c
	Chaplain III	23013	7c
	Charge Nurse III	20043	4b
	Charge Nurse Supervisor V	S20045	4b
	Chemist II	12022	5c
	Chemist III	12023	5c
	Chief Medical Technologist III	20123	5c
	Chief Pharmacist II	12072	5a
	Clin Nurse Special III	20183	4b
	Clin Pharmacy Aide IV	50114	5b
	Clinical Associate V	13045	7h
	Community Service Director III	14193	7e
	Community Service Director IV	14194	7e
	Dental Assistant IV	50054	9
	Dental Assistant V	50055	9
	Dental Hygienist	20105	9
	Dentist E V	E20015	1c
	.	.	.
	.	.	.
	.	.	.
Program			
Personnel			
2. Administrative	Superintendent E I	E00001	11
& Clerical	Superintendent E III	E00003	11
(Program	Switchboard Operator Supervisor VII	S64077	11
Code = B2)	Switchboard Operator V	64075	11
	Switchboard Operator V/Work Leader	W64075	11
	Tabulating Machine Clerk IV	65054	11
	Teleprocessing Operator IV	65044	11
	Teleprocessing Operator V	65045	11

Table B.1. continued

D.M.H. Program Category	Job Title	Class Code	Occupational Group Codes
	Training Director V	S15035	11
	Training Officer III	15043	11
	Training Officer IV	15044	11
	Word Processor III	65063	11
	Word Processor IV	65064	11

Total number of job titles = 338

Appendix C

Annotated Bibliography on Human Resource Forecasting and Planning

Acton, Jan, and Levin, Robert. *State Health Manpower Planning: A Policy Overview.* Rand Report No. R-724-RC. Santa Monica, Calif.: Rand Corporation, 1971.
This report offers some good insights into forecasting, recruitment, and training.

Arnoff, Franklin N., and others. *Manpower for Mental Health.* Chicago: Aldine Publishing, 1979.
Deals with manpower trends, utilization, motivation, models, economics, and theory.

Aronson, R. L. (ed.). *The Localization of Federal Manpower Planning.* Ithaca, N.Y.: Cornell University, 1973.
Eleven articles about organizing manpower delivery systems in large cities. The role of forecasting, and manpower and economic planning are offered as two perspectives.

Bartholomew, D. J. *Stochastic Models for Social Sciences.* (2nd ed.) New York: Wiley, 1973.
An application of stochastic models—especially Markov chain processes—to social and occupational mobility, education and manpower systems, and recruitment, promotion, and turnover in organizations of constant and changing size.

Bartholomew, D. J., and Forbes, Andrew F. *Statistical Techniques for Manpower Planning.* New York: Wiley, 1979.

A comprehensive supply-side approach to workforce planning, complete with mathematics, illustrated examples, and applications. Lots of exercises and solutions provided. Book concludes with a short chapter on demand forecasting. Heavily mathematical.

Bartholomew, D. J., and Smith, A. R. (eds.). *Manpower and Management Science*. Lexington, Mass.: Lexington Books, 1971. Edited papers delivered at the seventeenth International Conference of The Institute of Management Sciences (TIMS), held at Imperial College, London, July 1970.

Bennison, M., and Casson, J. *The Manpower Planning Handbook*. London: McGraw-Hill (U.K.), 1984. A largely supply-side discussion of planning technique. Focuses on nonmathematical depiction, discussion, and illustration of planning models.

Burack, Elmer H. *Strategies for Manpower Planning and Programming*. Morristown, N.J.: General Learning Press, 1972. Develops an overall logic for understanding workforce planning and converting plans into decisions.

California Department of Mental Hygiene. *Mental Health Manpower*. Vol. 1: *An Annotated Bibliography and Commentary*. Vol. 2: *Recruitment, Training, and Utilization*. Sacramento: California Department of Mental Hygiene, 1965. A two-volume set. Volume 1 contains an extensive annotated review of the literature up to 1965 and includes a topical index. Volume 2 is a compilation of articles and surveys on the use of practitioners, and an annotated review of related literature up to 1965.

Charnes, A., Cooper, W. W., and Niehaus, R. J. *Studies in Manpower Planning*. Washington, D.C.: Office of Civilian Manpower Management, U.S. Department of Navy, July 1972. A comprehensive decision analysis that applies formal mathematical models to workforce planning and management. The analysis develops a multilevel model that links more than one management level of decision making and ties top-level resource planning to the career-planning process. Markovian models, linear and goal programming models, and spectral analysis are used.

Clark, Harry L., and Thurston, Dona L. *Planning Your Staffing Needs: A Handbook for Personnel Workers.* Washington, D.C.: U.S. Civil Service Commission, 1977.

A "how-to-do-it" handbook that focuses on the key issue of planning staffing needs: estimating future vacancies caused by employee turnover. Techniques described include the graphical, log-probability nomograph, and the use of least square techniques for curve fitting.

Doeringer, Peter B., and Piore, M. J. *Internal Labor Markets and Manpower Analysis.* Lexington, Mass.: Lexington Books, 1970.

Deals with manpower issues in the context of "internal labor markets," such as hospitals and administrative divisions where the pricing and allocation of labor are governed by administered rules and procedures rather than markets.

Goldstein, Harold M., and Horowitz, Morris A. *Utilization of Health Personnel: A Five Hospital Study.* Germantown, Md.: Aspen, 1978.

Title speaks for itself.

Graduate Medical Education Advisory Committee. *Estimating Manpower Requirements.* Washington, D.C.: Department of Health, Education, and Welfare, 1977.

Discusses the history of health manpower requirements; dimensions of requirements estimation; theoretical and practical concepts for quantification; factors affecting requirements; estimation and forecasting; development of research strategy.

Greer, Charles R., Jackson, Dana L., and Fiorito, Jack. "Adapting Human Resource Planning in a Changing Business Environment." *Human Resource Management* (Spring 1989), *28* (1), 105–123.

A 1984 survey of human resource planning practices among 137 firms responding to a mail questionnaire regarding practices on both the supply and demand sides of human resource forecasting and planning. Findings note the effects of environmental turbulence and the direct involvement of line managers in human resource planning.

Gringold, R. C., and Marshall, K. T. *Manpower Planning Models.* New York: North-Hollard, 1977.

Mathematical discussion of basic manpower planning concepts, cross-sectional models, longitudinal models, optimization models, and validation.

Hall, Kathleen. *A Markovian Flow Model: The Analysis of Movement in Large-Scale (Military) Personnel Systems.* Rand Report No. R-514-PR, Santa Monica, Calif.: Rand Corporation, March 1971.

Application of a Markovian mathematical model to the forecasting of personnel mobility and supplies over time.

Hall, Kathleen. *A Markovian Flow Model: The Analysis of Movement in Large-Scale (Military) Personnel Systems—Program Reference Manual.* Rand Report No. R-534-PR. Santa Monica, Calif.: Rand Corporation, March 1971.

Programmer documentation and illustrations for implementing a system of Markovian model programs described in R-514-PR, *A Markovian Flow Model: The Analysis of Movement in Large-Scale (Military) Personnel Systems.*

Hall, Kathleen. *A Markovian Flow Model: The Analysis of Movement in Large-Scale (Military) Personnel Systems—Program Listing.* Rand Report No. Rp-535-PR. Santa Monica, Calif.: Rand Corporation, PR, March 1971.

FORTRAN listings of the subroutines described in R-514-PR and R-534-PR. Subroutines were compiled and executed on an IBM 360/65 using a FORTRAN H compiler.

Health Manpower Council of California. *1970 California Health Manpower: Four Major Approaches to Determining Health Manpower Requirements and Ways to Meet Them.* Orinda: Health Manpower Council of California, 1970.

Presents a "numbers," "utilization," "consumer," and a "total health care" approach to determining health workforce requirements and recommends using all four approaches together. Deals with the particular strengths and weaknesses of each approach.

Jakubauskas, Edward B., and Palomba, N. A. *Manpower Economics.* Reading, Mass.: Addison-Wesley, 1973.

A basic text, covering supply, demand, and policy. A chapter is given to the specifics of manpower planning.

Katz, Lawrence B. *A Markovian Model for Assessment of Personnel Hiring Plans.* Washington, D.C.: NASA Technical Note, NASA Ind-7640, June 1974.

Application of a Markovian model for assessment of personnel hiring plans. Initially developed to assess hiring at the directorate level at the Goddard Space Flight Center in Greenbelt, Maryland.

Lester, R. A. *Manpower Planning in a Free Society.* Princeton, N.J.: Princeton University Press, 1966.

Discusses how markets affect manpower planning; also covers demand forecasting and supply factors.

Levine, Rachael A. "Consumer Participation in Planning and Evaluation of Mental Health Services." *Social Work, 15* (2), 41–46.

Case studies and analysis of consumer input to mental health planning. Concludes that consumer participation plays an important role in breaking down hostility and effecting behavioral change.

Lewis, C. B. (ed.). *Manpower Planning: A Bibliography.* London: English Universities Press, 1969.

Extensive list of basic literature prior to 1969. Includes summary essays on manpower planning at the national, industrial, and firm levels.

McGregor, Eugene B., Jr. "Issues and Problems in Applying Quantitative Analysis to Public Sector Human Resource Management." In Charles H. Levine (ed.), *Managing Human Resources: A Challenge to Urban Governments.* Newbury Park, Calif.: Sage Publishers, Annual Reviews, 1977.

A discussion of workforce forecasting, planning, and programming. Problems and assumptions associated with applying quantitative tools to substantive workforce management problems are considered. Emphasis is given to modes of analysis actually or potentially useful in public agencies.

Moskow, Michael H. *Strategic Planning in Business and Government.* New York: Committee for Economic Development, 1978.

A brief summary of the logic and essential characteristics of strategic planning. A comparison of important differences and similarities between business and government planning. Case examples are cited in an appendix.

National Institute of Mental Health. *Development of a Micro Simulation Model of Health Manpower Demand and Supply.* Washington, D.C.: DHEW Publication No. HRP-0016347, 1970.
Description of a manpower planning model that is composed of three modules: service, manpower, and education. A section on technical and data problems is included.

National Institute of Mental Health. *The Mental Health of Rural America.* Washington, D.C.: DHEW Publication No. (HSM) 73-9035, 1973.
Describes the rural programs of the National Institute of Mental Health, focusing on epidemiological and demographic studies, rural attitudes, urbanization, American Indians, rural delinquents, approaches to providing services, case studies of rural mental health centers, and manpower supplies.

National Institute of Mental Health. *Needs Assessment Approaches: Concepts and Methods.* Washington, D.C.: DHEW Publication No. (ADM) 77-472, 1977.
A very basic manual on needs assessment. This little book is divided into sections on theory and methodology.

National Institute of Mental Health. *A Manual on State Mental Health Planning.* Washington, D.C.: DHEW Publication No. (ADM) 77-473, 1978.
Covers all main aspects of planning, including needs assessment methods.

Pettman, Barrie O., and Tavernier, Gerard. *Manpower Planning Workbook.* (2nd ed.) Brookfield, Utah: Gowen, 1984.
A step-by-step manual, including reporting shells.

Spulber, Nicholas, and Horowitz, Ira. *Quantitative Economic Policy and Planning: Theory and Models of Economic Control.* New York: Norton, 1976.
An application of the mathematics of balancing the supply and demand sides of labor markets.

Stangert, Per. *Information, Uncertainty, and Adaptive Planning.* Stockholm: Forsvarets Forskningsanstalt, 1974.

An investigation of the role and nature of formal criteria for the evaluation of planning strategies. A methodology is proposed for dealing with uncertainty. Probabilistic game theory, decision-making techniques, and forecasting are discussed. Key conclusions focus on the need for flexibility and adaptability in planning.

Taylor, Lord, and Chave, Sidney. *Mental Health and Environment.* London: Longmans, Green, 1964.

Analyses of various British surveys concerning mental health epidemiology, social indicators, hospital populations, and practitioner characteristics. Sample survey forms are included in the appendices.

U.S. Civil Service Commission. *Decision Analysis Forecasting for Executive Manpower Planning.* Washington, D.C.: Civil Service Commission, Bureau of Executive Manpower, June 1974.

Description of decision analysis forecasting to help determine executive manpower needs and resources at the agency level and below. Application of decision-tree analysis to an array of probable work force outcomes.

U.S. Department of Health, Education, and Welfare. *An Analysis of Health Manpower Models.* Washington, D.C.: Public Health Service, Health Resource Administration, DHEW Publication No. (HRA) 75-19, 1974.

A detailed description of fifty-six models. Most use regression analysis, other forms of linear programming, and some game theory. The usefulness of each model is considered.

U.S. Department of Health, Education, and Welfare. *Documents Related to Health Manpower Planning: A Bibliography.* Washington, D.C.: Public Health Service, Health Resource Administration, DHEW Publication No. (HRA) 75-14.012, 1974.

A large compendium of studies on all major types of planning activities. Includes many state and local reports.

U.S. Department of Health, Education, and Welfare. *An Inventory of Health Manpower Models.* Washington, D.C.: Public Health Service, Health Resource Administration, DHEW Publication No. 75-19, 1974.

A companion volume to *An Analysis of Health Manpower Models,* this book details the major mathematical models in terms of input variables, output variables, and data used.

U.S. Department of Health, Education, and Welfare. *Methodological Approaches for Determining Health Manpower Supply and Requirements.* Vol. 1: *Analytical Perspective.* Washington, D.C.: Public Health Service, Health Resource Administration, DHEW Publication No. (HRA) 76-14511, 1976.

An orientation guide for the health manpower planner. Details methods for estimating supply and demand, and deals critically with the issue of statistics.

U.S. Department of Health, Education, and Welfare. *Methodological Approaches for Determining Health Manpower Supply and Requirements.* Vol. 2: *Practical Planning Manual.* Washington, D.C.: Public Health Service, Health Resource Administration, DHEW Publication No. (HRA) 76-14512, 1976.

A description and evaluation of the major methods used to determine present and future health manpower supply and demand. Gives a good deal of attention to alternative methodologies; includes questionnaire samples and selected table formats.

U.S. Department of Health, Education, and Welfare. *Mental Health Planning: An Annotated Bibliography.* Washington, D.C.: Public Health Service, Health Resource Administration, DHEW Publication No. (HRA) 79-14001, 1978.

A broad but selective list of literature on all aspects of mental health planning. Includes a chapter on manpower resources.

U.S. Department of Transportation. *FAA Aviation Forecasts: Fiscal years 1978–1989.* Washington, D.C.: Federal Aviation Administration, FAA-AVP-77-32, September 1977.

One of the more sophisticated examples of federal agency attempts to project levels of aviation activity and work load from which the demand for an aviation safety workforce can be measured for use by the budget and constituent units of the agency.

Vroom, V. H., and MacCrimman, K. R. "Toward a Stochastic Model of Managerial Careers." *Administrative Science Quarterly,* June 1968, 26–46.

Early example of a Markovian model applied to administrative career planning.

Walker, James W. *Human Resource Planning.* New York: Wiley, 1983.

A basic text covering the practical approaches and processes employed in human resource forecasting and planning. Emphasizes a corporate-based, supply-side approach to human resource management.

Appendix D

Human Resource Forecasting and Planning Example

Ultimately, the goal of forecasting is to support a planning process. To illustrate the kind of calculations involved in workforce planning, we return to the case of mental health care. The workforce management logic requires that planners define the personnel requirements for an operating system and then derive staffing needs by comparing requirements with on-board personnel projections. As indicated earlier, personnel requirements are defined by the formula,

$$M_{ij}w = r$$

where

M_{ij} = the staffing standards matrix of mental health occupations (i) and mental health providers (j);
w = a vertically arrayed work-load vector;
r = the derived vertical vector of personnel requirements.

The derivation of statewide mental health requirements is found as the product of staffing standards and work load. For the sake of illustration, assume that the staffing standards taken from a recent study of state institutions (McGregor, 1984) yield the following matrix of coefficients for the state's mental illness (M.I.) and mental retardation and developmental disability (M.R.D.D.) hospitals, respectively:

		M.I. Hospitals	M.R.D.D. Hospitals
	Psychiatrists	.019	.005
	Psychologists	.012	.007
	Social workers	.022	.015
	Nurses	.063	.024
M_{ij} =	Therapists	.029	.022
	Other direct care personnel	.560	.632
	Support staff	.294	.294

Clearly, the M.I. case is staffed on a medical model with relatively large numbers of doctors, nurses, and psychiatric attendants. The M.R.D.D. institutions are training and development centers that employ large numbers (not shown explicitly here) of education and training personnel classified here as "other direct care." These fractions are based on the percent each occupational category is of the total workforce for each type of institution. In effect, each patient in a mental illness hospital requires, *assuming that the M_{ij} coefficients are appropriate*, .019 FTE of psychiatrist time, .012 of clinical psychologist effort, and so forth. Thus,

$$
\begin{pmatrix}
.019 & .005 \\
.012 & .007 \\
.022 & .015 \\
.063 & .024 \\
.029 & .022 \\
.560 & .632 \\
.294 & .294
\end{pmatrix}
\begin{pmatrix}
\text{ADPP} \\
2,400 \\
2,000
\end{pmatrix}
=
\begin{pmatrix}
55.6 \\
42.8 \\
82.8 \\
199.2 \\
113.6 \\
2608.0 \\
1293.6
\end{pmatrix}
$$

M.I.	M.R.D.D.		Total Requirements
		55.6	Psychiatrists
		42.8	Psychologists
		82.8	Social workers
		199.2	Nurses
		113.6	Therapists
		2608.0	Other direct care
		1293.6	Support staff

If we say that the average daily patient population (ADPP) is 2,400 patients in the M.I. hospitals and 2,000 in the M.R.D.D. hospitals, the result is a vertical vector (r) that enumerates the workforce requirements by occupational category. In effect 56 psychiatrists, 43 clinical psychologists, and so forth, will be required. In sum, a total workforce of 4,397 employees to care for 4,400 patients is said to be "required." The totals result from standard matrix and vector multiplication 45.6 psychiatrists (2,400 times .019) are required for the M.I. hospitals and 10 psychiatrists (2,000 times .005) for the M.R.D.D. hospitals, for a total of 55.6 psychiatrists. The same multiplication (row vector times a column vector) can be used to derive all requirement totals. The reader will note that the quantitative analysis is very simple compared to the real question, which is: Who is qualified to be a psychiatrist? Do these requirements mean senior, board-certified psychiatrists? Can they include cross-trained physicians? Board eligible, but not certified? Practitioners trained only in established American medical schools? Clearly, there is room for much massaging of data bases and professional clinical judgment. Nevertheless, as these numbers were based on state employment data, it is clear that institutional care is an expensive proposition; there is nearly a one-to-one staff to patient ratio programmed into this particular definition of workforce requirements. Public managers and policymakers horrified by the cost implications of such requirements definitions may well wish to try out other acceptable staffing in a computerized simulation format before buying the results as definitive.

Regardless of the precise figures, if staffing requirements can somehow be derived, what, then, are the staffing needs? The extent to which current on-board strength diverges from operational requirements is defined as the difference between the requirements vector (r) and the current on-board strength vector (s). Thus,

$$r - s = \text{staffing needs}$$

where a negative number means there are too many staff employed and a positive number indicates an unsatisfied operating requirement. In the former case, employment levels should logically be reduced. In the latter case, personnel recruitment is implied.

The staffing logic can also be reversed. Analysts can take

on-board personnel strength as given and derive the patient capacity of a mental health facility or system. This can be computed as:

$$M^{-1}sI = C,$$

where

m − 1 = the inverse of a staffing coefficient vector
s = the on-board staffing vector
I = an identity matrix
C = the patient capacity matrix.

In descriptive terms, the vector M^{-1} defines the number of patients one FTE employee can effectively treat. Thus, staffing standard of .019 psychiatrists per patient means that one FTE psychiatrist can effectively treat 53 patients (1/.019). The patient capacity of each personnel classification can be calculated where personnel are the constraining resource input. For example, if for some reason, such as a hiring freeze, a mental illness hospital staffing vector were found to be:

$$s = (50, 40, 70, 200, 100, 1500, 1000)$$

then the patient capacity of the mental illness hospitals can be computed for each staffing level as follows, using the staffing coefficients discussed earlier. The use of the identity matrix is a manipulative convenience that produces a diagonal vector of employment totals arrayed in a format compatible with further analysis; for example, personnel costs can be projected as the product of the employment matrix (containing the nonzero diagonal) and an average salary vector.

$$
\begin{pmatrix} .019 \\ .012 \\ .022 \\ .063 \\ .029 \\ .56 \\ .294 \end{pmatrix}^{-1} \quad (50, 40, 70, 200, 100, 1500, 1000) \qquad I = C
$$

$$
= \begin{pmatrix} 53 \\ 83 \\ 45 \\ = 16 \\ 35 \\ 2 \\ 3 \end{pmatrix} \quad (50, 40, 70, 200, 100, 1500, 1000) \quad \begin{pmatrix} 1\,0\,0\,0\,0\,0\,0 \\ 0\,1\,0\,0\,0\,0\,0 \\ .\ \ 1\ \ \ \ . \\ .\ \ \ 1\ \ \ . \\ .\ \ \ \ 1\ . \\ .\ \ \ \ \ 1. \\ 0\,0\,0\,0\,0\,0\,1 \end{pmatrix}
$$

$$
= \begin{pmatrix} 2650 & 0 & 0 & 0 & 0 & 0 & 0 \\ 0 & 3320 & 0 & 0 & 0 & 0 & 0 \\ 0 & 0 & 3150 & 0 & 0 & 0 & 0 \\ 0 & 0 & 0 & 3200 & 0 & 0 & 0 \\ 0 & 0 & 0 & 0 & 3500 & 0 & 0 \\ 0 & 0 & 0 & 0 & 0 & 3000 & 0 \\ 0 & 0 & 0 & 0 & 0 & 0 & 3000 \end{pmatrix}
\begin{matrix} \text{Psychiatrists} \\ \text{Psychologists} \\ \text{Social workers} \\ \text{Nurses} \\ \text{Therapists} \\ \text{Other direct care} \\ \text{Support staff} \end{matrix}
$$

The calculations are presented above in vector and matrix form so the possibilities for computerized computation can be easily envisioned. In this example, the result is a main diagonal defining the total patients a given staffing level can serve. Thus, a given facility has a sufficient number of therapists to care for 3,500 patients on an average daily patient population basis, followed in order by clinical psychologists, nurses, and social workers who can serve a maximum of 3,320, 3,200, and 3,150 patients, respectively. The staffing levels for psychiatrists, however, are sufficient to cover only 2,650 patients. The result is a staffing bottleneck. If each patient must be covered by *all* seven staffing levels, the capacity of the mental illness system is fixed at 2,650. It can be raised to 3,000—the next staffing bottleneck caused by support staff levels—simply by hiring 6.6 FTE psychiatrists, each of whom, according to the staffing standards used in this exercise, can manage a case load of 53 patients.

The results are illustrative only. The point is to show how the workforce management logic might be applied to workforce systems in order to project numerical staffing requirements, staffing needs, and patient treatment capacities under stated assumptions. Such analysis does *not* supplant or subvert the importance of experienced clinicians and managers making clinical and managerial judgments at the facility level about the quality of patient care. Leaving aside clinical issues, the core *management* question is whether workforce acquisitions and losses move an institution *over time* in a direction deemed desirable by those responsible for managing a state mental health system. The planning issue, then, is to discover what effect current and future decisions and actions have for the improvement of mental health care, the overall competence of the state's workforce, and the ability of the state's institutions to compete effectively in a changing system of mental health care delivery.

Appendix E

The Learning Curve
Illustrated

The general phenomenon of the learning curve is based on an insight that is both very simple and very powerful: people learn while working and the learning effect on productivity can be mathematically estimated. The practical application of the learning curve is nicely captured in a quotation taken from David Halberstam's assessment of the problems plaguing American automobile manufacturing (1986, pp. 307–308):

> There was what the consultant groups liked to call a learning curve in an industry. In its most elemental phrasing it went like this: The more cars you manufactured, the better you became; your engineers got better and your processes got better. Thus as you produced more and better cars, the cost of each car not only went down but went down sharply. In a way this was what had happened to the Ford Motor Company in its early years, when Henry Ford had systematically upgraded his assembly line without really changing his car. Now this was happening in Japan, with one major difference: Again and again Henry Ford had had to wait for technology to catch up with his dreams, but the Japanese were going through

their growing period when the technology, often foreign-developed, was already available and was fifty years more advanced than in Ford's day. That meant the race was even faster and the speed of the learning curve was even quicker. The Boston Consulting Group, of which Abegglen [*Note:* the reference is to Professor James Abegglen, a student of Japanese industrial management] was a founder, had figured out that in Japan, for each doubling in the learning curve, or in accumulated experience (the accumulated experience was the total number of cars manufactured), the cost in real terms dropped somewhere between 20 and 30 percent. Since in the days of explosive growth a company might go through a doubling every year, that meant that its costs were coming down at an astonishing rate. The stress in a period like this was immense, for the only way to win was to pour money back in, expand some plants, build others, and keep them running two or three shifts. Abegglen, who had watched Japan come into industry after industry, doubted that the American auto companies had any idea of what this might mean to them, and of how good the Japanese would quickly become. The Japanese might make an appalling number of mistakes in the beginning, but they would not make mistakes very long, and their quality would soon be very high.

A decade later, a study done by two of Abegglen's colleagues in the Boston Consulting Group . . . showed how right he had been. The study compared the prices of similar Japanese and American cars. In 1952 the American car had cost $1500, the Japanese car $2950; by 1959 the gap had begun to close, roughly $1900 for the American car, $2100 for the Japanese. By 1961 the Japanese car was slightly cheaper, $1750, as opposed to $1850 for the American. By 1964 the econo-

mies of scale had had a clear effect; a Japanese car
cost $1400, an American $1900. By 1970 the difference was dramatic, $1210 for the Japanese,
$2215 for the American.

Learning curve analysis has been applied to many industries: supercomputers (Kozmetsky, 1985), aircraft (Andress,
1954; Argote, Beckman, and Epple, 1990), and shipbuilding
(Argote, Beckman, and Epple, 1990). Obvious extensions of
learning-curve analysis include government contracting for
manufactured products (Andress, 1954) as well as production
operations of government itself, although I was unable to discover any research on the application of learning-curve analysis to public services delivered by government. In addition,
learning-curve analysis has been used to assist decision making
with respect to pricing, hiring policy, and antitrust decisions
(Argote, Beckman, and Epple, 1990).

The classic learning curve is calculated with the assistance of natural logarithms that have the effect of allowing any
doubling of product output (2 to 4, or 1,000 to 2,000) to be
plotted against the reduction in the direct labor hours required
(see Figure 11.3). The hourly input requirement can be expressed in terms of the *total* hourly requirement to produce a
given total output, or the *incremental* hours required to produce one additional unit of output, or the *average* hours required to produce a cumulative total output. The use of logarithms converts to a straight line a downward-sloping curvilinear
(exponential) function expressing the relationship between total hours of direct labor and the cumulative units produced.
The equation for the *cumulative average hours* is

$$Y = ax^b,$$

where

Y = the cumulative average hours for any number of units
a = the number of hours required to build the first unit
x = any number of completed units

$b = \ln(LR)/\ln(2)$, where LR is the learning rate expressed as a percentage reduction in cumulative average hours for each doubling of production.

Thus, at $LR = 80\%$ (an 80 percent reduction in direct labor hours required for each doubling), the value of the negative slope of b is calculated as: $b = \ln(.8)/\ln(2) = -.0223/.693 = -0.322$. As a result, it is possible to calculate the total number of hours required to produce T cumulative units of output as: $T = (x)ax^b$. In addition, the number of hours (U) required to build a specific *additional* unit is calculated as: $U = (b + 1)ax^b$.

The following table (E.1) is calculated to show the hourly requirements obtained when an 80 percent learning rate is assumed. Alternative calculations can be developed either by plugging into the formulae the log of alternative learning rates or by consulting tables where the calculations have already been made (Belkaoui, 1986).

Table E.1. Illustrated Hourly Labor Requirements at Different Productivity Levels: 80 Percent Learning Rate.

No. Units	x^b	$(x)\,ax^b$ Total Hours (T)	$(b+1)\,ax^b$ Incremental Hours (U)	ax^b Average Hours (Y)
1	—	12	12	12
2	.8	19.2	6.5	9.0
3	.7	25.3	5.7	8.42
4	.64	30.72	5.21	7.68
10	.48	57.18	3.88	5.72
20	.38	92.02	3.13	4.60
50	.29	171.58	2.33	3.43
100	.23	274.90	1.87	2.75
150	.20	358.70	1.62	2.39
1500	.045	1710.0	.77	1.14

Source: Andress, 1954.

References

Allison, G. T. "Public and Private Management: Are They Fundamentally Alike in All Unimportant Respects?" Paper presented to Public Management Research Conference, The Brookings Institution, Washington, D.C., 1979. Reprinted in J. L. Perry and K. L. Kraemer (eds.), *Public Management: Public and Private Perspectives.* Mountain View, Calif.: Mayfield, 1983.

"Amendment of Demonstration Project." *Federal Register,* July 28, 1981, *46* (144), 38660–38661.

"Amendment of Demonstration Project." *Federal Register,* Sept. 24, 1982, *47* (186), 42306–42312.

Andress, F. "The Learning Curve as a Production Tool." *Harvard Business Review,* Jan./Feb. 1954, *32,* 87–97.

Applegate, L. M., and Cash, J. I. "GE Canada: Designing a New Organization." Cambridge, Mass.: Harvard Business School, Case no. N9-189-138, 1989.

Argote, L., Beckman, S. L. and Epple, D. "The Persistence and Transfer of Learning in Industrial Settings." *Management Science,* Feb. 1990, *36,* 140–154.

Armstrong, J. A. *The European Administrative Elite.* Princeton, N.J.: Princeton University Press, 1973.

Avellar, J. W. "Virginia: The Development of Facility Staffing Standard for a State System." In J. P. A. Leopold and J. S. McCombs (eds.), *Job Analysis and Staffing Standards: Methods and Uses in Mental Health Services.* Baltimore, Md.: Department of Mental Hygiene, School of Hygiene and Public Health, Johns Hopkins University, 1982, 149–158.

Backoff, R. W., and Rainey, H. G. "Technology, Professionalization, Affirmative Action, and the Merit System." In C. H. Levine (ed.), *Managing Human Resources: A Challenge to Urban Governments.* Newbury Park, Calif: Sage, 1977, 113–139.

Bailey, J. *Job Design and Work Organization.* Englewood Cliffs, N.J.: Prentice-Hall, 1983.

Bartholomew, D. J., and Forbes, A. F. *Statistical Techniques for Manpower Planning.* New York: Wiley, 1979.

Becker, G. S. *Human Capital: A Theoretical and Empirical Analysis, with Special Reference to Education.* New York: National Bureau of Economic Research, 1964.

Beer, M., and others. *Managing Human Assets.* New York: Free Press, 1984.

Belkaoui, A. *The Learning Curve: A Management Accounting Tool.* Westport, Conn.: Quorum Books, 1986.

Bell, J. R., and Steedman, L. B. "Personnel Problems in Converting to Automation." In F. C. Mosher (ed.), *Governmental Reorganizations: Cases and Commentary.* Indianapolis, Ind.: Bobbs-Merrill, 1967.

Bennison, M., and Casson, J. *The Manpower Planning Handbook.* London: McGraw-Hill, 1984.

Benveniste, G. *Professionalizing the Organization: Reducing Bureaucracy to Enhance Effectiveness.* San Francisco: Jossey-Bass, 1987.

Blau, P. M. *The Dynamics of Bureaucracy.* Chicago: University of Chicago Press, 1955.

"Blue Shield of Massachusetts." Boston: Harvard Business School, Case Program no. 9-184-018, 1983.

Boulding, K. E. "The Economics of Knowledge and the Knowledge of Economics." *American Economic Review,* 1966, *56,* 1–13.

Brady, R. H. "MBO Goes to Work in the Public Sector." *Harvard Business Review,* Mar./Apr. 1973, *51,* 65–74.

Bragaw, L. *Managing a Federal Agency: The Hidden Stimulus.* Baltimore, Md.: Johns Hopkins University Press, 1980.

Brickner, W. H. "Innoventures: A Case for Public Policy Reforms." *Columbia Journal of World Business,* Fall 1981, *16,* 77–90.

Briefs, U., Kjar, J., and Rigal, J. *Computerization and Work: A Reader on Social Aspects of Computerization.* Berlin: Springer-Verlag, 1985.

Briscoe, D. R., O'Neil, R. F., and Cook, E. "Strategic Human Resources Decision-Making: An Economic Lesson." *Human Resource Management,* Summer 1982, 7, 2–5.

Brock, J. *Managing People in Public Agencies.* Boston: Little, Brown, 1984.

Brown, R. G. S. *The Administrative Process in Britain.* London: Methuen, 1971.

Bulkeley, W. M. "PC Networks Starting to Oust Mainframes in Some U.S. Firms." *Wall Street Journal Europe,* May 29, 1990, pp. 1, 10.

Burack, E. H. *Strategies for Manpower Planning and Programming.* Morristown, N.J.: General Learning Press, 1972.

Bureau of Policies and Standards. *Handbook of Occupational Groups and Series of Classes.* Washington, D.C.: U.S. Civil Service Commission, reprinted Sept. 1973.

Butterfield, B. D. "Companies Seek to Bolster Workers' Math, Science Skills." *Boston Globe,* June 19, 1989, p. 1.

Camillus, J. C., and Lederer, A. L. "Corporate Strategy and the Design of Computerized Information Systems." *Sloan Management Review,* Spring 1985, p. 26.

Campbell, A. K. "Testimony on Civil Service Reform and Reorganization." Testimony Before the Committee on Post Office and Civil Service, U.S. House of Representatives, March 14, 1978. In R. J. Thompson (ed.), *Classics of Public Personnel Policy.* Oak Park, Ill.: Moore Publishing, 1979, 77–102.

Carnevale, A. P. *Human Capital: A High Yield Corporate Investment.* Washington, D.C.: American Society for Training and Development, National Issues Series, 1983.

Castro, L., Hanson, J., and Rettig, T. *Advanced Programmer's Guide: Featuring dBASE III and dBASE II.* Culver City, Calif.: Ashton-Tate, 1985.

Ceriello, V. R. "Computerizing the Personnel Department: Make or Buy?" *Personnel Journal,* Sept. 1984, *63,* 44–49.

Chapman, R. L., Maharay, G. S., and McGregor, E. B., Jr. *Re-*

lating the Federal White-Collar Occupational Coding Structure to the Standard Occupational Classification System. Washington, D.C.: National Academy of Public Administration, 1979.

Child, J. "Managerial Strategies, New Technology, and the Labor Process." In J. M. Pennings and A. Buitendam (eds.), *New Technology as Organizational Innovation: The Development and Diffusion of Microelectronics.* Cambridge, Mass.: Ballinger, 1987.

Chorafas, D. N. *The Knowledge Revolution.* London: Allen & Unwin, 1968.

Ciborra, C. U. "Research Agenda for a Transactions Costs Approach to Information Systems." In R. J. Boland, Jr. and R. A. Hirschheim (eds.), *Critical Issues in Information Systems Research.* London: Wiley, 1987.

Clark, H. *Planning Your Staffing Needs.* Washington, D.C.: U.S. Civil Service Commission, 1977.

Clark, H. L., and Thurston, D. R. *Planning Your Staffing Needs: A Handbook for Personnel Workers.* Washington, D.C.: Bureau of Policies and Standards, U.S. Civil Service Commission, 1977.

Cleveland, H. "The Twilight of Hierarchy: Spectulations on the Global Information Society." *Public Administration Review,* Jan./Feb. 1985a, *45,* 185–195.

Cleveland, H. *The Knowledge Executive.* New York: Dutton, 1985b.

Cohen, M. D., March, J. G., and Olsen, J. P. "A Garbage Can Model of Organizational Choice." *Administrative Science Quarterly,* 1972, *17,* 1–25.

Coleman, J. S., and others. *Equality of Educational Opportunity.* Washington, D.C.: Office of Education, U.S. Department of Health, Education, and Welfare, 1966.

Colvard, J. E. "Federal Managers and the Civil Service Simplification Act." *The Federal Managers Quarterly,* Jan. 1987a, *5,* 21.

Colvard, J. E. "The Office of Personnel Management Work Force Agenda." Paper prepared for the National Conference on Public Administration, Boston, Mar. 30, 1987b.

Comfort, L. K. "Action Research: A Model for Organizational Learning," *Journal of Policy Analysis and Management,* Fall 1985, *5,* 100–118.

Cook, D. S., and Ferris, G. R. "Strategic Human Resource Management and Firm Effectiveness in Industries Experiencing Decline." *Human Resource Management,* Fall 1986, *25,* 441–458.

Couturier, J., and others. *Government Labor Markets.* Evanston, Ill.: Northwestern University, 1979.

Cyert, R. M., and March, J. G. *A Behavioral Theory of the Firm.* Englewood Cliffs, N.J.: Prentice-Hall, 1963.

Denison, E. F. *Why Growth Rates Differ: Postwar Experience in Nine Western Countries.* Washington, D.C.: The Brookings Institution, 1967.

Devanna, M. A., Fombrun, C. J., and Tichy, N. M. "A Framework for Strategic Human Resource Management." In C. J. Fombrun, N. M. Tichy, and M. A. Devanna, *Strategic Human Resource Management.* New York: Wiley, 1984.

Dimock, M. "Revitalized Program Management." *Public Administration Review,* May/June 1978, *38,* 199–204.

Doeringer, P. B., and Piore, M. J. *Internal Labor Markets and Manpower Analysis.* Lexington, Mass.: Lexington Heath Books, 1971.

Douglas, J., Klein, S., and Hunt, D. *The Strategic Managing of Human Resources.* New York: Wiley, 1985.

Downs, A. *Inside Bureaucracy.* Boston: Little, Brown, 1967.

Drexler, E. K. *Engines of Creation.* New York: Anchor Press, 1986.

Drucker, P. F. *The Age of Discontinuity.* New York: Harper & Row, 1968.

El Sawy, O. A. "Personal Information Systems for Strategic Scanning in Turbulent Environments: Can the CEO Go On-Line?" *MIS Quarterly,* Mar. 1985, *9,* 53–60.

Evans, P. A. L. "The Strategic Outcomes of Human Resource Management." *Human Resource Management,* Spring 1986, *25,* 149–167.

Fiedler, F. *A Theory of Leadership Effectiveness.* New York: McGraw-Hill, 1967.

Fine, S. A. "The 1965 Third Edition of the Dictionary of Occupational Titles—Content, Contrast and Critique." Kalamazoo, Mich.: W. E. Upjohn Institute for Employment Research, 1968.

Flamholtz, E. G. *Human Resource Accounting: Advances in Concepts, Methods, and Applications.* (2nd ed.) San Francisco: Jossey-Bass, 1985.

Foegen, J. H. "Too Much Negative Training." *Business Horizons,* Sept./Oct. 1987, pp. 51–53.

Fombrun, C., Tichy, N. M., and Devanna, M. A. *Strategic Human Resource Management.* New York: Wiley, 1984.

Forman, S. "Job Enrichment in the Bureau of Workman's Compensation (A)." In J. Brock, *Managing People in Public Agencies: Personnel and Labor Relations.* Boston: Little, Brown, 1984.

Fossum, J. A., Arvey, R. D., Paradise, C. A., and Robbins, N. E. "Modeling the Skills Obsolescence Process: A Psychological/Economic Integration." *Academy of Management Review,* 1986, *11,* 362–374.

Frantzreb, R. B. *Microcomputers in Human Resources Management: A Directory of Software.* Roseville, Calif.: Advanced Personnel Systems, 1985.

Fredericks, P., and Venkatraman, N. "The Rise of Strategy Support Systems." *Sloan Management Review,* Spring 1988, *13,* 47–54.

French, W. L. *The Personnel Management Process.* (5th ed.) Boston: Houghton Mifflin, 1978.

Galbraith, J. R. *Designing Complex Organizations.* Reading, Mass.: Addison-Wesley, 1973.

Geneen, H. *Managing.* New York: Avon Books, 1984.

Ghemawat, P. "Building Strategy on the Experience Curve." *Harvard Business Review,* Mar./Apr. 1985, *63,* 143–149.

Golzen, G. "Flexible Networks Keep Costs Low." *The Sunday Times* (London), Jan. 28, 1990, p. F1.

Gore, A., Jr. "China Lake." *The Federal Managers Quarterly,* Jan. 1987, *5,* 22–23.

Grace, P. J. *War on Waste.* New York: Macmillan, 1984.

Greer, C. R., Jackson, D. L., and Fiorito, J. "Adapting Human Resource Planning in a Changing Business Environment." *Human Resource Management,* Spring 1989, *28,* 105–123.

Gringold, R. C., and Marshall, K. T. *Manpower Planning Models.* New York: North-Holland, 1977.

Gupta, A. K., and Wilemon, D. L. "Accelerating the Development of Technology-Based New Products." *California Management Review,* Winter 1990, *32,* 24–44.

Hadden, S. G. "Intelligent Advisory Systems for Managing and Disseminating Information." *Public Administration Review,* Nov. 1986, *46,* 572–578.

Halberstam, D. *The Reckoning.* New York: Morrow, 1986.

Hall, R. H. *Dimensions of Work.* Englewood Cliffs, N.J.: Prentice-Hall, 1985.

Hall, R. "The Management of Intellectual Assets: A New Corporate Perspective." *Journal of General Management,* Autumn 1989, *15,* 53–68.

Hatry, H. P. "Issues in Productivity Measurement for Local Governments." *Public Administration Review,* Nov./Dec. 1972, *32,* 776–784.

Heclo, H. *A Government of Strangers: Executive Politics in Washington.* Washington, D.C.: The Brookings Institution, 1977.

Heiken, B. E., and Randall, J. W., Jr. "Customizing Software for Human Resources." *Personnel Administrator,* Aug. 1984, *29,* 43–48.

Held, W. G. "Decision Making in the Federal Government: The Wallace A. Sayre Model." In F. S. Lane (ed.), *Current Issues in Public Administration.* (2nd ed.) New York: St. Martin's Press, 1982.

Hellriegel, D., and Slocum, J. W., Jr. *Management: A Contingency Approach.* Reading, Mass.: Addison-Wesley, 1974.

Heneman, H. G., Jr., and Seltzer, G. *Employer Manpower Planning and Forecasting.* Washington, D.C.: U.S. Department of Labor, Manpower Research Monograph No. 19, 1970.

Herzberg, F. *Work and the Nature of Man.* Cleveland, Ohio: World Publishing, 1966.

Huber, G. P. "Issues in the Design of Group Decision Support Systems." *MIS Quarterly,* Sept. 1984, *8,* 195–204.

Hudson Institute. *Workforce 2000: Work and Workers for the Twenty-first Century.* Indianapolis, Ind.: Hudson Institute, June 1987.

Hufnagel, E. M. "Developing Strategic Compensation Plans." *Human Resource Management,* Spring 1987, *26,* 93–108.

Hyde, A. C., and Shafritz, J. M. "HRIS: Introduction to To-morrow's System for Managing Human Resources." *Public Personnel Management,* Mar.–Apr. 1977, *6,* 71–77.

James, H. L. "Nine Major Trends in HRM." *Personnel Administrator,* Nov. 1986, *31,* 102–109.

Joint Commission on Accreditation for Hospitals. *Consolidated Standards for Child, Adolescent, and Adult Psychiatric, Alcoholism, and Drug Abuse Programs.* Chicago: Joint Commission on Accreditation for Hospitals, 1979.

Joint Financial Management Improvement Program. *Report on Federal Productivity: Productivity Trends FY 1967–1973.* Vol. 1. Washington, D.C.: U.S. General Accounting Office, 1974.

Joskow, P. L., and Rose, N. L. "The Effects of Technological Change, Experience, and Environmental Regulation on the Construction Cost of Coal-Burning Generating Units." *Rand Journal of Economics,* 1985, *16,* 1–27.

Judson, A. S. "The Awkward Truth About Productivity." *Harvard Business Review,* Sept./Oct. 1982, *60,* 93–97.

Kanter, R. M. "The New Workforce Meets the Changing Workplace: Strains, Dilemmas, and Contradictions in Attempts to Implement Participative and Entrepreneurial Management." *Human Resource Management,* Winter 1986, *25,* 515–537.

Karna, K. (ed.). *Expert Systems in Government Symposium.* Washington, D.C.: IEEE Computer Society, 1985.

Kaufman, H. *Are Government Organizations Immortal?* Washington, D.C.: The Brookings Institution, 1976.

Kaufman, H. *Time, Chance, and Organizations.* Chatham, N.J.: Chatham House Publishers, 1985.

Keen, P., and Scott-Morton, M. S. *Decision Support Systems: An Organizational Perspective.* Reading, Mass.: Addison-Wesley, 1978.

Keen, P. G. W. *Competing in Time: Using Telecommunications for Competitive Advantage.* Cambridge, Mass.: Ballinger, 1986.

Kettl, D. F. *Government by Proxy: (Mis?)Managing Federal Programs.* Washington, D.C.: Congressional Quarterly Press, 1988.

King, J. L., and Kraemer, K. "Information Systems and Intergovernmental Relations." In Trudi C. Miller (ed.), *Public Sector Performance: A Conceptual Turning Point.* Baltimore, Md.: Johns Hopkins University Press, 1984.

King, W. R., and Cleland, D. I. "Information for More Effective Strategic Planning." *Long Range Planning,* Feb. 1977, *10,* 59–65.

Kooiman, J., and Eliassen, K. A. *Managing Public Organizations: Lessons from Contemporary European Experience.* Newbury Park, Calif.: Sage, 1987.

Kozmetsky, G. *Transformational Management.* Cambridge, Mass.: Ballinger, 1985.

Kustoff, M. "Assembling a Micro-Based HRIS: A Beginner's Guide." *Personnel Administrator,* Dec. 1985, *30,* 29–36.

Lamberton, D. M. (ed.). *Economics of Information and Knowledge.* New York: Penguin, 1971.

Lambright, H. L., and Teich, A. H. "The Organizational Context of Scientific Research." In P. C. Nystrom and W. H. Starbuck (eds.), *Handbook of Organizational Design.* Vol. 2, *Remodeling Organizations and Their Environments.* London: Oxford University Press, 1981, pp. 305–319.

Larson, R. W., and Zimney, D. J. *The White-Collar Shuffle.* New York: American Management Association, 1990.

Lawrence, P. R., and Lorsch, J. *Organization and Environment.* Cambridge, Mass.: Harvard Graduate School of Business Administration, 1967.

Lawrence, R. Z. *Can America Compete?* Washington, D.C.: The Brookings Institution, 1985.

Leavitt, H. J. "Applied Organizational Change in Industry: Structural, Technological, and Humanistic Approaches." In J. G. March (ed.), *Handbook of Organizations.* Chicago: Rand McNally, 1965, 1114–1170.

Leich, H. "Rank in Man or Job? Both!" *Public Administration Review,* Spring 1960, *20,* 92–99.

Leontief, W. *Input-Output Economics.* New York: Oxford University Press, 1966.

Levine, C. H. (ed.). *The Unfinished Agenda for Civil Service Reform: Implications of the Grace Commission Report.* Washington, D.C.: The Brookings Institution, 1985.

Levine, C. H. "The Federal Government in the Year 2000: Administrative Legacies of the Reagan Years." *Public Administration Review,* May/June 1986a, *46,* 195–206.

Levine, C. H. "The Quiet Crisis of the Civil Service: The Federal Personnel System at the Crossroads." Occasional Paper No. 7. Washington, D.C.: National Academy of Public Administration, 1986b.

Likert, R. *New Patterns of Management.* New York: McGraw-Hill, 1961.

Likert, R. *The Human Organization: Its Management and Values.* New York: McGraw-Hill, 1967.

Lindblom, C. E. "The Science of 'Muddling Through,' " *Public Administration Review,* 1959, *19,* 79–88.

Lindblom, C. E. *Politics and Markets: The World's Political Economic Systems.* New York: Basic Books, 1977.

Louis, K. S., and Sieber, S. D. *Bureaucracy and the Dispersed Organization: The Educational Extension Agent Experiment.* Norwood, N.J.: Ablex Publishing, 1979.

"Low-Tech Education Threatens the High-Tech Future." *Business Week,* Mar. 28, 1983, pp. 95, 98.

Lubin, J. S. "Legal Challenges Force Firms to Revamp Ways They Dismiss Workers." *Wall Street Journal,* Sept. 13, 1983, pp. 1, 16.

Ludwin, W. G. "Simple Models for Powerful Results." *Administration and Society,* Feb. 1988, *19,* 479–492.

Lynn, F. "An Investigation of the Rate of Development and Diffusion of Technology in Our Modern Industrial Society." *Report of the National Commission on Technology, Automation and Economic Progress.* Washington, D.C.: U.S. General Printing Office, 1966.

McGill, M. E., and Wooten, L. M. "Management in the Third Sector." *Public Administration Review,* Sept./Oct. 1975, *35,* 444–445.

McGregor, D. *The Human Side of Enterprise.* New York: McGraw-Hill, 1960.

McGregor, E. B., Jr. "Problems of Public Personnel Administration and Manpower: Bridging the Gap." *Public Administration Review,* Nov./Dec. 1972, *32,* 889–899.

McGregor, E. B., Jr. "Politics and the Career Mobility of Bureaucrats." *American Political Science Review,* Mar. 1974, *68,* 18–26.

McGregor, E. B., Jr. "Issues and Problems in Applying Quantitative Analysis to Public Sector Human Resource Management." In C. H. Levine (ed.), *Managing Human Resources: A Challenge to Urban Governments.* Vol. 13, *Urban Affairs Annual Review.* Newbury Park, Calif: Sage, 1977, 225–252.

McGregor, E. B., Jr. *A Strategy for State-Wide Mental Health Work Force Planning and Management.* Bloomington, Ind.: School of Public and Environmental Affairs, Indiana Mental Health Work Force Planning Project, Mar. 1984.

McGregor, E. B., Jr. "The Grace Commission's Challenge to Public Personnel Administration." In C. H. Levine (ed.), *The Unfinished Agenda for Civil Service Reform: Implications of the Grace Commission Report.* Washington, D.C.: The Brookings Institution, 1985.

McGregor, E. B., Jr. "The Public Sector Human Resource Puzzle: Strategic Management of a Strategic Resource." *Public Administration Review,* Nov./Dec. 1988, *48,* 941–950.

McGregor, E. B., Jr. "The Evolving Role of the Federal Government." In J. L. Perry (ed.), *Handbook of Public Administration.* San Francisco: Jossey-Bass, 1989.

McGregor, E. B., Jr., and Daly, J. "The Strategic Implications of Automation in Public Sector Human Resource Management." *Review of Public Personnel Administration,* Fall 1989, *10,* 29–47.

Machlup, F. *The Production and Distribution of Knowledge.* Princeton, N.J.: Princeton University Press, 1962.

Magee, J. R. "What Information Technology Has in Store for Managers." *Sloan Management Review,* Winter 1985, *10,* 45–49.

Magnus, M., and Grossman, M. "Computers and the Personnel Department." *Personnel Journal,* Apr. 1985, *64,* 42–48.

March, J. G. "The Business Firm as a Political Coalition." *Journal of Politics,* 1962, *24,* 662–678.

March, J. G. "Ambiguity and Accounting: The Elusive Link Between Information and Decision-Making." *Accounting, Organizations and Society,* 1987, *12,* 153–168.

March, J. G. *Decision and Organizations.* London: Blackwell, Oxford, 1988.

March, J. G., and Simon, H. A. *Organizations.* New York: Wiley, 1958.

Markus, M. L., and Robey, D. "Information Technology and Organizational Change: Causal Structure in Theory and Research." *Management Science,* May 1988, *34,* 583–598.

Martin, S. *Managing Without Managers: Alternative Work Arrangements in Public Organizations.* Newbury Park, Calif.: Sage, 1983.

Meier, G. *Leading Issues in Economic Development.* (5th ed.) New York: Oxford University Press, 1989.

Mensch, G. *Stalemate in Technology.* Cambridge, Mass.: Ballinger, 1979.

Mercer, M. W. *Turning Your Human Resources Department into a Profit Center.* New York: American Management Association, 1989.

Meshoulam, I., and Baird, L. S. "Proactive Human Resource Management." *Human Resource Management,* Winter 1987, *26,* 483–502.

Messner, H. "The Environment Inside EPA." *The Bureaucrat,* Spring 1986, *15,* 55–59.

Meyer, D. N. "The Office Automation Cookbook: Management Strategies for Getting Office Automation Moving." *Sloan Management Review,* Winter 1983, *8,* 51–60.

Meyer, H. E. "Personnel Directors Are the New Corporate Heroes." *Fortune,* Feb. 1978, pp. 84–88.

Miller, A. R., Treiman, D. J., Cain, P. S., and Roos, P. A. *Work, Jobs, and Occupations: A Critical Review of the "Dictionary of Occupational Titles."* Washington, D.C.: National Academy Press, 1980.

Miller, K. D. *Retraining the American Workforce.* Reading, Mass.: Addison-Wesley, 1989.

Mintzberg, H. *The Structuring of Organizations: A Synthesis of the Research.* Englewood Cliffs, N.J.: Prentice-Hall, 1979.

Mosher, F. C. *Governmental Reorganizations: Cases and Commentary.* Indianapolis, Ind.: Bobbs-Merrill, 1967.

Mosher, F. C. *Democracy and the Public Service.* New York: Oxford University Press, 1968.

Murname, R. J. "Education and the Productivity of the Work Force." In R. E. Litan, R. Z. Lawrence, and C. E. Schultze (eds.), *American Living Standards: Threats and Challenges.* Washington, D.C.: The Brookings Institution, 1988, 215–245.

Murray, M. A. "Comparing Public and Private Management: An Exploratory Essay." *Public Administration Review,* 1975, *35,* 364–371.

Myers, S., and Marquis, D. G. *Successful Industrial Innovations.* NSF 69-71. Washington, D.C.: National Science Foundation, 1969.

Nardoni, R. "Piecing Together a Micro-Based HRIS." *Personnel Journal,* Feb. 1985, *64,* 38–43.

National Alliance of Business. *Employment Policies: Looking to the Year 2000.* Washington, D.C.: National Alliance of Business, 1986.

National Manpower Council. *Government and Manpower.* New York: Columbia University Press, 1964.

"New Pay Bill Aims at Turnover." *Federal Times,* Apr. 27, 1987, p. 12.

Newland, C. A. "Management by Objectives in the Federal Government." *Bureaucrat,* Winter 1974, 349–426.

Niehaus, R. J. (ed.). *Human Resource Policy Analysis: Organizational Applications.* New York: Praeger Special Studies, 1985.

Nkomo, S. M. "Strategic Planning for Human Resources—Let's Get Started." *Long Range Planning,* Feb. 1988, *21,* 66–72.

Nonaka, I. "Toward Middle–Up–Down Management: Accelerating Information Creation." *Sloan Management Review,* Spring 1988, *13,* 9–18.

Norkett, P. *Accountancy for Non-Accountants.* Vol. 2, *Management Accounting.* London: Longman, 1982.

Odiorne, G. S. *Strategic Management of Human Resources: A Portfolio Approach.* San Francisco: Jossey-Bass, 1984.

Odiorne, G. "Strategic Management of Human Resources for the '80s and '90s: The Concept of HRD and Its Key Role in

Public Mental Health Agencies." Keynote Address at the Eighth National Assembly of State Mental Health Human Resource Development Programs, Portland, Maine, Aug. 27–29, 1986.

Oka, H., and Tanimitsu, T. "A Short History of Mitsubishi Electric Corporation's Basic Philosophy of Semiconductor R & D and Its Related Human Resource Management." In R. J. Niehaus (ed.), *Human Resource Policy Analysis: Organizational Applications.* New York: Praeger, 1985.

Osigweh, C. A. B. "Collective Bargaining and Public Sector Union Power." *Public Personnel Management Journal,* Spring 1985, *14,* 75–84.

Ost, E. J. "Team-Based Pay: New Wave Strategic Incentives." *Sloan Management Review,* Spring 1990, *31,* 19–27.

O'Toole, J. *Work and the Quality of Life: Resource Papers for Work in America.* Cambridge, Mass.: MIT Press, 1974.

Ouchi, W. G. "Markets, Bureaucracies and Clans." *Administrative Science Quarterly,* Mar. 1980, *25,* 129–141.

Pascale, R. T., and Athos, A. G. *The Art of Japanese Management.* New York: Simon & Schuster, 1981.

Perrow, C. "A Framework for Comparative Organizational Analysis." *American Sociological Review,* Apr. 1967, *32,* 194–208.

Perrow, C. *Complex Organization: A Critical Essay.* Glenview, Ill.: Scott, Foresman, 1973.

Perry, J. L. (ed.), *Handbook of Public Administration.* San Francisco: Jossey-Bass, 1989.

Perry, J. L., and Kraemer, K. L. (eds.). *Public Management: Public and Private Perspectives.* Mountain View, Calif.: Mayfield, 1983.

"Personnel Widens Its Franchise." *Business Week,* Feb. 26, 1979, pp. 116, 121.

Peters, T. J., and Waterman, R. H., Jr. *In Search of Excellence: Lessons from America's Best-Run Companies.* New York: Harper & Row, 1982.

Peterson, R. B., Tracy, L., and Cabelly, A. *Readings in Systematic Management of Human Resources.* Reading, Mass.: Addison-Wesley, 1979.

Prien, E. P. "The Function of Job Analysis in Content Validation." *Personnel Psychology*, Summer 1977, *30*, 167–174.

"Proposed Demonstration Project: An Integrated Approach to Pay, Performance Appraisal, and Position Classification for More Effective Operation of Government Organizations." *Federal Register*, Apr. 18, 1980, *45* (77), 26505–26543.

Public Service Research Council. *Public Sector Bargaining and Strikes*. Vienna, Va.: Public Service Research Council, 1982.

Pyhrr, P. A. "The Zero-Base Approach to Government Budgeting." *Public Administration Review*, Jan./Feb. 1977, *37*, 1–8.

Quinn, J. B. *Strategies for Change: Logical Incrementalism*. Homewood, Ill.: Irwin, 1980.

Rainey, H. G., Backoff, R. W., and Levine, C. H. "Comparing Public and Private Organizations." *Public Administration Review*, 1976, *36*, 223–244.

Rajan, A. "The Skill Gap That Could Be Lethal." *The Sunday Times* (London), Apr. 29, 1990, p. F1.

Ramo, S. "SMR Forum: America's Technology Slip—A New Political Issue." *Sloan Management Review*, Summer 1980, *21*, 77–85.

Rathwell, M. A., and Burns, A. "Information Systems Support for Group Planning and Decision-Making Activities." *MIS Quarterly*, Sept. 1985, *9*, 255–271.

Reich, R. B. "Why the U.S. Needs an Industrial Policy." *Harvard Business Review*, Jan./Feb. 1982, *60*, 74–81.

Reich, R. B. *The Next American Frontier*. New York: Penguin Books, 1983.

Ridgway, V. F. "Dysfunctional Consequences of Performance Measurements." *Administrative Science Quarterly*, Sept. 1956, *1*, 240–247.

Rockart, J. R., and Flannery, L. S. "The Management of End User Computing." *Communication of the ACM*, Oct. 1983, *26*, 776–784.

Rockart, J. R., and Scott-Morton, M. S. "Implications of Changes in Information Technology for Corporate Strategy." In A. Hax (ed.), *Readings on Strategic Management*. Cambridge, Mass.: Ballinger, 1984.

Rockart, J. R., and Treacy, M. E. "The CEO Goes On-Line." *Harvard Business Review*, Jan./Feb. 1982, *60*, 82–88.

Roethlisberger, F. J., and Dickson, W. J. *Management and the Worker*. Cambridge, Mass.: Harvard University Press, 1939.

The Roosevelt Center. *The High Flex Society*. Chicago: The Roosevelt Center, Sept. 1987.

Rosen, H. *The Merit System in the United States Civil Service*. Washington, D.C.: U.S. House of Representatives, Post Office and Civil Service Committee, 1975.

Rosen, H. *Servants of the People: The Uncertain Future of the Federal Civil Service*. Salt Lake City, Utah: Olympus Publishing, 1985.

Rosenthal, E. A. "Productivity in Procurement: Measures and Results." Greenbelt, Md.: Goddard Space Flight Center, Summer Institute in Public Administration, 1973.

Rosenthal, S. R. *Managing Government Operations*. Glenview, Ill.: Scott, Foresman, 1982.

Savas, E. S. *Privatization: The Key to Better Government*. Chatham, N.J.: Chatham House Publishers, 1987.

Sayre, W. S. "The Triumph of Techniques Over Purpose." *Public Administration Review*, Spring 1948, *8*, 134–135.

Sayre, W. S. "Bureaucracies: Some Contrasts in Systems." *The Indian Journal of Public Administration*, Apr.–June 1964, *10*, 219–229.

Schick, A. "The Road to PPB: The Stages of Budget Reform." *Public Administration Review*, Dec. 1966, *26*, 243–258.

Schneider, B., and Konz, A. M. "Strategic Job Analysis." *Human Resource Management*, Spring 1989, *28*, 51–63.

Schuler, R. S., and Jackson, S. E. "Linking Competitive Strategies with Human Resource Management Practices." *Academy of Management Executive*, 1987, *1*, 207–219.

Schultz, T. W. *Investment in Human Capital: The Role of Education and Research*. New York: Free Press, 1971.

Scientific American, special issue on "The Mechanization of Work," Sept. 1982.

Scoville, J. G. *The Job Content of the U.S. Economy, 1940–1970*. New York: McGraw-Hill, 1969.

Scoville, J. G. *Manpower and Occupational Analysis: Concepts and Measurements.* Lexington, Mass.: Lexington Books, 1972.

Second Public Management Research Conference. *The Changing Character of the Public Work Force: Conference Report.* Washington, D.C.: U.S. Office of Personnel Management, Mar. 1981, OPM document no. 134-59-7.

Seidman, H. "Government-Sponsored Enterprise in the United States." In B. L. R. Smith (ed.), *The New Political Economy: The Public Use of the Private Sector.* New York: Wiley, 1975.

Seidman, H., and Gilmour, R. *Politics, Position, and Power: From the Positive to the Regulatory State.* (4th ed.) New York: Oxford University Press, 1986.

Sharp, C. *The Economics of Time.* New York: Wiley, 1981.

Shenkar, O., and Chow, I. H. "From Political Praise to Stock Options: Reforming Compensation Systems in the People's Republic of China." *Human Resource Management,* Spring 1989, *28,* 65–85.

"The Shrinking of Middle Management." *Business Week,* Apr. 25, 1989, pp. 54–80.

Simon, H. A. *Models of Man.* New York: Wiley, 1957.

Simon, H. A. "Decision Making as an Economic Resource." In L. H. Seltzer (ed.), *New Horizons for Economic Progress.* Detroit: Wayne State University Press, 1964.

Simon, H. A. *The Sciences of the Artificial.* Cambridge, Mass.: The MIT Press, 1969.

Smith, B. L. R. *The New Political Economy: The Public Use of the Private Sector.* New York: Wiley, 1975.

Spencer, L. M., Jr. *Calculating Human Resource Costs and Benefits: Cutting Costs and Improving Productivity.* New York: Wiley, 1986.

Spencer, W. J. "Research to Product: A Major U.S. Challenge." *California Management Review,* Winter 1990, *32,* 45–53.

Stahl, O. G. *Public Personnel Administration.* (7th ed.) New York: Harper & Row, 1976.

Stalk, G., Jr. "Time—The Next Source of Competitive Advantage," *The McKinsey Quarterly,* Spring 1989, 28–41.

Stanley, D. T. *Managing Local Government Under Union Pressure.* Washington, D.C.: The Brookings Institution, 1971.

Starling, G. *Managing the Public Sector.* (3rd ed.) Homewood, Ill.: Dorsey Press, 1986.

Stout, R., Jr. *Management or Control? The Organizational Challenge.* Bloomington: Indiana University Press, 1980.

Suleiman, E. N. *Politics, Power, and Bureaucracy in France: The Administrative Elite.* Princeton, N.J.: Princeton University Press, 1974.

Szewczak, E. J. "Building a Strategic Data Base." *Long Range Planning,* Apr. 1988, *21,* 97–103.

Taylor, E. "Suggested Formula for Staffing of 24-Hour Positions Where Shifts Are Utilized." Indianapolis, Ind.: Indiana Department of Mental Health, Nov. 4, 1981.

Taylor, F. W. *The Principles of Scientific Management.* New York: Norton, 1947.

Thierauf, R. J. *Decision Support Systems for Effective Planning and Control.* Englewood Cliffs, N.J.: Prentice-Hall, 1982.

Thompson, F. J. *Personnel Policy in the City.* Berkeley: University of California Press, 1975.

Thurow, L. *Investment in Human Capital.* Belmont, Calif.: Wadsworth, 1970.

Tichy, N. M., Fombrun, C. J., and Devanna, M. A. "Strategic Human Resource Management." *Sloan Management Review,* 1982, *7,* 47–61.

Tolchin, M., and Tolchin, S. *To the Victor: Political Patronage from the Clubhouse to the White House.* New York: Random House, 1971.

Trento, J. J. *Prescription for Disaster.* New York: Crown, 1987.

Trist, E. L. "The Sociotechnical Perspective." In A. Van de Ven and W. Joyce (eds.), *Perspectives on Organization Design and Behavior.* New York: Wiley, 1981.

Tsui, A. S. "Defining the Activities and Effectiveness of the Human Resource Department: A Multiple Constituency Approach." *Human Resource Management,* Spring 1987, *26,* 35–69.

Tushman, M. L., and Nelson, R. R. "Introduction: Technology, Organizations, and Innovation." *Administrative Science Quarterly,* Mar. 1990, *35,* 1–8.

Ulrich, D., Geller, A., and DeSouza, G. "A Strategy, Structure,

Human Resource Database: OASIS." *Human Resource Management*, Spring 1984, *23*, 77–90.

U.S. Bureau of the Census. *City Employment in 1976.* Washington, D.C.: U.S. Bureau of the Census, GE 76, no. 2, July 1977.

U.S. Bureau of the Census. *Statistical Abstract of the United States: 1989.* (109th ed.) Washington, D.C.: U.S. Department of Commerce, 1989.

U.S. Department of Labor. *Dictionary of Occupational Titles.* Washington, D.C.: Bureau of Labor Statistics, 1977.

U.S. General Accounting Office. *General Management Review Issue Area Plan.* Washington, D.C., Aug. 1986.

U.S. General Accounting Office. *Managing Human Resources: Greater OPM Leadership Needed to Address Critical Challenges.* Washington, D.C.: GAO/GGD-89-19, Jan. 1989.

U.S. General Accounting Office. *Observations on the Navy's Managing to Payroll Program.* Washington, D.C.: GAO/GGD-90-47, Mar. 1990.

U.S. House of Representatives, 95th Congress, 2nd session. *Civil Service Reform Act of 1978, Conference Report* (to accompany S.2640). Washington, D.C.: Report No. 95-1717, Oct. 5, 1978, 4 and 5.

U.S. Office of Personnel Management. *Management Reports I– IX: Evaluation of the Navy Personnel Management Demonstration Project.* Washington, D.C.: Office of Performance Management, Research and Demonstration Division, 1984 to 1986.

U.S. Office of Personnel Management. *1989 Personnel Research Conference Proceedings.* Aug. 16–17, 1989, at Chevy Chase, Md.

van Gunsteren, L. A. "Information Technology: A Managerial Perspective." In I. M. Pennings and A. Buittendame (eds.), *New Technology as Organizational Innovation.* Cambridge, Mass.: Ballinger, 1987, pp. 277–290.

Vroom, V. H., and MacCrimman, K. R. "Toward a Stochastic Model of Managerial Careers." *Administrative Science Quarterly,* June 1968, *13*, 26–46.

Walker, J. W. "Forecasting Manpower Needs." *Harvard Business Review,* Mar./Apr. 1969, *47*, 152–164.

Walker, J. W. *Human Resource Planning.* New York: McGraw-Hill, 1980.

Wallace, M. J., Jr. "Rewards and Renewal: America's Search for Competitive Advantage Through Alternative Pay Strategies." In *Personnel Research Conference Proceedings* (Aug. 16–17, 1989, Chevy Chase, Md.). Washington, D.C.: U.S. Office of Personnel Management, 1989. Conference held Aug. 16–17, 1989, at Chevy Chase, Maryland.

Walton, R. E. *Innovating to Compete: Lessons for Diffusing and Managing Change in the Workplace.* San Francisco: Jossey-Bass, 1987.

Ward, S. C. "How to Computerize Your Personnel Planning." *Long Range Planning,* Aug. 1987, *20,* 88–101.

Webb, J. E. *Space Age Management.* New York: McGraw-Hill, 1969.

Weidenbaum, M. L. *The Modern Public Sector: New Ways of Doing the Government's Business.* New York: Basic Books, 1969.

White, H. C. *Chains of Opportunity: System Models of Mobility in Organizations.* Cambridge, Mass.: Harvard University Press, 1970.

Wildavsky, A. *The Politics of the Budgetary Process.* Boston: Little, Brown, 1964.

Wildavsky, A. *Speaking Truth to Power: The Art and Craft of Policy Analysis.* Boston: Little, Brown, 1979.

Williamson, O. E. *Markets and Hierarchies: Analysis and Antitrust Implications.* New York: Free Press, 1975.

Wilson, J. Q. *Varieties of Police Behavior.* Cambridge, Mass.: Harvard University Press, 1968.

Wilson, L. J. "The Navy's Experiment with Pay, Performance, and Appraisal." *Defense Management Journal,* Third Quarter 1985, pp. 30–40.

Wise, C. R., and McGregor, E. B., Jr. "Government Productivity and Program Evaluation Issues." *Public Productivity Review,* Mar. 1976, *1,* 5–19.

Woodward, J. *Industrial Organization: Theory and Practice.* New York: Oxford University Press, 1965.

Yelle, L. E. "The Learning Curve: Historical Review and Comprehensive Survey." *Decision Sciences,* 1979, *10,* 302–328.

Zand, D. *Information, Organization, and Power.* New York: McGraw-Hill, 1981.

Zuboff, S. *In the Age of the Smart Machine: The Future of Work and Power.* New York: Basic Books, 1988.

Index